D0098651

NO LONGER PROPERTY OF
SEATTLE PUBLIC LIBRARY

BY DAVID SIROTA

Back to Our Future: How the 1980s Explain the World We Live in Now—
Our Culture, Our Politics, Our Everything

Hostile Takeover

The Uprising

B A C K
TO **O**UR
FUTURE

BALLANTINE BOOKS
NEW YORK

BACK TO OUR FUTURE

HOW THE 1980s EXPLAIN THE WORLD WE LIVE IN NOW— OUR CULTURE, OUR POLITICS, OUR EVERYTHING

DAVID SIROTA

Copyright © 2011 by David Sirota

All rights reserved.

Published in the United States by Ballantine Books, an imprint of The Random House Publishing Group, a division of Random House, Inc., New York.

BALLANTINE and colophon are registered trademarks of Random House, Inc.

Library of Congress Cataloging-in-Publication Data

Sirota, David (David J.)
Back to our future : how the 1980s explain the world we live in now—
our culture, our politics, our everything / David Sirota.
p. cm.
Includes bibliographical references.
ISBN 978-0-345-51878-1 (hardcover : acid-free paper)—
ISBN 978-0-345-51880-4 (ebook)
1. United States—Civilization—1970– 2. United States—Social conditions—
1980– 3. Popular culture—United States. 4. Political culture—United States.
5. Nineteen eighties. I. Title.
E169.12.S5188 2011
973.92—dc22   2010041627

Printed in the United States of America on acid-free paper .

www.ballantinebooks.com

2 4 6 8 9 7 5 3 1

First Edition

Book design by Susan Turner

To Jeff and Steven—beloved brothers,
best friends, fellow children of the 1980s

"What happens to us in the future?
Do we become assholes or something?"

—MARTY McFLY, 1985

CONTENTS

INTRODUCTION xiii

PART I · LIKING IKE, HATING WOODSTOCK 1

DIE, HIPPIE, DIE! 7

PART II · THE JUMP MAN CHRONICLES 31

THE JOHN GALT OF OCEANIA 36

JUST DO IT 52

OUTLAWS WITH MORALS 75

PART III · WHY WE (CONTINUE TO) FIGHT 105

KICKING THE VIETNAM SYNDROME 112

OPERATION RED DAWN 139

PART IV · THE HUXTABLE EFFECT 171

MOVIN' ON UP? 180

THE END OF HISTORY? 214

ACKNOWLEDGMENTS 221

NOTES 223

GLOSSARY 261

INTRODUCTION

For as long as I can remember, I have never seen the 1980s as an "era" or a "historical moment" or, God forbid, a "period." To me, the decade has always been a language. I don't remember the 1980s as much as I speak it and think in it. As anyone who has seen me around my two brothers knows, I mean this quite literally.

As typical kids growing up in the suburbs, my siblings and I were pretty different from one another. We had different tastes, jobs, interests, attitudes, and politics, and we always had our fair share of fights, including one featuring a flying *Karate Kid* kick to the throat (alas, I have yet to mete out my wedgie revenge for that one). But through it all, we patched together a common dialect of eighties references that served as a diplomatic Morse code-bridging conflict, forging compromise, and filling uncomfortable silence.

In the Sirota household, you could garner forgiveness with a proper mimic of *Planes, Trains and Automobiles* ("Sorry," whispered like a pajama-clad Del Griffith), demand someone do something by quoting Indiana Jones ("Do it, now!" with a clenched fist), lament an oddity with a line from *Coming to America* ("That's *real* fucked up."), describe the weather in *The Empire Strikes Back* terms ("It's like Hoth out there!"), and tell anyone to do just about anything with the generic mantra of *Rocky III* ("Go for it," mumbled with the Italian Stallion's guttural inflection). If you didn't understand something, you said, "Whatchoo talkin' bout, Willis?" like Arnold Jackson in *Diff'rent Strokes*. If you were sick of being told to do a chore too many times, you mimicked Walter Fielding in *The Money Pit* by saying, "I know where the bucket is," through clenched underbite. If you were planning on eating a big meal, you told Mom you were ready for "The Ol' 96er" from *The Great Outdoors*. If you needed to take a dump, you politely excused yourself by saying you had to go be the "administrator of this facility" à la Lando Calrissian. If you were trying to describe a cool car that just drove by, you would characterize it as some iteration of *Knight Rider*'s KITT, *The Dukes of Hazzard*'s General Lee, or *Uncle Buck*'s transmission-exploding jalopy. For everything else, you simply whipped out *Superman II*'s überversatile command: "Kneel before Zod."

To outsiders, it must have seemed as if my parents had conceived a trio of Tourette's cases and subsequently strapped us, *Clockwork Orange*-style, to our hulking Zenith television and its wheezing Panasonic VCR.

Our extended family was for the most part bemused or only mildly irritated by our vernacular. Strangers were bewildered, freaked-out, or both—and we didn't care.

By the time we hit our college years, my brothers and I saw this language as epistemology. To us, nothing could not in some way trace its provenance to an obscure eighties movie, sitcom, toy, video game, song, commercial, or athlete. But as more self-aware adults, we pledged to conceal this view in mixed company, for fear of total social alienation. While steadfast in our enthusiasm for our formative decade, we learned to keep our eighties religion to ourselves for fear of being socially ostracized.

Which was fine with me. Frankly, I did not aspire to a sad, celibate life making my name as the Cliff Clavin of 1980s trivia. And to us Sirota boys, that's what our encyclopedic knowledge of the Reagan-Era's cultural esoterica was: an amusing and fun patois appropriate for inside jokes and barroom theorizing, but not much more.

But then, a little while ago, something weird started happening— something "heavy," as Marty McFly might say. The 1980s began becoming cool. Not just VH1 *Big 80s* ironic cool—like, really, *actually* cool. More cool than the decade ever was in its own time. Cool, as in a legitimate *phenomenon*.

Suddenly, *The Karate Kid* and *The A-Team* were fighting for the number one spot atop the movie charts, and *Hot Tub Time Machine*'s journey back to the 1980s was the leading comedy in America. At the same time, *Red Dawn, Short Circuit, Tron, Ghostbusters, Clash of the Titans, Footloose,* and *Arthur* were being remade; brands such as *Transformers, G.I. Joe, Predator, Star Wars, The Equalizer,* and *Nightmare on Elm Street* were being resurrected; video games such as *Missile Command* and *Asteroids* were becoming feature-length films; classics such as *Zelda* were being rereleased; and the *Los Angeles Times* blared the headline "Atari Reboot Is Underway."

Suddenly, Bruce Springsteen, Bon Jovi, and Devo were back on tour, and Gene Simmons and Dee Snider had their own A&E reality shows. Without warning, you could be at a public event (such as me at the last Denver Brewfest) and find yourself engulfed by a throng of drunk twentysomethings earnestly rocking out to cover bands playing Eddy Grant's "Electric Avenue," the Eurythmics "Sweet Dreams," and the Talking Heads' "Once in a Lifetime"—and playing that eighties Velveeta in a straight, nonironic fashion.

Suddenly, Hulk Hogan, Jerry Seinfeld, and William Shatner— William fucking Shatner!—were back to being major TV stars, Meryl Streep was once again winning Academy Awards, and one of the Golden Girls—Betty White—was hosting *Saturday Night Live.*

Suddenly, Apple was again the rage in the computer industry, Nintendo was dominating the video-game market, Tories were winning British elections, and Russians were spying on the United States.

Suddenly, the Philadelphia Phillies were World Series contenders, the Philadelphia Flyers were fighting for a Stanley Cup, and the Los Angeles Lakers were playing the Boston Celtics in the NBA finals.

In an America whose 1980s destroyed the boundaries between entertainment, news, and politics, this bizarre déjà vu could be seen in even the most deadly serious stuff.

Once again, we were funding a proxy war in Afghanistan, rattling our sabers at Iran, getting fleeced by Gordon Gekkos on Wall Street, and talking about poverty in Reaganesque "welfare queen" terms. In this cauldron of nostalgia, George W. Bush started explaining complex geopolitical issues by going *Top Gun* with aircraft-carrier landings and one-liners such as "Bring it on"—all while his partner, Dick Cheney, became universally referred to as eighties villain Darth Vader. After that, Barack Obama achieved international celebrity discussing race in "Cosby moments," and then, when running for president, was regularly likened to Cliff Huxtable. During that campaign, his opponents became yet more eighties archetypes—Sarah Palin was the authentic *Roseanne* who pledged to "go rogue" like an eighties action star, all while ticketmate John McCain—who has basically the same name as *Die Hard*'s protagonist—obsessed over which Muslim country we should designate as the next target of Chuck Norris's *Delta Force.*

In short, America abruptly started speaking the ancient 1980s language of my youth—and continues to speak it to this day. The critical question is, why?

Part of it is the sheer magnitude of everything associated with a time that epitomized the opposite of the old Small Is Beautiful idea. The 1980s was the primogenitor of the supersize concept. Everything was big—really big. Like, Big John Studd big. Big hair. Big defense budgets. Big tax cuts. Big shoulder pads. Big blockbuster movies. Big sports stars. The Big Gulp. Even the decade's most endearing tale of youthful innocence was about a grade-schooler asking an arcade machine to make him *Big.* And all that bigness made a correspondingly immense psychological impression on America at precisely a time when that impression could be made to last.

Remember, just as the mythology of the 1960s was boosted by occurring in the first decade of Baby Boom activism and television ubiquity, the 1980s came during a uniquely explosive confluence of mind-blowing multimedia revolution and sociopolitical transformation.

The decade was the first in which the majority of American households possessed a television, a VCR, and cable service—and nearly half had video-game systems. Everything from consumer products manufacturers to fast-food chains to retail outlets were vertically integrating themselves—as was the all-important telecom industry. By 1983, just fifty conglomerates controlled the vast majority of the newspaper, broadcast, magazine, movie, and publishing firms. Such a consolidated megaphone was no longer merely able to produce diffuse and diverse noise. It was perfectly constructed to reinforce narrow cultural memes, and in the eighties those were the ones emanating from an ultra-conservative Reagan Revolution, a growing Me Generation, a racist reaction to the civil rights movement, and a bitterly nationalistic backlash to the Vietnam disaster.

So, for example, you didn't see *E.T.: The Extra-Terrestrial* just in your movie theater. You saw that antigovernment parable about children having to flee faceless, jackbooted federal agents in your Atari cassettes, your Happy Meals, your board games, your action-figure sets, and your Reese's Pieces wrappers. You didn't see Mr. T's minstrel act just in Hollywood bit parts, you saw it in the cereal you were eating, the Saturday-morning cartoons you were watching, the Trapper Keeper you were using, and the professional wrestling matches you were cheering. In short, you no longer received disparate bits of information about the world; the 1980s was the first time the tools existed to provide you with an entire way of thinking.

Having never before been subjected to such a powerful propaganda machine, we were a tabula rasa without today's well-honed bullshit detectors, and the first imprint on our psychological blank slate—the pulverizing imprint of 1980s pop culture—has naturally been the most lasting.

Aiding this 1980s legacy were the structural economic changes of the Reagan era. With wages stagnating and families struggling to sustain incomes in the 1980s, more women entered the workforce and more employees began spending longer hours on the job. Left with less adult attention and supervision, eighties kids started spending much more time hanging out in the basement with their new popculture pedagogues: the television, VCR, Atari, and Apple IIe.

This goes a long way to answering why the 1980s resurrection is taking place at this exact moment.

"Show me the games of your children," goes the anthropologists' refrain, "and I'll show you the next hundred years." That aphorism is particularly important when we consider entertainment media. As *The Boston Globe* reported in 2009, "a wave of sociological research is showing" that "TV and movie characters can shape how we look at real-world events" and that "fiction, in fact, can shape our perceptions of the world even more than reality."

If that's true, then it's no shock the 1980s is on the ascent right now. After all, World War II vets brought up on old-time radio and sixties hippies raised on *Ed Sullivan* are currently being replaced in society's culture-shaping positions by eighties kids. From cable hosts such as Glenn Beck and Rachel Maddow to CEOs such as Bill Gates and Steve Jobs to House and Senate chairmen, to President Obama himself, our world is increasingly run by the prepubescents, teenagers, college kids, and young ladder-climbers who were originally indoctrinated and inculcated in the 1980s—and they are bringing that decade's values, worldviews, and attitudes back.

But what does it mean to "bring the 1980s back"? This is a tougher question to answer than it may appear, because "the 1980s" is a difficult concept to define.

Most decades have, of course, been fastidiously filed away and organized by a searchable keyword in our mental hard drive:

- 1930s: The Great Depression
- 1940s: The Greatest Generation
- 1950s: Postwar Prosperity, Joe McCarthy, Black-and-White Television
- 1960s: Woodstock, I Have a Dream, The Beatles, Sex
- 1970s: Oil Embargo, Watergate, The Bee Gees, More Sex, Porn
- 1990s: *Friends,* Dot-Com, "I Did Not Have Sex with That Woman"
- 2000s: W.

The 1980s, though, defies taxonomy. Depending on the age, race, sexual orientation, geography, and sports-team affiliation of the person you are reminiscing with, the decade was hilarious, awful, or totally rad and the beginning of America's rebirth, the beginning of the end of the world, or perhaps—not coincidentally—all of the above. Not surprisingly, there are just no short catchphrases or grand unifying theories to sum up such a monumental late-century clusterfuck. Seriously—what succinct terms adequately explain the conflicting phenomena of Just Say No, Just Do It, Michael Jackson, Boy George, Oliver North, Super Mario Brothers, Teenage Mutant Ninja Turtles, and Alf—all grandly presided over by a Democrat-turned-Republican actor-turned–Cold Warrior? There are none, which is why whenever you try to explain the 1980s, you end up sounding as if you're karaokeing "We Didn't Start the Fire."

That said, for all the decade's hard-to-quantify contradictions, broad themes from the 1980s clearly still influence our thinking, govern our worldview, and direct our actions.

Today, we still see economics through *Wall Street*'s eyes and government through *The A-Team*'s garage goggles, confident that a few "greed is good" tweaks and hired mercenaries can save our economy and foreign policy. We still view race through the *Diff'rent Strokes* and *Cosby Show* living rooms, differentiating between the acceptable "transcendent" minorities and unacceptably ethnic ones.

When we consider ourselves on the global stage, we still imagine Sergeant Slaughter. When we look at the rest of the world, we still scowl at the Iron Sheik. When we think about how our society defines community, responsibility, and personal success, we may think we see the ancient hyperindividualistic, up-by-the-bootstraps hero from a 19th century Horatio Alger novel or a mid 20th-century Marlboro ad. Yet, what we're really looking at is a far more supercharged version of those archetypes from the 1980s. Every public-policy, competition, and entertainment plot worships the Michael Jordan ideal originally popularized in sneakers, T-shirts, animated movies, and McDonald's commercials in the 1980s—the solitary megastar, the one-man team, the silhouette of a single individual soaring split-legged over everyone else.

Knowing this, it's no accident that those with the most acute interest in shaping contemporary opinion speak to us in Twiggy's dumbed-down 1980s dialect, as if we're Buck Rogers just waking up from a two-decade slumber.

In matters of national security, politicians dress up like Maverick and do their best impression of Christopher Lloyd in *Back to the Future* precisely *because* they know that invoking *Top Gun* bravado and screaming about Middle Eastern terrorist cells preparing to rampage suburban shopping malls is a language we were preprogrammed to understand. Same thing for economics—in the face of recession, we keep being told we can all be Brantley Foster because the 1980s embedded that *Secret of My Success* fantasy in our minds. And same thing for government itself—as environmental catastrophes and financial crises make the case for stronger public institutions, we nonetheless still hear that the government is evil and that only the "rogue" can save us because that's the *Rambo* theory we long ago learned to revere.

In that sense, the eighties fixation in our current culture and politics may not really be a resurrection at all. Just as I never stopped speaking 1980s with my brothers, our 1980s fetish may actually be the intensification of an ethos that never actually went extinct, in part because no epochal force ever intervened to kill it.

Think about it: the first half of the 1990s were largely "about nothing," as *Seinfeld* seemed to predict, and the second half's dot-com euphoria was a cheap repeat of Wall Street's go-go days during the decade prior, only with fewer pin-striped cocaine freaks and more jeans-and-T-shirt potheads. Then came the post-9/11 era, which was basically a return to America circa 1986, only with Libya, Michael Milken, and *Who's the Boss?* replaced by Iraq, Ken Lay, and *The Family Guy*.

Now today, almost every major cultural touchstone is rooted in the 1980s—whether obviously or subtly. *The Sopranos* was an update of a 1980s Scorsese flick. *The Wire* was Baltimore's own *Colors*. *Curb Your Enthusiasm* is a Los Angeles–set *Seinfeld*. *American Idol* is *Star Search*. Kobe is MJ. Mahmoud Ahmadinejad is the Ayatollah Khomeini. Brad and Jen are Sean and Madonna. David Cameron is Margaret Thatcher. Barack Obama is, according to Republicans, Jimmy Carter. The BP spill is the Exxon Valdez disaster. The Wii is the NES. *Twilight* is *The Lost Boys*. Even the whole weird New Jersey obsession—from *Jersey Shore* to *Jersey Couture* to *Jerseylicious* to *Jersey Girl* to *Garden State*—is happening because the land of Springsteen and Bon Jovi and Trump casinos remains synonymous with the eighties mullets, hairsprays, and styles that are now so retro-chic.

Writing all that, I must confess, is not easy for me. It evokes stomach pangs and a quickening pulse rate and sweat beads, some of which are dripping onto the keyboard as I bang out this sentence. The truth is, I feel that I'm violating the promise that my brothers and I made when we became adults—our pledge to stop publicly conversing in 1980s-ese, so as to avoid looking like freaks. Breaking that vow of silence is a little bit scary.

However, I've got a rationale for doing so. I figure if everyone is now conversing in that dialect, then I can break my familial pact—in fact, as a journalist, I feel that I am obligated to. In this present moment of national confusion and chaos, we must not shy away from the truly tough (and simultaneously fun) issues. Specifically, we must not only examine why a twenty-first-century nation is still a 1980s society, but how that anachronistic reality is affecting us right now and how it will impact our world in the years ahead.

That's what this book is all about, with these pages aiming to be an update of Doc Brown's flux-capacitor-powered time machine. Granted, this particular Delorean is only made out of paper and ink. And granted, it doesn't require 1.21 jigowatts. But rest assured, like Doc's original its time circuits are programmed to take us to the past, which means we will indeed be going back to our future.

PART I

LIKING IKE, HATING WOODSTOCK

It is impossible to consider the enduring legacy of the 1980s without first returning to and prostrating ourselves at the altar of Michael J. Fox.

More than the name before Robert Goulet and Wayne Gretzky on an alphabetical list of the most famous. Canadians, Fox was the Spud Webb of 1980s Hollywood—a freakishly short, explosive phenom whose talents were forever immortalized on the poster-covered walls of teenage bedrooms. But unlike his kindred spirit, who was merely dunking basketballs for the Atlanta Hawks and starring in Paul Simon videos, Fox in the 1980s was helping concoct the indelible generational fantasies that still dictate America's sense of possible and impossible, desirable and undesirable.

Fox's initial break came in 1982, when as a little-known actor he scored the role of Alex P. Keaton in *Family Ties*. From the beginning, the central "situation" in this sitcom was explicitly decade-driven in its obsession with "rejecting the counterculture of the 1960s and embracing the wealth and power that came to define the '80s," as the Baltimore *Sun* put it.

The Thursday-night NBC show focused on the friction between Steven and Elyse Keaton, two hippie caricatures clinging desperately to their sixties outlook, and their son Alex, a portrait of eighties ambition whose coat-and-tie wardrobe and Reagan worship were a big middle finger to his parents' Woodstock generation.

The show was a top-five-rated program for four years of its seven-year run, and some of its best-known episodes centered on the adult-minded Alex lambasting the 1960s and trying to personify everything his still-juvenile parents marched against back in their pot-and-protest youth.

The program's introductory montage, for instance, features photos of Steven and Elyse organizing a campus rally in their college years, decked out in bell-bottoms, vests, and long, flower-specked hair. In the show's pilot, the Keatons huddle on the living room couch watching Steven's home movies of peace marches, only to have Alex tell him, "The sixties are over, Dad." (Steven later wonders, "Do you think he was switched at birth and the Rockefellers have our kid?"). A few episodes later, when Steven and Elyse are jailed for marching against nuclear proliferation, Alex comes to bail them out with the rejoinder, "You know what's wrong with parents today? They still think they can change the world."

Later, when Steven asks Alex to help him finish a documentary on poverty at the local public television station, Alex says, "I don't think it would look good—me working for a nonprofit organization . . . the whole concept of nonprofit is . . . ew."

Fox was never supposed to occupy the central role in *Family Ties*—his endearingly clownish parents were. But his character's Brooks Brothers conservatism and, more important, his ridiculing of his elders' sixties disposition proved so appealing to the Reaganized audience of the 1980s that NBC had its screenwriters revamp the program's entire structure.

"All the elements of Alex's character that I regarded as liabilities, the young people immediately saw as strengths," says Gary David Goldberg, the recovering hippie who created the show. "They loved his fascination with money, loved how he dressed, and really respected that he fights for his [conservative] position, knows what he wants, and has a plan."

Fox became so iconic via Alex that after just three years as a full-time television actor, he landed the part of Marty McFly in *Back to the Future*—the only entertainment product that arguably rivals *Family Ties* for mass success predicated on intergenerational friction.

When you dig beneath the film's Huey Lewis ballads and its lightning-bolt pyrotechnics, you find in *Back to the Future* a timeless fable about retreat into nostalgia.

Robert Zemeckis's film, which ended up grossing more than a quarter billion dollars, features a typically spoiled and cynical suburban teenager escaping America's most hysterical fears (e.g., corrupted youth, family dysfunction, wild-eyed, bazooka-wielding Libyans, etc.) by fleeing to an idyllic 1950s—a time when (supposedly) the kids were all clean-cut, innocent, and optimistic; every home sported a white-picket fence and fluttering American flag; and the only major threats to tranquillity were Peeping Toms like George McFly, leather-jacket hoodlums like Biff Tannen, and slacker-loathing high-school principals like Mr. Strickland.

Marty flees, in other words, the sixties-soiled present that Alex P. Keaton instructed us to despise and escapes into a 1950s Americana we were being taught to see as one big *Saturday Evening Post* illustration.

Pitting that bleached snapshot of an arcadian, patriotic, benevolently capitalist, conservative, Caucasian, and therefore good fifties against the psychedelic cartoon of an anti-American, malevolently collectivist, permissive, diverse, and thus awful sixties came to be far more than an overused cliché of Hollywood scriptwriters (though it certainly remains that). Thanks to the 1980s, it has become the foundational allegory in our red-white-and-blue theology—the creation tale subsequently referenced by every shaman, prophet, and zealot in our civic religion.

Admittedly, the semiotics were supposed to change with the 2008 election. John McCain, a stiff, stodgy Dwight Eisenhower wannabe replete with war-hero status and glimmering medals, was soundly defeated by the picture of generational transcendence. Barack Obama, the kind of postmodern sensation that Andy Warhol could only fantasize about, continually boasted that his youth and cosmopolitan background would allow him to rise above the sixties-flavored conflict that had come to define politics. Yet, even a victor seemingly immune from generational stereotype is now depicted in 1980s-style caricatures of the fifties and sixties. His liberal proponents portray his glamour and "best and brightest" smarts as JFK-esque, while his conservative enemies channel Joe McCarthy and George Wallace by alternately labeling him a dangerous communist and/or a menacing black nationalist.

Today, these eighties-composed memories of the mid-twentieth century are everywhere, and certainly not limited to the dialogue of *That '70s Show* or the pot jokes of Seth Rogan flicks. The quadrennial struggle for our now-celebritized presidency is only one of many battles in which those manipulated memories are still used as rhetorical weapons against each other—and against a more nuanced understanding of our world.

DIE, HIPPIE, DIE!

Every time one of these ex-hippies comes prancing in from yesteryear, we gotta get out the love beads and pretend we care about people. —ALEX P. KEATON, 1986

For the past several days I've been noticing a steep rise in the number of hippies coming to town. . . . I know hippies. I've hated them all my life. I've kept this town free of hippies on my own since I was five and a half. But I can't contain them on my own anymore. We have to do something, fast! —ERIC CARTMAN, 2005

In 1975, a Democratic Party emboldened by civil rights, environmental, antiwar, and post-Watergate electoral successes was on the verge of seizing the presidency and a filibuster-proof congressional majority. That year, *The Rocky Horror Picture Show* and *One Flew Over the Cuckoo's Nest* were two of the three top-grossing films—the former a parody using the late-sixties sexual revolution to laugh at the puritanical fifties, the latter based on the novel by beat writer Ken Kesey. Meanwhile, three of the top-rated seven television shows were liberal-themed programs produced by progressive icon Norman Lear, including *All in the Family*—a show built around a hippie, Mike Stivic, poking fun at the ignorance of his traditionalist father-in-law, Archie Bunker.

A mere ten years later, Republican Ronald Reagan had just been reelected by one of the largest electoral landslides in American history, and his party had also gained control of the U.S. Senate. Two of the top three grossing films were *Back to the Future,* which eulogized the fifties, and *Rambo: First Blood Part II,* which blamed sixties antiwar activism for losing the Vietnam conflict. Most telling, *All in the Family*'s formula of using sixties-motivated youth and progressivism to ridicule fifties-rooted parents and their traditionalism had been replaced atop the television charts by its antithesis: a *Family Ties* whose fifties-inspired youth ridicules his parents' sixties spirit.

The political and cultural trends these changes typified were neither coincidental nor unrelated, and their intertwined backstories explain why we're still scarred by the metamorphosis.

The late 1970s and early 1980s marked the birth of an entire industry organized around idealized nostalgia, and particularly midcentury, pre-1965 schmaltz. You likely know this industry well—it survives in everything from roadside Cracker Barrel restaurants to the Jersey shore's Old Time photo stands to Michael Chabon's novels to *Band of Brothers*–style miniseries glorifying the valor of World War II vets—and it first found traction in the 1980s creation of The Fifties™.

Turning a time period into a distinct brand seems common today, what with the all-pervasive references to generational subgroups (Gen X, Gen Y, etc.). But it was a new marketing innovation back in the 1980s. As Temple University professor Carolyn Kitch found in her 2003 study of mass-circulation magazines, generational labeling is "primarily a phenomena of the last quarter of the 20th century," and it began (as so many things have) as an early-1980s ad strategy aimed at selling products to Baby Boomers and their parents.

Like all sales pitches, fifties hawking employed subjectivity, oversimplification, and stereotypes. For eighties journalists, advertisers, screenwriters, and political operatives seeking a compelling shorthand to break through the modern media miasma, that meant making The Fifties into much more than the ten-year period between 1950 and 1959. It meant using pop culture and politics to convert the style, language, and memories of that decade into a larger reference to the entire first half of the twentieth century, all the way through the early

1960s of the New Frontier—those optimistic years "before President Kennedy was shot, before the Beatles came, when I couldn't wait to join the Peace Corps, and I thought I'd never find a guy as great as my dad," as Baby from the classic eighties film *Dirty Dancing* reminisced.★

Why The Fifties, and not the 1930s or '40s, as the face of the entire pre-sixties epoch? Because that decade was fraught with far less (obvious) baggage (say, the Depression or global war) and hence was most easily marketed in the saccharine entertainment culture of the devil-may-care 1980s.

Indeed, as the Carter presidency started to crumble in 1978 and Reagan began delivering fiery speeches in preparation for his upcoming presidential run, the crew-cut-and-greaser escapades of *Happy Days* and the poodle skirts of *Laverne & Shirley* overtook the sixties-referencing urbanity, ethnicity, and strife of Norman Lear's grittier sitcoms. In movie theaters, *Animal House* and *Grease* hit classic status almost instantly. These successes encouraged the culture industry to make the eighties the launching point for a self-sustaining genre of wildly popular back-to-the-fifties productions.

There were retrospectives such as *Diner, Stand By Me,* and *Peggy Sue Got Married* and biopics of fifties icons such as *The Right Stuff, La Bamba,* and *Great Balls of Fire!* There was *Hoosiers,* with its bucolic small towns, its short shorts, and its nonbreakaway rims. There were Broadway plays such as *Brighton Beach Memoirs* and *Biloxi Blues,* commemorating the honor, frugality, and innocence of the World War II years. And there was a glut of new Eisenhower biographies.

Even 1980s productions not overtly focused on decade nostalgia were decidedly recollective of fifties atmospherics.

There was *Witness,* which used the story of a Philadelphia cop's voyage into lily-white Amish country to juxtapose the simplicity of America's pastoral heritage against the crime-ridden anarchy of the black inner city.

There was *Superman* and *Superman II*—films that reanimated a TV

★For this reason, "the fifties" refers in this chapter to the entire cultural era after World War II through the 1963 assassination of President John F. Kennedy. Similarly, "the sixties" refers to the cultural era from the Kennedy assassination through the mid-1970s.

hero of the actual 1950s, idealized Clark Kent's midcentury youth, and depicted his adulthood as the trials of a fedora-wearing anachronism trying to save modern Metropolis from postfifties peril.* And there were the endless rip-offs—the Jets-versus-Sharks rivalry of *West Side Story* ripened into the socs-versus-greasers carnage of *The Outsiders,* while the hand-holding of *Grease* became the ass-grabbing of *Dirty Dancing.*

Through it all, pop culture was manufacturing a *Total Recall* of the 1950s for a 1980s audience—an artificial memory of The Fifties that even came with its own canned soundtrack.

Though we tend to think of the late 1970s and early 1980s as the glory days of punk rock and the primordial soup of what would become rap, Wurlitzer-ready rockabilly and doo-wop were the rage. This was the heyday of the Stray Cats and their standing base, the moment when Adam Ant released the jukebox jam "Goody Two Shoes," and Queen's rockabilly hit "Crazy Little Thing Called Love" hit number one on the charts. As the Hard Rock Cafe and Johnny Rockets franchises created a mini-fad of fifties-flavored restaurants, the B-52s' surf rock was catching a new wave; Meat Loaf was channeling his Elvis-impersonation act into the absurdist 1950s tribute "Paradise by the Dashboard Light"; and ZZ Top was starring in music videos featuring a muscle car that Danny Zuko might have driven at Thunder Road. Even Billy Joel, until then a folksinger, was going all in with a blatant teenybopper tribute, "Uptown Girl."

This sonic trend wasn't happening in a vacuum—it was thrumming in the shadow of the chief missionary of 1950s triumphalism, Ronald Reagan.

The Gipper's connection to The Fifties wasn't just rooted in his success as a midcentury B-movie actor nor in his *American Graffiti* pompadour. The Fifties had long defined his persona, career, and message. Here was "the candidate of nostalgia, a political performer whose be-bop instrument dates from an antediluvian choir," as *The*

---

*In *Superman,* the enemy was the crime and terrorism of Lex Luthor. In the sequel, it was the triumvirate of General Zod's Soviet-style authoritarianism, Ursa's overaggressive feminism, and Non's George W. Bush–esque mix of swagger and ignorance.

Washington Post wrote in 1980. Here was a man campaigning for president in the late 1970s and early 1980s calling for the country to go back in time. And not just a few years back in time—*way* back in time to the dreamy days before what he called the "hard years" of the late 1960s.

"Not so long ago, we emerged from a world war," Reagan said in a national address during his 1980 presidential campaign. "Turning homeward at last, we built a grand prosperity and hopes, from our own success and plenty, to help others less fortunate. Our peace was a tense and bitter one, but in those days, the center seemed to hold."

Writing to a campaign contributor, Reagan said he wanted to bring forth a "spiritual revival to feel once again as [we] felt years ago about this nation of ours." And when he won the White House, his inauguration spelled out exactly what he meant by "years ago": The lavish celebration dusted off and promoted fifties stars such as Frank Sinatra and Charlton Heston.

This wasn't a secret message or a wink-and-nod—it was the public theme of Reagan's political formula. In a *Doonesbury* comic about the 1980 campaign, cartoonist Gary Trudeau sketched Reagan's mind as "a storehouse of images of an idyllic America, with 5 cent Cokes, Burma Shave signs, and hard-working White People." When naming him 1980 "Man of the Year," *Time* said, "Intellectually, emotionally, Reagan lives in the past." The article added that the new president specifically believes "the past"—i.e., the The Fifties—"is his future." And as both the magazine and America saw it, that was the highest form of praise—just as it is today.

This all might have gone the way of New Coke if the early-1980s celebration of The Fifties™ was happening in isolation. But those Bob Ross paintings of happy Levittown trees and Eisenhower-era blue skies only became salient because the eighties placed them in the American imagination right next to sensationalized images of Woodstock and the Kent State massacre.

Securing that prime psychological real estate meant simultaneously doing to the sixties what was being done to the fifties—only with one twist: Instead of an exercise in idealization, The Sixties™ brand that came out of the 1980s was fraught with value judgments downplaying the decade's positives and emphasizing its chaos.

Through politics and mass media, a 1960s of unprecedented social and economic progress was reremembered as a time of tie-dye, not thin ties; burning cities, not men on the moon; LBJ scowls, not JFK glamour; redistributionist War on Poverty "welfare," not universalist Medicare benefits; facial-haired Beatles tripping out to "Lucy in the Sky with Diamonds," not bowl-cut Beatles chirping out "I Want to Hold Your Hand."

Some of the sixties bashing in the 1980s came from a media that earnestly sought to help Baby Boomers forgive themselves for becoming the buttoned-down adults they had once rebelled against. Some of it was the inadvertent side effect of an accelerating twenty-four-hour news cycle that historian Daniel Marcus notes almost always coupled references to the sixties with quick "shots from Woodstock of young people cavorting in the mud, perhaps discarding various parts of their clothing or stumbling through a drug-induced haze."

And some of it was just the uncontrived laziness of screenwriters and directors.

"Getting a popular fix on the more elusive, more complicated, and far more common phenomena of the sixties is demanding because a lot of it isn't photogenic," says Columbia professor Todd Gitlin, the former leader of Students for a Democratic Society and author of *The Sixties.* "How easy it was to instead just make films about the wild people, because they are already an action movie, and their conception of themselves is already theatrical."

The revisionism and caricaturing revolved around three key themes, each of which denigrated the sixties as 100 percent awful.

The first was the most political of all—patriotism. Love of country, loyalty to America, national unity—these were memes that Reagan had been using to berate the sixties since his original jump from Hollywood to politics.

During his first campaign for California governor, he ran on a platform pledging to crush the "small minority of beatniks, radicals, and filthy speech advocates" at Berkeley who were protesting the Vietnam War. As president, he railed on nuclear-freeze protesters (like Steven and Elyse Keaton in that first season of *Family Ties*) as traitors "who would place the United States in a position of military and moral inferiority."★

The media industry of the time followed with hypermilitarist films blaming antiwar activists for America's loss in Vietnam (more on that in the chapter "Operation Red Dawn"), and magazine retrospectives basically implying that sixties social movements were anti-American. As just one example, a 1988 *Newsweek* article entitled "Decade Shock" cited the fact that "patriotism is back in vogue" as proof that the country had rejected the sixties—the idea being that the sixties was wholly unpatriotic.

But while flag-waving can win elections and modify the political debate, it alone could not mutate the less consciously political, more reptilian lobes of the American cortex. So the 1980s contest for historical memory was also being waged with more refined and demographically targeted methods.

For teenagers, The Fifties™ were used to vandalize The Sixties™ through a competition between the Beatnik and the Greaser for the mantle of eighties cool. As historian Daniel Marcus recounts, the former became defined as "middle-class, left-wing, intellectual and centered in New York City and San Francisco"—that is, defined as the generic picture of weak, effete, snobbish coffeehouse liberalism first linked to names such as Hart and Dukakis, and now synonymous with Kerry, Streisand, and Soros. Meanwhile, the Greaser came to be known as an urbanized cowboy—a tough guy who "liked cars and girls and rock and roll, was working class, usually non-Jewish 'white ethnic' and decidedly unintellectual."

This hero, whose spirit we still worship in the form of Joe the Plumber and "Bring it on" foreign policy, first stomped the Beatnik through the youth-oriented iconography of the 1980s—think idols such as the Fonz, Bruce Springsteen, and Patrick Swayze; movies like *Staying Alive, Rocky,* and *The Lords of Flatbush;* bands such as Bon Jovi, Guns N' Roses, and Poison; and, not to be forgotten, the chintzy clothing fad of ripped jeans and tight white T-shirts.

★In a sense, Reagan sounded just like Alex P. Keaton ripping on his parents, which might explain why the president told reporters *Family Ties* was his favorite program and why he offered to appear on an episode—an offer the show's writers rejected.

For adults who experienced the real fifties and sixties, the propaganda had to be a bit less overt to be convincing. So their memories were more subtly shaped with the arrival of a life-form whose mission was to absolve the hippie generation for becoming the compromised and depoliticized elders they had once railed on and protested against.

This seductive species became known as yuppies—short for young urban professionals.

The invasion of the yuppies and all of their requisite tastes, styles, and linguistic inflections officially commenced when *Newsweek* declared 1984 the Year of the Yuppie, following the publication of *The Yuppie Handbook* and the presidential campaign of Gary Hart—a New Agey candidate who looked as if he carried a dog-eared copy of the tome around in his breast pocket. A few months later, *Adweek* quoted executives from the major television networks saying their goal in coming years would be to "chase yuppies with a vengeance"—a prediction that came true, according to *Rolling Stone*'s 1987 report on a series of hit shows that the magazine called Yuppievision. By 1988, a suited Michael J. Fox eating sushi was on the cover of an *Esquire* magazine issue devoted entirely to "Yupper Classmen." Fittingly, one of the articles noted a poll showing that 60 percent of Americans could identify the word *yuppie*—almost twice the number that could identify the nation's secretary of state.

While *yuppie* certainly evoked supermodern feelings in the 1980s, the concept was etymologically rooted in a politicized past. The word made its public debut in a 1983 newspaper column about Jerry Rubin, the leader of the Youth International Party (yippies) who had abandoned his sixties radicalism for the 1980s world of business. His life story was a textbook yuppie parable of sixties rejection: He was a member of the "vanguard of the baby-boom generation," which had "march[ed] through the '60s" but was now "advancing on the 1980s in the back seat of a limousine," as *Newsweek* put it.

University of Pittsburgh cultural-studies scholar Jane Feuer says that through precisely this historiography, yuppie lore spurred a national "self distancing" from the sixties by justifying "the former flower children laughing at their own [80s] materialism."

The mythology pervaded the national media. For instance, in

its obsessive coverage of the Baby Boomers' evolution, a 1986 article in *Time* seeded its prose with asides about a "dogmatic" and overly "headstrong" sixties "generation that has made a pastime out of prolonged adolescence" but is now facing "up to the responsibilities of adulthood." Likewise, *Newsweek* in 1988 berated a "failed" sixties that proved "the more things change, the more they remain the same" and cheered on eighties hyperconsumerism and conservatism.

That metastasized into hit-you-over-the-head television such as the *Family Ties* installment called "My Back Pages." The episode, whose name cheekily recalls a Bob Dylan song, shows Steven reconnecting with a colleague named Matt from their days writing for a left-wing magazine. Matt looks and sounds as if he hasn't changed his hippie wardrobe or belief system since Woodstock. Following Alex's obligatory insults ("Every time one of these ex-hippies comes prancing in from yesteryear, we gotta get out the love beads, put on the ponchos, and pretend we care about people"), Steven goes to work with Matt on reviving the publication, only to have Matt yell at him for writing a "reactionary" article daring to "suggest people actually go out and vote for one of the two prevailing parties."

Steven responds with a slogan of yuppie apologism: "Things aren't as black-and-white as they used to be."

That line could have been the subtitle for *thirtysomething*—an eighties program so intent on preaching the yuppie gospel that it licensed a consumer catalog to showcase its yuppie characters' chic clothing. *thirtysomething* centered around Michael, a hippie turned ad executive, and his grown-up frat-house friends, as they reminisced about—and chuckled at—their long-haired sixties antics. By the time *thirtysomething* was airing, this sixties-ridiculing tripe had become such a reliable comedic formula that the show's writers insisted on flashing characters back to cartoonish sixties memories, even though by the show's own chronology they would have been too young to be in those settings in the actual 1960s.

Of course, many believe yuppie historiography was originally distilled into its purest form in *The Big Chill,* one of the highest-grossing movies of 1983. The film, which was a bigger-budget version of John Sayles's *Return of the Secaucus Seven,* revolves around a group of college buddies turned yuppies who reunite at the funeral of Alex, a man who has committed suicide because he couldn't let go of the 1960s and join his friends' yuppified stratosphere.

The reunion participants embody what historian Gil Troy calls "The Great Sellout" of the 1980s—Harold, the college liberal, has corporatized his undergraduate dalliance with radicalism by using the Marxist idiom "Running Dog" as the name of his Wal-Mart-size shoe company; Michael, the idealistic college-newspaper reporter, has become a *People*-magazine hack; Nick, the psychology major, is a Porsche-driving drug addict; Sam, the activist who once delivered fiery speeches to thousands of fellow students, is now the star of an inane *Magnum, P.I.* rip-off called *J. T. Lancer;* Meg, the law student who started out as a public defender because she wanted to defend "Huey and Bobby" (i.e., Black Panther leaders Huey Newton and Bobby Seale), came to view her indigent clients as "scum" and consequently moved to a high-priced corporate law firm.

With sixties rock music playing in the background, the weekend gathering is punctuated by jokes about the group's campus rallies, "marches on Washington," "ideological fanaticism," and belief that "property was a crime." But unlike the eighties pop culture that glorified the fifties, this trip down memory lane wasn't dramatized as a voyage of wistful nostalgia—it was a jaunt into a sixties past that the wizened yuppies came to see as patently ridiculous, as displayed by the movie's climactic dinner scene.

During the meal, Meg, the business lawyer, dares to pine for a feeling of altruism and activism she felt in the sixties. That prompts the shoe company CEO, Harold, to snap, "We were great then and we're shit now? I don't buy that." When he is challenged by his own wife, who says, "I'd hate to think [our past commitment] was all just fashion," she is literally laughed at when he begs the others to "help me with these bleeding hearts!"

The Big Chill's emblematic message was the opposite of a lamentation—it was a fist-pumping endorsement of the sixties' demise, a celebration that depicted the era's goals as unrealistic, its ethos as unserious, its politics as unsuccessful, and therefore its abandonment in favor of eighties conservatism as perfectly responsible.

That yuppie-absolving parable was irresistibly alluring, as it provided a moral explanation for yippie organizer Jerry Rubin to jump ship for corporate life, SDS activist David Stockman to become Ronald Reagan's archconservative budget director, and millions of other sixties participants to similarly discard their collegiate values for a less utopian adulthood. Indeed, if one scene sums up the yuppies' repudiation of their youth, it is the consolation Karen offers to Sam when he fears his schlocky *J. T. Lancer* television show "is just garbage" compared to his past activism.

"Not true," she says. "You're entertaining people!"

That's the same debasement of sixties values and aggrandizement of eighties culture photographed on the cover of *Esquire's* yuppie issue, captured in the chic sets of *L.A. Law* and *Miami Vice,* and forever memorialized on yuppie nostalgia outlets such as Lifetime TV. It is the same snobbery delivered by the *thirtysomething* suburbanite who joked, "If we can't have the revolution, we might as well have a great breakfast room"; and it is the same consolation Elyse offers Steven when she insists his pursuit of upper-middle-class comforts "are political acts as strong as anything you ever did back at Berkeley."

Yuppie deification in the 1980s provided America with the same "massive rationalization" that the Big Chillers momentarily worried about and then laughed off—the very rationalization that still makes denigrating the sixties seem altogether justified.

Despising the sixties is now as much a part of twenty-first century Americana as *South Park.* When in the cartoon's renowned "Die, Hippie, Die!" episode Eric Cartman combats those who "smoke pot, wear crap, and smell bad" with a loud recitation of granola-wilting death metal, we laugh with the fat little ball of spite because it is funny to watch the nation's pervasive sixties antipathy be so poignantly satirized.

However hilarious, though, Cartman's taboo humor ridicules an authentic animus—the kind typically delivered today through shrieked euphemisms like "socialist," "tree hugger," or "liberal," from snarling middle-aged white men in Fox News studios or on the steps of Southern state capitals—and these guys rarely have their tongue in their cheek. Yes, "Die, Hippie, Die!" is no laughing matter for many Americans; it is a deadly serious clarion call anchored in eighties pop culture and—as importantly—eighties politics.

The pitting of the idealized fifties directly against the tarnished sixties and then making that battle America's central political cause started right at the beginning of the 1980s, thanks to events at once calculated, chronological, and coincidental—events that symbolized a monumental changing of the guard.

In the months after the 1980 election, two central figures in sixties folklore were shoved off the American stage: John Lennon, icon of radicals' resistance to authority, was assassinated, and Walter Cronkite, forever associated with Vietnam-era truth-telling, retired from anchoring the *CBS Evening News.* Months later, *Raiders of the Lost Ark* and its fifties heroics was packing seats at movie theaters—and, of course, the Reagan Revolution was sweeping the land.

No single force more intensely crystallized these crosscurrents into a cogent fifties-versus-sixties message than this volcanic eruption of anger that equated support for conservative Republicanism with the incineration of the sixties.

The magma of resentment politics that had been simmering underground since the late 1970s exploded during the stretch run of the 1980 presidential campaign. In August of that year, Reagan channeled white rage at the civil rights movement by endorsing the racist euphemism *states rights,* an endorsement that came during a speech to a Confederate-flag-waving audience in the same Mississippi town where three civil rights workers had been murdered by the Ku Klux Klan. Days later, he lashed out at opponents of the Vietnam conflict, saying the invasion was a "noble cause" and suggesting that war critics made America "afraid to let [U.S. soldiers] win." Then in October, Reagan pitted the social conservatism of The Fifties against the secular progressivism of The Sixties by telling the National Religious Broadcasters' convention, "I don't think we should have ever expelled God from the classroom."

"These [were] implicit attacks on three of the most salient political incursions in the Sixties—the civil rights movement, the antiwar movement, and the Warren Court's invalidation of traditional political and social practices," says historian Daniel Marcus.

Not surprisingly, Reagan built his two terms around a nonironic version of the "Die, Hippie, Die!" rallying cry that Eric Cartman later poked fun at. On Capitol Hill, Reagan bashed "welfare queens" and affirmative action while pushing bills to gut the Great Society and War on Poverty programs of the sixties. On the international stage, the veteran Cold Warrior channeled his forty-year legacy of anti-communist histrionics into an arms race with the Soviets and into covert military operations against leftists in Latin America. And on hot-button social and regional issues, Reagan's administration went out of its way to wage high-profile campaigns that inherently lampooned hippies.

In the schools, First Lady Nancy Reagan's Just Say No crusade indicted sixties drug culture. Out west, Interior Secretary James Watt framed his assault on environmental regulations as a fifties-versus-sixties war to "restore America's greatness" against a green movement that he called "a left-wing cult" plotting "to bring down the government." At GOP rallies, it was all red meat: Republicans were fighting The Sixties freaks who "blame America first," as Reagan's United Nations Ambassador Jeane Kirkpatrick bellowed at the 1984 Republican National Convention.

Reagan's followers made sure to put all of this sixties bashing within a back-to-the-future narrative of fifties restoration. Speaking to a 1980s gathering of the Heritage Foundation—a conservative think tank whose very name references midcentury sentimentality—a minister said, "We're here to turn the clock back to 1954 in this country." Similarly, right-wing columnists Rowland Evans and Robert Novak said Reagan revolutionaries were trying to "return the republic to the status quo of an earlier day [that] might be fixed at 1955"—the exact year Marty McFly famously revisited.

Democrats for the most part had no idea how to respond. Walter Mondale's 1984 campaign, for instance, aired an ad that walked into the sixties stereotype by playing Crosby, Stills, and Nash's hippie anthem "Teach Your Children"—as if to say, yes, a vote for Mondale is a vote for the counterculture. Other Democratic presidential candidates such as Hart, John Glenn, and Jesse Jackson tried to lash themselves to the positive legacies of the sixties, only to get eviscerated by its negatives.

By the time Reagan was leaving office, this fifties-glorifying jihad against the sixties hadn't just become one front in scorched-earth election campaigns—it had become the raison d'être of American politics itself.

As *Newsweek* noted in its 1988 cover story on the "Sixties Complex," "Gary Hart lost his chance to be president when his admiration for the '60s style of Jack Kennedy led him to Bimini with Donna Rice [and] Douglas Ginsburg's Supreme Court prospects went down the rabbit hole after someone remembered his youthful experiments with pot." Meanwhile, Republican vice-presidential nominee Dan Quayle was a "fraternity man in the heyday of SDS, a Goldwaterite in the year of LBJ," a hippie-hating square who "smoked no dope [and] dropped no acid"—a draft-dodger who was "catalyzing" a "fundamental re-examination of the '60s" in the middle of a presidential race.

This "sixties complex," which should have been a sideshow in the face of 1988's oncoming recession and imminent Soviet collapse, quickly became the main event as George H. W. Bush's post-Reagan campaign incited a further generational tit-for-tat.

At their party's national convention, Republicans aired a Bush biopic that intertwined images of Bush's fifties heritage, sixties riots, and the supposed unity and prosperity of the Reagan years. That was followed up by Bush's acceptance speech. Standing before the nation, this Ivy League scion, Kennebunkport aristocrat and son of a U.S. Senator boldly presented his life as an up-by-the-bootstraps success story, allegedly typical of the "old-fashioned common sense" of The Fifties.

"We moved from a shotgun [house], to a duplex apartment, to a house and lived the dream," he said. "High school football on Friday night, Little League, neighborhood barbecue. People don't see their experience as symbolic of an era—but of course we were."

From there, it was on to slandering Massachusetts Governor Michael Dukakis—a genuine first-generation, up-by-the-bootstraps fifties success story—as a sixties radical. Early on, Republicans accused the Democratic presidential nominee's wife, Kitty, of burning flags at antigovernment rallies during the Vietnam conflict. Forced to respond to the baseless charges in the same demeaning language of generational warfare, she asserted that far from being a hippie in the sixties, she was actually carrying the torch of The Fifties™ by "having babies and raising a family."

Emboldened, the GOP moved to successfully portray the historical symbol of red-white-and-blue patriotism as a seditious rogue state. Massachusetts, once venerated as the colonial cradle of the nation and populated mostly by working-class fifties archetypes à la Archie Bunker—this same place was reimagined by the GOP as Haight-Ashbury circa 1967 through a campaign that slandered Boston, Cambridge, Harvard University, and by extension Dukakis as "elitist" and unpatriotic.

Most remember the last weeks of the 1988 campaign as the moment when Bush's team reached back to the anti-civil-rights backlash of fifties-versus-sixties politics with the famed Willie Horton ads. But that was only part of it. While making his television attack campaign the political equivalent of a blaxploitation film, Bush was also touring the country promoting his fifties heritage—specifically, his World War II service and what he called his "Norman Rockwell vision of America, the vision of kids and dogs and apple pie and flags on parade."

Bush's astounding come-from-behind victory, built on fifties-versus-sixties attacks, subsequently turned intergenerational low blows into the most oft-used moves in politics' Cobra Kai dojo. To truly destroy an opponent, you sweep the leg by tying him to the sixties.

This was the go-to cheap shot of the election that capped off the 1980s as a political era—the 1992 battle between Bush and Bill Clinton. Before most Americans knew anything about the Democrat's policy positions, his experience, or even his womanizing, the sixties-obsessed Republican Party made sure people knew that he had called the military draft "illegitimate," worked for George McGovern's 1972 campaign, organized a protest march against the Vietnam War during his Rhodes Scholarship days in England, and once smoked weed but "did not inhale" (a line that "made it into the national conversation overnight," as ABC's Peter Jennings chuckled at the time). By the time Clinton stumbled into the general election, *Saturday Night Live* was, quite literally, satirizing him as a tie-dyed hippie—a depiction Republicans tried to capitalize on.

In what may be history's most succinct and pure example of the

"Die, Hippie, Die!" ethos, Dan Quayle's wife, Marilyn, delivered a headline-grabbing speech at the 1992 Republican National Convention, saying, "Not everyone joined in the sexual revolution or dodged the draft. . . . Not everyone concluded that American society was so bad that it had to be radically remade by social revolution. . . . Not everyone joined the counterculture."

This didn't stop with Clinton's victory, partly because Clinton joined the fifties-versus-sixties war himself. Though grassroots activists were hoping Clinton would "go in there and redeem the sixties generation," as one 1992 Democratic volunteer was quoted in *Rolling Stone* as saying, Clinton did the opposite with his triangulating politics, deregulatory agenda, declarations that "the era of Big Government is over," and insistence that we're "ending welfare as we know it."

Two years after his election, those same sixties-rebuking themes were picked up by soon-to-be Speaker of the House Newt Gingrich, who started telling audiences that the Democrats had become a party of "traitors," "total bizarreness, total weirdness," "countercultural McGovernicks," and, therefore, the "enemy of normal Americans."

In 1996, it was Bob Dole, the World War II veteran from Kansas—thanks to *The Wizard of Oz* the geographic location most associated with prefab fantasies of fifties Americana—promising to "be the bridge to an America that only the unknowing call myth." In 2000, it was George W. Bush's campaign "to *restore* honor and dignity" to an America that supposedly had it taken away by Al Gore and his pot-smoking, Earth Day–loving sixties youth. And through it all conservative activists were steadily beating the generational drum— from Christian conservative leader Gary Bauer saying his movement was advocating "not a single public-policy goal [that] was not understood as necessary for a healthy society when Eisenhower was president," to conservative scholar Charles Murray saying America should be restored to "as it was in 1960."

Then came 2004—a contest many thought would, if not end the eighties death match between the fifties and sixties, then at least turn the tables on it. In those post-9/11 days of hypermilitarism, John Kerry, who spent the sixties getting shrapnel fired into his ass in Vietnam, was running against Bush, who spent the sixties partying at home in the Alabama National Guard. Yes, the Democrat was the war hero and the Republican was the guy who had lived the 1980s caricature of the sixties' countercultural lifestyle.

Yet, the television airwaves teemed with a doctored photo of Kerry at a sixties antiwar rally with Hanoi Jane Fonda, then with allegations that he threw his military medals at the U.S. Capitol, and then, finally, with clips of a long-haired Kerry testifying against the Vietnam War at a congressional hearing.

"It's never stopped being 1968," said one senior Bush adviser summing up the whole assault.

In short, Kerry became the 1980s cartoon of the sixties, and that was that.

With politics and popular culture becoming one and the same in the 1980s, the "Die, Hippie, Die!" crusade of the electoral arena was simultaneously amplified in entertainment.

During the mid-1980s, Pat Robertson's Family Channel joined Nick at Nite in the cable lineup, bookending its religious and political shows with black-and-white reruns from The Fifties. In 1990, there was Madonna's craving The Fifties vogue and its penchant for giving "good face." In 1994, it was *Forrest Gump* parables about The Fifties™ guy who never changes his fifties ways, being heartbroken by the hippie whose involvement in The Sixties™ results in drug abuse, venereal disease, and tragic death. In the late 1990s, it was *Swingers* and Big Bad Voo Doo Daddy resurrecting fifties bowling-shirt loungewear and big-band swing music—and now it's *Mad Men* making fifties narrow suits and thin ties cool again. And, of course, it's *Saving Private Ryan*, the *Band of Brothers* miniseries, *Castle Wolfenstein* video games, and all of the products that formed what Temple professor Carolyn Kitch calls today's "full-blown World War II nostalgia industry"—an industry whose promotion of the "good war" is used to counter bad memories of Vietnam and its sixties discontents.★

That last phenomenon exemplifies how so many of these trends,

★Writing in *In These Times* in 2006, journalist Christopher Hayes examined this World War II nostalgia industry in detail, noting it's breathtaking scope. Among

their subjective opinions and their generational politics, made the crucial jump from entertainment to news media—and blurred the distinction between the two. Recall that NBC News anchor Tom Brokaw hit paydirt in recent years by recasting himself as the planet's leading fifties auteur with a book he called *The Greatest Generation*. By definition, this now omnipotent superlative assumes a fifties generation that is *greater* than the others that followed—greater because, as Brokaw asserts, The Fifties generation exhibits "a strong sense of loyalty and service, modesty and achievement," which its offspring "were distanced from . . . during the sixties."

Now today, the 1980s has all but guaranteed that any remaining positive attributes of the sixties are kept alive—if at all—via trivialized movies about Woodstock, hippie Halloween costumes, Phish shows, The Gap's 1969 jeans line, and Ben & Jerry's ice cream. As a real political movement, sixties ardor was commodified—and therefore diluted—in the 1980s by spectacles such as We Are the World, Hands Across America, and Live Aid. These became today's Katrina telethons, Farm Aid concerts, and euphoric election rallies—causes and events that portray grassroots activism merely as momentary bursts of celebrity-driven entertainment and engagement. And in 2008, that's exactly what the Obama campaign understood so well.

Republicans that year were doing what they've been doing since the 1980s. Their convention's relentless harping on Obama's background as a Chicago "community organizer" tried to tie him to sixties radical Saul Alinsky, label his church a radical institution, portray his pastor as a black nationalist, and lash Obama to Bill Ayres of the Weather Underground. It was all part of a multifaceted effort to make the country see the candidate and his wife as Black Panthers from the sixties. And the GOP's campaign to label him a foreign-born,

---

the products he examines are "a book about veterans of the Pacific Theater called *Flags of Our Fathers*"; "a clunking Bruce Willis vehicle called *Hart's War*"; 2001's "summer blockbuster *Pearl Harbor*"; historian Stephen Ambrose's ten "books between 1994 and 2001, including a distilled history of the war for 'young readers' called *The Good Fight*"; the ongoing transformation of Tom Hanks into "a kind of WWII commemoration crusader, cutting a series of radio ads that advocated for a World War II memorial to be built on the Mall"; and what Hayes calls pure "kitsch: In 1999, *People* named 'The World War II Soldier' one of its '25 Most Intriguing People,' right next to Ricky Martin and Ashley Judd."

madrassa-trained Muslim was a way to question Obama's American-ness in a post-9/11 world, in the same way conservatives have been questioning liberals' patriotism since the sixties.★

For its part, the media amplified The Sixties whenever it could. In the lead-up to the Democratic National Convention in Denver, reporters showered a tiny protest group called Re-create '68 with undue attention. In a typical dispatch a full six months before the convention, *Politico* published a breathless story about event organiz-ers "wrestl[ing] with 1968" because Americans "are loath to revisit what they see as a disastrous time for both the anti-war movement and the Democratic Party."

A month later, the *Guardian* in the UK headlined its own story "Echoes of 1968 Return to Haunt the Divided Democrats," noting that two documentary films (*The Chicago 10* and *The Great Chicago Conspiracy Circus*) had just been released, and that *West Wing* creator Aaron Sorkin was working on a movie about Abbie Hoffman. By summer, the din had gotten so loud, *The New Yorker* published a cover showing Michelle Obama as Angela Davis and Barack Obama as a terrorist, lampooning a country fixated on trying to turn anything and everything into a vaudeville of sixties malevolence.

Obama saw the spectacle in front of him, and rather than muddle through a generational war that had been going on since the 1980s, he circumvented the battlefield entirely, repeatedly telling Americans he had no connection at all to the fight.

Obama's campaign stressed his Establishment credentials—his Ivy League résumé and his time in the Illinois legislature—before it ever talked about his brief stint as a community organizer. Obama fled from Jeremiah Wright, Jesse Jackson, and any other black leader who had roots in the sixties or sixties-esque politics. Of the Ayres connec-tion, he reminded reporters that the radical "did something that I de-

---

★Just look at the trajectory of this political tactic: Reagan implicitly questioned sixties liberals' loyalty to country in 1983 by saying they want to "place the United States in a position of military and moral inferiority." Republican Party chairman Rich Bond opened his party's 1992 convention by saying, "We are America, these other people are not America." John McCain in 2008 aired a television ad calling himself "an American president Americans have been waiting for"—the message being that Obama wasn't just un-American in his liberal beliefs, but actually not an American.

plore forty years ago when I was six or seven years old"—the message being that he was way too young to even remember the sixties. Most prominently, he packaged his campaign as a cause of transcendence that would finally end all the sixties-obsessed strife that had been roiling politics since the 1980s.

At the same time, though, Obama harnessed the surviving tatters of the activist sixties by using his media superstardom to turn his candidacy into a presidential campaign version of Live Aid—big crowds, lots of excitement, and kinda sorta that vague feeling of something momentarily Woodstocky. Through social-networking sites, blogs, T-shirts, posters, and appearances on entertainment television shows, Obama did transcend—he transcended not so much generation, but politics, becoming a powerful mass cultural brand.*

This wasn't merely Bill Clinton and the saxophone—this was a candidate so omnipresent in so many spheres that many Americans knew him by a Shepard Fairey pastel that didn't even have the candidate's name on it.

The brilliance was in the marketing. Unlike past Democrats, who tried the impossible contortion of simultaneously tying themselves to positive sixties policies (Medicare, women's rights) while distancing themselves from the 1980s image of The Sixties™ (riots, busing, drugs), Obama conjured that sixties energy by shunning ideology and promoting a pastiche "movement" that was unthreateningly fashionable, consumerist, and safe. His campaign wasn't Woodstock, it was a Las Vegas Woodstock revue—glitzy, exciting, and reminiscent, but with all the security, order, and clean bathrooms of a corporate-owned casino—and none of the danger, dirt, or commitment of old times. As Obama himself said while planning his run, he knew he could use his "fifteen minutes of fame" to be "a stand-in for that desire" by many for the gauzy glory and excitement of sixties activism

---

*Obama was actually named Brand of the Year by *Advertising Age* in 2008. In its essay explaining the award, the magazine specifically highlighted his brand's transcendence, noting it was "big enough to be anything to anyone yet had an intimate enough feel to inspire advocacy. . . . Mr. Obama somehow managed to be both Coke and Honest Tea, both the megabrand with the global awareness and distribution network and the dark-horse, upstart niche player."

without the hard-edged stands and intimidating repercussions that actually came with genuine engagement.

To be part of the Obama "movement," the campaign didn't ask you to demonstrate or stage sit-ins or mount constant pressure for the passage of legislation—you could show up with fifteen thousand other people to hear the candidate speak and then go home. To waft that sweet smell of sixties communalism without the era's corresponding commitment, you could don an Obama T-shirt, forward an Obama email, or post an Obama image on your Facebook page—and not have to think of yourself as the awful hippie you learned to hate in the eighties.

"Obama won office by capitalizing on our profound nostalgia [for] social movements [but he] decisively parted ways with [those] movements from which he has borrowed so much," wrote cultural critic Naomi Klein, noting that Obama specifically employed sixties imagery—"Pop Art posters from Che, his cadence from King, his Yes We Can! slogan from the migrant farmworkers' *Sí, Se Puede!*"

Now, during the Obama presidency, the Tea Party opposition is an exact analogue to the Reagan vanguard, all the way down to the latter-day roots of its very name—in the late 1970s and early 1980s, the *The New York Times* labeled what were then the first contemporary antigovernment/antitax revolts "modern Boston Tea Parties." Not surprisingly, the goal of today's Tea Party protesters is a return to the politics of the fifties-worshiping, sixties-bashing 1980s.

Tea Party protesters and their leaders in the conservative movement acknowledge this intrinsically in their choice of language and extrinsically in their most unfiltered declarations. For example, an essay posted on the website of FreedomWorks, the organization that sponsors Tea Party demonstrations, says protesters are enraged by "the sense that the country that they grew up in is *slipping away* right before their eyes."

House Republican leader John Boehner (R-OH) says today's Tea Party rallies are organized by people who are saying "wait a minute, this is not where we're going, *my kids and grandkids are going to grow up in a different country than I grew up in.*" It's a line that went from his lips to the rank and file's mouth, as local media filled up with quotes like the one delivered by a California protester who told her newspaper, "We're here to keep America *the way it was* when we grew up."

Glenn Beck, the Tea Party's media field general, says it is about "real outrage from real people who just want their country back"—and he's very clear that "back" means before The Sixties™. In one recent diatribe, Beck praised Joe McCarthy for "shin[ing] the spotlight on the Communist Party" in the 1950s. In another, he insisted "fifty years ago people felt happier" than they do today because today "we have less God," prompting his guest to agree by saying, "Something happened in the 1950s where everything went down . . . that's when they started taking God"—"they" being the hippies, "God" presumably being a reference to mid-twentieth-century courts barring prayer in school.

This kind of nostalgia now slashes its way through today's politics and policy debates, and its lack of connection to specific issues betrays its eighties-crafted anchor in intergenerational conflict.

"This is nothing at all to do with health care," said Tea Party leader Mark Williams in a CNN interview. "It's about this nation deviating from, or this government more accurately, deviating from this nation's legacy."

"Things we had in the fifties were better," another Tea Party leader told *The New York Times.*

"What we want is to get back to where our country was one hundred years ago," said an Oklahoma Tea Party leader on CNN.

"It's kind of a time for another Eisenhower," Bob Dole told *Politico* in a discussion about 2012 presidential candidates.

The language—"back," "real people," "deviating from," "slipping away," "the way it was," "different country than I grew up in," "legacy," "better time"—underscores the fierce yearning for a fantastical authenticity and conformity of old-time fifties America, sans the real-world downsides like lynch mobs, religious bigotry, burning crosses, chauvinism, union-busting, and smokestack pollution that plagued the mid-twentieth century. Whether or not Tea Party leaders are specifically pointing to the actual 1950s is less important than that the broader movement is advocating that bigger, 1980s-manufactured concept of The Fifties™.

The tragedy, of course, is the elimination of the kind of moderate Republicanism that once played a pivotal political, cultural, and legislative role in the real 1950s and 1960s. Conservatives today accept no compromise positions on taxes, national security, social issues, or anything else, because to Republican leaders, conceding such middle ground is akin to aiding and abetting the hippies—an unthinkable proposition, but not just to them.

Let's be honest—since the 1980s, Democrats have largely surrendered the memory of the sixties, placating—rather than challenging— the "Die, Hippie, Die!" frame. This—not just campaign contributions and corruption—explains why they have refused to champion a wildly popular Medicare for Everybody idea—they simply don't want to re-litigate the sixties. This too helps explain why President Obama has refrained from cracking down on exorbitant Wall Street pay—he fears being called a "redistributionist" and being lumped in with the sixties radicals he spent his campaign fleeing from.

No doubt, the dynamic is most pronounced on issues of war and peace. The 1980s lampooned antiwar activists as a modern sixties counterculture disciples whose unrealistic pacifism endangered the country. Yet, rather than using the Iraq War to change this image and remind the country that the Vietnam protests of the sixties stopped a similarly wrongheaded policy, most congressional Democrats simply validated the sixties hatefest by supporting the invasion, fearing "no" votes would get them tarred and feathered as hippies, just as they had been in the Reagan years. When Iraq turned into a Vietnam-like quagmire, the process just picked up where it had left off—even as the antiwar movement was proven correct, conservatives nonetheless vilified the left as hippies driven by blind anger and ideology, and Democrats responded by essentially agreeing.

A back-and-forth during the conflict's bloody months in the summer of 2007 tells the tale. Writing in the *The New York Times Magazine,* war proponent Michael Ignatieff summed up the hawks' argument, saying that while progressive antiwar protesters may have "correctly anticipated catastrophe," they did so "not by exercising judgment but by indulging in ideology." Putting forward Jeane Kirkpatrick's "blame America first" argument, he added that antiwar voices are motivated by a sixties-hatched belief that "America is always and in every situation wrong."

That same week, influential Democratic politicians made head-lines echoing the same argument. In a story headlined "Centrist Democrats Take on Left over Iraq," *Politico* reported that leading law-makers warned the supposedly all-powerful hippies that they would risk losing the presidency "if they present a face to the public that is too angry in tone" in opposing the war.

The volleys and countervolleys exposed what, on the merits, should be unimaginable oxymorons. To continue a perpetual back-lash, conservatives since the 1980s have developed a vested interest in preserving the memory of a 1960s that was, in reality, the historic apex of progressive achievement. At the same time, progressives now flee from that era as if it were their dark ages. Even more absurd, the right, through the Tea Party movement, now uses the very sixties protest tactics that ended the fifties to make its case for ending The Sixties and bringing back The Fifties—for fear of a new sixties they believe is on the horizon.

"As a veteran of the political and cultural wars of the Sixties," wrote Norman Podhoretz, "I knew from my own scars that no mat-ter how small and insignificant a group the anti-Americans of the left might for the moment look to the naked eye, they had it in them to rise and grow again."

As an author and magazine editor, Podhoretz grew into a Mt. Rushmore–size political icon in those early years of the 1980s when the fifties-versus-sixties war for the American memory was just be-ginning. Yet, that quote is not from one of his Reagan-era mani-festos, but from an article he published in the 2007 *Wall Street Journal*—an article that came a year after CNN's election website asked, "What Would Alex P. Keaton Do?" and two years after Eric Cartman warned that if South Park doesn't "do something fast" about the hippies, it will be "the end of all life as we know it."

In that way, Podhoretz's eighties-infused rhetoric of generational combat was as up-to-date and as culturally resonant as the latest iPhone commercial.

And that is the problem.

PART II

THE JUMP MAN CHRONICLES

George Orwell authored *1984* in 1949, which suggests the British novelist was a Jedi Knight, or, at minimum, a Jedi Knight in training. For Orwell's prophecies were at least as prescient as Luke Skywalker's apocalyptic visions in *The Empire Strikes Back.*

Though his home was not in a galaxy far, far away, Orwell was writing his novel a long time ago—sixty years before America was consumed by the Great Summer Camp Color War of the 21st Century. It would be a Manichaean struggle whose marquee blood feuds would make the Socs-versus-Greasers rumbles seem downright friendly. The late 2000s would kick off the age of the Keith Olbermann–Bill O'Reilly vendetta, the era of screaming matches between Glenn Beck followers and Ed Schultz listeners—the epoch of bleating competitions between media shepherds and their particular flocks of sheeple and brawls between zombie disciples of this or that television ayatollah.

Orwell had forecasted it all when he envisioned a future in which "the whole climate of thought will be different."

He wrote, "There will be no thought, as we understand it now. Orthodoxy means not thinking—not needing to think. Orthodoxy is unconsciousness."

Giving Orwell's premonition the same benefit of the doubt that, say, the History Channel affords Nostradamus's predictions, it's no stretch to believe this Englishman had the Force. We may not be fully "unconscious" but we're damn close.

Consider, as just one example, the loyalty oaths of the Palinites and the Obamabots.

During a packed 2009 Palin appearance at a Borders bookstore in Columbus, Ohio, supporters professed fervent love of Alaska's half-term governor and proudly acknowledged that their fealty is rooted in theocratic worship. In a YouTube video attracting more than a million page views in its first month, one Palinite after another was asked to explain his or her devotion, and one Palinite after another openly admitted it had nothing to do with any of Palin's positions on issues.

One said Palin "stands for what America is," then offered up no specifics.

Another said, "[Palin is] someone who can make a difference," adding that, on particular policies, "I don't know . . . I guess I never really thought about it."

Still another cited Palin's "fairness and realness," but when pressed to cite a Palin legislative position epitomizing those traits, the Palinite said, "I can't think of a policy."

The Obamabots can be just as mindlessly entranced—the difference is that some of them are famous.

"I'll collect paper cups off the ground to make [Obama's] pathway clear," says actress Halle Berry. "I'll do whatever he says."

"[Obama] walks into a room and you want to follow him somewhere, anywhere," says actor/director George Clooney.

Condensing this pro-Obama sentiment, Craigslist founder Craig Newmark told *Fast Company* in 2008, "I'm still struggling to articulate what it is about [Obama]," finally blurting out, "I see him as a leader."

If these were Branch Davidians in Waco, Texas, talking about David Koresh, they might find themselves at the barrel-end of FBI assault rifles. Instead, this is what America has become: a miasma of mobs hidebound by our respective color captains.

As I said, this isn't unconsciousness, but it's close. More and more of us are outsourcing critical contemplation, vesting complete faith in others, and letting them do the thinking for us. It is an anti-ideology ideology—ideological devotion to individual deities, almost wholly irrespective of the deities' belief systems. And while this is happening most prominently in politics, it is also happening everywhere else.

Look and listen carefully to your interpersonal interactions—and you'll inevitably find a warehouse full of talking points shrink-wrapped by the celebrity gods to whom we have bequeathed our cognition.

We read from Oprah's book-club list and get life tips from her magazine. We imbibe Perez Hilton's gossip and pass on Matt Drudge's headlines—and we do it all without question. We look to Jim Cramer and Suze Orman for investment buy and sell orders, we turn to Deepak Chopra or Dr. Phil for happiness directives—and when we discuss and disagree, we marshal our arguments like Chris Matthews or Lou Dobbs or Rush Limbaugh, depending on whichever icon we've decided to idolize in any given week.

In our celebrity polytheism, What Would Jesus Do? is now What Would the Famous Do?—whichever of the famous we choose to follow.

Is this new? Well, no and yes.

No, role models are not new, they've been around in some shape or form since cavemen anointed tribal leaders. And, no, it's not new for millions of people to loyally worship individuals they've never met or seen in person.

But, yes, there is something new about the intense, personal quality of today's hero worship, and how it is leading a (theoretically) democratic society to back a social religion that sees merit only in the Great Individuals. It is a pernicious dogma whose ancient forms began their modern-day conquest in 1984.

Just as Jedi Master George Orwell predicted.

THE JOHN GALT OF OCEANIA

It could easily be a matter of timing, where society was looking for something positive. —MICHAEL JORDAN EXPLAINING HIS CELEBRITY ASCENT, 1998

People are very hungry for something new . . . I think I'm a stand-in for that desire. —BARACK OBAMA EXPLAINING HIS POLITICAL ASCENT, 2006

Nineteen eighty-four was more artificially predestined to become an Important Year than any other single twelve-month period before it, and not just because it was the first year in a half century the United States would host the Summer Olympic Games. Nineteen eighty-four was, well, *1984*. Thanks to the folklore erected by Orwell's novel, the mystical expectations of real-life 1984 became an early-eighties version of the doomsday hoopla that would later surround the other potential human-created Armageddon, Y2K. Things were bound to go bonkers in both years, if only because the buildup was so great.

Ultimately, though, only 1984 delivered exactly what was promised.

Nineteen eighty-four set the conditions for an almost perfectly calibrated system of cultural indoctrination—one that blended Orwellian totalitarianism with Ayn Rand's notions of individualism. From then on, newspeak and doublethink taught America to worship single, godlike individuals above all else.

On the campaign trail that year, Ronald Reagan's aides were busy using his reelection effort to make the office of the presidency into a full-fledged Mt. Olympus, portraying the sole commander in chief "as the personification of all that is right with or heroized by America," as one strategy memo noted.

In the publishing industry, bestseller lists teemed with self-aggrandizing tomes by larger-than-life personalities such as Lee Iacocca and Jane Fonda. In Washington, a new Ayn Rand Institute for public policy was finalizing its plans to seed high school and college curricula with pro-individualist propaganda. In Hollywood, *Lifestyles of the Rich and Famous* began celebrating plutocrats' wealth and power, while Arnold Schwarzenegger was launching *The Terminator* franchise by portraying an indestructible antihero who singularly carried the planet's destiny in his steroid-engorged arms.

But most significant of all, in packed arenas, Michael Jordan was making his National Basketball Association debut.

Jordan's professional career became the tale of the broader cult of the individual, in part because his personal story fit so easily into every individual-glorifying myth the biggest Ayn Rand fan could ever hope to invent.

The most prominent narrative projected Jordan as Howard Roark from *The Fountainhead,* the underdog whose steadfast fidelity to self-expression is ultimately vindicated as moral and just and good. Here was the working-class kid from North Carolina, who initially gets cut from his high school basketball team, then sees his individual talents inhibited by an overly structured college offense at University of North Carolina, then gets relegated to one of the NBA's worst franchises, the Chicago Bulls. When he tries to finally break out, exploit his personal talents, and create a unique image in his rookie year, league officials first ban him from wearing his specially designed red-and-black shoes, and then jealous veteran players George Gervin, Magic Johnson, and Isiah Thomas allegedly conspire to ruin his first All-Star game by preventing him from getting the ball. Soon, NBA coaches are criticizing him for destroying old-fashioned team sports. One Bulls assistant says bluntly, "We would be a better team . . . if he didn't try to score every time he touched the basketball."

Nonetheless, Jordan perseveres, and the Roarkian sensibility doesn't kill him or his team—on the contrary, he goes on to win five Most Valuable Player awards, six NBA championships, and billing as the greatest athlete in sports history. His success convinces the league to drop its team-oriented traditionalism in favor of individualist spectacles such as dunk contests and marketing schemes that promote high-profile games as one-on-one, star-on-star grudge matches. Jordan even convinces the skeptical coaching class that hyperindividuality is a virtue. One coach of a Bulls rival waxes nostalgic about watching Jordan refuse to pass, then "put the ball on the floor and [go] through all five" defenders on his own. Another Bulls coach trumpets the "Archangel Offense," whereby teammates are ignored; "we give Jordan the ball and say, 'Michael, save us.'"

Out of this mythology came the spin-off tale of Jordan as Rand's Atlas, who easily lifts the weight of the entire sport of basketball on his shoulders.

In this legend, the phenom enters an NBA that saw seventeen of its twenty-three teams lose money in his rookie year, a league whose biggest championship games were only being aired on tape-delayed television after local stations' late-evening news broadcasts. Jordan's squad is a particularly bad joke; suffering from poor attendance, the Bulls are worth just $19 million in his rookie season. But after four years of the shooting guard's gravity-defying performances, the Bulls have tripled their audience and the NBA is crediting Jordan alone for one-third of the league's entire attendance increase. Within the decade, the Bulls will be worth close to $200 million and the NBA will be one of the most successful sports businesses in the world.

Yet, if all of this happened only in the vacuum of athletics, Jordan would be a source of fascination just for hard-core NBA fans, but not much for most of the rest of us. If his spectacular play had merely lifted his own sport out of its financial doldrums, he'd be Dr. J or Willie Mays or Jack Nicklaus—well remembered by the elder generation, but a cultural afterthought. If he were merely history's greatest basketball player, the religion of individual deification may have remained buried in Rand's thousand-page books, only to be studied by those bug-eyed freaks in college Objectivist clubs, and narcissism's favorite question, "Who is John Galt?" would never have become "Who is Michael Jordan?"★

But that's where Nike comes in.

In 1983, Nike "displaced Adidas as the world's top athletic footwear company," wrote *Washington Post* sportswriter Jim Naughton. It was a seemingly impossible achievement, and one that Nike founder and CEO Phil Knight had been dreaming about since the early 1970s when he first began selling running shoes at local track-and-field meets in Oregon. His firm's rise was truly spectacular. For the five years prior to overtaking Adidas, Nike was reporting an annual earnings growth rate of nearly 100 percent, leading *Forbes* magazine to list it as one of the most profitable businesses in America.

But Nike stumbled just as quickly as it ascended. By the middle of 1984, the company was tanking. In a scathing article headlined "Nike Loses Its Footing on the Fast Track," *Fortune* said Nike's "earnings are dismal, management is shuffling, and many wonder if founder Philip Knight has run out of breath."

That's when Knight made two bold business decisions. First, he signed Jordan to a five-year, $2.5 million contract, a stunningly large payout for an as-yet-untested rookie. Knight then shifted his company into what journalist Donald Katz calls "a hero business," applying "in full measure his hunch that if a company could somehow manage to project everywhere his own incorrigible sports-fan's urge to ascribe glory to gifted athletes, the results could be magical."

Within a year, things took off. Nike launched its seminal "Flight 23" ad, which played the sound of jet engines behind a shot of a slow-motion Jordan soaring split-legged toward a basket. The image of this silhouette flying through the air—now immortalized as Nike's

---

★For those who didn't go through a silly late-teens/early-twenties Ayn Rand phase, "Who is John Galt?" is the opening line of Rand's book *Atlas Shrugged*. In the story, Galt is an inventor and industrialist—the quintessential Great Individual. Rather than succumb to any notions of "common good," he organizes other Great Individuals to go on strike and withhold their singular greatness from society, so as to show the world that it can only survive by letting the Great Individuals do whatever they want, and never subjecting them to any communal or team sensibilities.

ubiquitous orange "Jump Man" logo—was interrupted only by Jordan's dunking the ball and by a tagline equating his talents with superhuman powers of levitation. ("Who says man was not meant to fly?" asks the final voice-over.)

This initial spot incited pandemonium. In the first year, 2.3 million pairs of Air Jordan basketball shoes were sold, generating $130 million in sales (for comparison, Naughton notes that "had Air Jordan been its own company, that figure would have made it the fifth-largest sneaker firm in the world").

Then came the second, even more famous round of ads in 1986 that not only exalted Jordan as sports' embodiment of Yahweh, but went further by sanctifying Jordan worship. The new campaign featured actor/director Spike Lee as a fictional Jordan cultist named Mars Blackmon (a character from Lee's inaugural movie, *She's Gotta Have It,* who is so obsessed with the Bulls star he refuses to take off his Air Jordans, even during sex). In various ads, Mars pays homage to Jordan, and the most famous of the series has Jordan calmly asserting that his basketball superpowers are a product of individual, nontransferrable awesomeness.

"You sure it's not the shoes?" Mars stutters.

"No, Mars," Jordan repeatedly replies, as if to say, "It's just that I'm superhuman."

In Jordan's first few years of NBA play, sportscasters started calling him Superman in Shorts, *Sports Illustrated* said he was prepared to "conquer the world," and local reporters often described him in biblical terms (one Chicago newspaper, for instance, demanded the Bulls hang "a halo atop Chicago Stadium" because "the celestial Jordan alleviated Chicago's spiritual malaise"). Meanwhile, his fellow players early on referred to him as "Jesus in Nikes" or even the Almighty himself.

"I think he's God disguised as Michael Jordan," said Larry Bird after Jordan poured in forty-nine points against the Celtics in a 1986 play-off game.

Air Jordans were this deity's most visible talisman—the Jesus sandals for walking on water or, as it were, dunking from the free-throw line. The shoes would go on to not only lift Nike into the financial stratosphere, but also synthesize an entire new basis for advertising.

Nike's creative team—and soon, most of Corporate America's—would come to believe that in the 1980s and beyond, "the unique selling proposition" (the industry term for the central marketing pitch) for all products would revolve less around the specific widgets being peddled than the image of the single godlike individuals selling them.

To be sure, both the marketing of iconoclastic individuality and its symbiosis with endorsement-based advertising had been around well before Nike. Jordan's Jump Man was, in a sense, just an offspring of 1954's Marlboro Man, the original blend of hard-sell marketing and ode to "rugged individualism." And all of Nike's hyperindividualized spokesgods of the Jordanized 1980s—whether Charles Barkley, John McEnroe, Andre Agassi, Bo Jackson, Wayne Gretzky, or Jordan himself—were walking in the footsteps of Arnold Palmer, the golf star who in 1960 became the first client of sports-marketing behemoth IMG and whose endorsement contracts pioneered "the idea of an athlete as a global brand," as *Golf* magazine noted.

But there was a difference: Jordanization was happening in the culture and technology of the 1980s, not Palmer's 1960s.

As Jordan began his rise in 1984, other Big Brothers and their Nike-like support systems were already helping him and Nike transform modern society into a version of Orwell's absolutist vision. Only rather than emulating the dystopian communism of *1984*'s Oceania, America was organizing itself around a devout reverence for hyper-individualism.

The sporting world—Jordan's home—was the first to succumb. As the Bulls guard gained prominence, his feats were rewarded by ESPN. In the 1980s, the then fledgling network and its show *Sports-Center* was beginning to addict fans every night to highlight clips of individual brilliance, creating "a culture where players practice their dunks instead of their back-door passes," as sports columnist Neil Hayes wrote.

At the same time, in communities all over America, baseball, basketball, and football fans of the 1980s started compiling their own lists of individual professional players and tabulating those players' com-

bined stats in various categories (RBIs, blocked shots, etc.). The winner of these "fantasy sports" competitions were those whose lists had
the highest totals, regardless of whether the players' real teams were
winning or losing games. The result is the now billion-dollar fantasy
sports industry, and a universe of fans more loyal to individual athletes
than to those athletes' teams.

The attitudinal shift was most prominently reflected in the way
the image of basketball changed in the 1980s. For instance, the early-
1980s NBA of fully functioning, multiple-passes-per-play teams such
as the Celtics and Lakers gave way to a late-1980s league that grabbed
fans' attention with Jordan acolytes refusing to pass and trying to
score every basket on their own.★

Even fictional basketball retrospectives like the 1986 classic
Hoosiers were compelled to attract audiences via Jordanization—or, in
its specific case, Jimmy-ization.

The film begins with Hickory, Indiana's high school coach Norman Dale making a point about selflessness when he benches a player
for violating his "four passes before a shot" rule. It's a heartwarming
moment, yet Dale is rewarded for his stand with a hysterical
pitchfork-wielding throng of local fans mounting a Tea Party–style
campaign to get him fired. Only when he abandons the rule and lets
his star forward Jimmy Chitwood go Jordan does the mob abate and
the team start winning. By the time Jimmy is breaking triple teams
against towering opponents in the championship game in Indianapo-
lis, a movie that began as a quaint lesson about the benefits of sharing
and team play becomes a parable celebrating individual selfishness and
the value of the Archangel Offense.

Sports, though, were just the beginning of Jordanization. In the
1980s, CEOs were being Jordanized on the covers of magazines and
in bestselling autobiographies as titans that saved entire industries.
Self-help gurus were starting to build Jordanized empires based on a
promise that loyalty to them and to their manufactured philosophies

---

★Such an approach now—predictably—dominates the lowest tiers of amateur basketball. As one high school coach told the *Seattle Post-Intelligencer* in 2001, grade-
schoolers have picked up "the idea that as long as they can establish themselves as
individuals, they'll make the pros."

could be the key to spiritual salvation (more on this in the next chapter). And for those who weren't being saved by the gurus, there were newly Jordanized religious prophets such as Jerry Falwell, Pat Robertson, Jimmy Swaggart, and Jim Bakker harnessing the burgeoning megachurch phenomenon to create a dual Christian worship of both Jesus and celebrity televangelists.

And, of course, the 1980s were becoming the Golden Age of Hollywood's Jordanized action heroes.

The stars of the 1980s screen weren't cowboys circa 1850, they were ultramodern comic-book caricatures such as Arnold Schwarzenegger's *Commando,* Richard Dean Anderson's *MacGyver,* and Carl Weathers's *Action Jackson.* These were characters with their own particular Jordan-esque supertalents.* Even the old Rocky Balboa was reimagined as a Jordan of boxing. Whereas 1970s Rocky from the series' first two installments had been a slow, regular-guy-with-heart *Sopranos* character living out of a dingy row house, 1980s Rocky from *III* and *IV* was reintroduced as a fleet-footed Lou Ferrigno–esque bodybuilder living in a robot-catered mansion and using his supertalents to singlehandedly save the free world from the Soviet menace.†

Unlike the Shanes and Lone Rangers of old, these 1980s heroes' ultracontemporary language, inflections, sartorial choices, and plot challenges made them seem just as genuine, current, and thus worthy of mass worship as those CEOs, self-helpers, and blow-dried reverends. These heroes' aura of authenticity was only helped by the president of the moment, Ronald Reagan. Having once portrayed silver-screen paladins as an actor, he became the real-life commander

---

*In case you're wondering, Schwarzenegger was an elite military agent, Anderson could save the planet with a paper clip, and Weathers could broil criminals with a grenade launcher and the pithy one-liner: "How do you like your ribs?"
†Interestingly, 1990s Rocky of *Rocky V* would be portrayed as the star who has everything unfairly stolen from him, and then beats up the guy who steals it from him. And then the 2000s Rocky of *Rocky Balboa* is a sad old man trying to reclaim a piece of his superstardom. In other words, Rocky goes from moron with nothing, to rich celebrity superstar, to rich celebrity superstar who loses all his money and is angry, to rich celebrity superstar who spends his old age desperately trying to get back some of his money and fame. So basically, Rocky is Wesley Snipes or Donald Trump . . . or America.

in chief and was prone to referencing 1980s movie fantasies when discussing issues facing the White House.★

Jordan, of course, became the best-known avatar of hyperindividualism—the John Galt of the new Oceania—because his specific talents weren't up for interpretation. Some might find CEOs boring, self-helpers and televangelists fake, action movies ridiculous, and chest-pounding politicians ideologically odious. But everyone could see that a guy with a forty-eight-inch vertical leap and a thirty-plus points-per-game average was divine. He was able to take the cult of the individual global with something previously unavailable to icons in his position: synergy.

Starting in the mid-1980s, Jordan's agent, David Falk, inked multiple endorsement deals that not only put Jordan's face everywhere, but everywhere *at the same time*. This idea of building global brand unity between an endorser's cross-platform and cross-product exposure would become the norm in advertising.

Nike naturally led the way, first launching an Entertainment Promotions department to seed movie and television scripts with Nike products, then teaming with Hollywood superagent Michael Ovitz on a joint "sports entertainment" venture, and ultimately launching Niketowns—giant stores that were one part retailer outlet, one part tourist-trap museum, one part Jordan shrine. As the 1980s became the early 1990s, journalist Donald Katz noted, "Murphy Brown's new baby would sport Air Jordan stuff, Whitney Houston would exercise in Nike gear in *The Bodyguard,* the young hero in *Free Willy* would bound around in a big black pair of Nikes, and Demi Moore would wear a pair of Tinker Hatfield's Air Huarache shoes in *A Few Good Men.*"

By the end of the 1980s, Nike had matured from a mere sporting goods company into one of the world's chief manufacturers of popular culture itself. Such a reach would make history's totalitarians blush. The firm wasn't just in the business of painting pastel murals of its Dear Leaders on the crumbling façades of apartment buildings in a

★Two examples: During the 1985 hostage crisis, Reagan said, "I saw *Rambo* last night. Now I know what to do next time this happens." In his 1986 State of the Union speech, Reagan described the coming years by parroting Dr. Brown's line from *Back to the Future:* "Where we are going, we don't need roads."

few isolated locales. Nike in the 1980s was the first to plumb the potential of individualism planetwide.

For Jordan, the corporation's chief sovereign, this meant no longer being just a basketball player. The face of Nike, Coca-Cola, McDonald's, Quaker Oats, Wilson, Sara Lee, Hanes, Ball Park franks, and Chevrolet (among others), he would end up one of the first to reach today's Famous for Being Famous classification.

In the U.S., polls at the end of the 1980s confirmed he had become the nation's most widely-recognized athlete, and its most-wanted product spokesman. In the early 1990s, when African American kids "were asked in a national survey to name two or three people they most admire, Michael Jordan tied with God," reported the Associated Press. On the world stage, Jordan achieved a similarly unimaginable cult status—the kind that would lead *The Washington Post* to call the Bulls star "the most famous man on Earth," and Chinese schoolchildren to list him next to Communist Party leader Zhou Enlai as one of the two greatest men in history.

"In cities he has never visited," the *Chicago Tribune* reported, "billboards [of Jordan's face] loom with no identification necessary."

Whereas such ubiquity had previously been achieved only by antiquity's theological patriarchs, Jordan, Nike, and a nine-figure-a-year ad budget were able to manufacture that reach in the post-modern 1980s. The Bulls guard and the Big Brothers in business and politics who followed him discovered that they could be Jesus sans Christianity. They could reign by selling a different but equally transcendent messianic religion—the cult of the individual.

In 2008, Michael Jordan appeared in a Hanes television ad. Ten years after his retirement from the NBA, he is shown at a country club getting into his car and driving away from Charlie Sheen as the actor fawns all over him à la Mars Blackmon. Other than Sheen at one point calling him "MJ," Jordan is not named or even vaguely linked to anything that might help identify him. Because Jordan is sitting down and alone in a sports car for almost the entire ad, you can't even detect his imposing height, which might have given him away as a hoops star.

And yet, whether you were a huge NBA fan or hated basketball, whether you were old enough to remember Jordan's 1980s rise or too young to remember his last rickety years with the Washington Wizards, the Hanes ad makers knew he *needed* no identification. Even more important, they knew Sheen's fawning required no explanation either. Michael Jordan, said the commercial, is a real-life god who deserves to be worshiped not only by regular peons, but even by famous people like Charlie Sheen—enough said, or, in this ad's case, unsaid.

As in so many of Jordan's original Nike ads, the Hanes spot devotes little time to the actual product being peddled. Though underwear is what the company wants you to buy, the "unique selling proposition" is almost exclusively Jordan, just as the unique selling proposition for everything now—clothes, electronics, cosmetics, religions, political ideologies—is almost always the sellers, regardless of what they are actually peddling.

Today, whether it's an athlete, actor, pundit, religious leader, New Age guru, or politician, we buy the celebrity pitchman, not the product being hawked—because that eighties-born cult of the individual has told us that the only way to make decisions is to trust, follow, mimic, and take orders from gods.

"You can't explain much in sixty seconds, but when you show Michael Jordan, you don't have to," said Nike CEO Phil Knight, explaining why his company spends three times as much on marketing its heroes as it does on basic capital expenditures. "People already know a lot about him. It's that simple."

Whereas we used to merely get our basketball entertainment from the actual Michael Jordan, we now also get our money advice from the Michael Jordans on CNBC; our ideological marching orders from pundit Michael Jordans on MSNBC and Fox News; and our psychological boosts from self-help Michael Jordans on late-night infomercials. For everything else, we rely on one of the two Chicagoans to rival Jordan for individual brand dominance: Oprah.

The other Chicagoan, of course, is Barack Obama—the reigning MVP of a politics and government that was first Jordanized in the 1980s.

Though the grassroots tumult of the 1960s began strengthening the notion of collective "people power," the general Jordanization of

1980s society helped permanently solidify America's political faith in the so-called Great Man Theory of History—i.e., that history is really the story of a few larger-than-life Michael Jordans (or Ronald Reagans, George W. Bushes or Barack Obamas), not mass movements of workmanlike Horace Grants (or local activists). The individualized mythology of Reagan as a Jordan was the start of this; so too was the depiction of our international enemies as Jordanized archenemies.

Since the 1980s, our politics have focused solely on the president, and both parties have vested more and more power in the executive branch as if it were the Almighty—as if the In God We Trust motto on our currency specifically references the presidency.

The constitutional theory of a "unitary executive"—originally a fantastical concoction of power-drunk Reagan aides—is now completely mainstream, as presidents issue signing statements and executive orders that overturn laws and start wars without congressional approval. If the legislative branch or local governments are considered at all in public policy matters, they are considered in the same way Michael Jordan once described his Bulls teammates: as a "supporting cast," and nothing more.

Consequently, whenever anything bad happens anywhere in America, we reflexively expect an immediate solution from whichever President Jordan is in office. When that president can't instantaneously break the opponent's defense and hit a basket, he inevitably appoints a special czar as his own personal mini-Jordan to try to dunk on the problem. And if anyone asks any questions or mentions such things as constitutional separation of powers (that is, something that mandates more of a governmental team game), the President Jordan and his entourage simply brag that he has every right to do whatever the hell he wants.

Recall that it was Vice President Dick Cheney who said public opinion "doesn't matter," and it was George W. Bush who, after once saying "God wants me to be president," asserted that he didn't need to justify his actions to anyone.

"I'm the commander—see, I don't need to explain," he said in 2002. "That's the interesting thing about being president. Maybe somebody needs to explain to me why they say something, but I don't feel like I owe anybody an explanation."

For the most part, Jordanized America doesn't just grudgingly tolerate this, we extol it by blessing it with the same labels we imparted to Jordan for his athletic attributes: "courage," "charisma," "resolve," "toughness," "strength," or—the biggest cliché of all— "leadership."

Consider the reaction to Bush's address to Congress in the immediate aftermath of 9/11. *The Wall Street Journal*'s Peggy Noonan called it "a God-touched moment and a God-touched speech," while *The Weekly Standard*'s Fred Barnes said "the stage was set for Bush to be God's agent of wrath," and the public rewarded Bush's subsequent power grabs with record-high approval ratings. If there's any criticism of any of this, it's usually shrouded in (albeit biting) satire, such as when *The Onion* in 2006 headlined a story "Bush Grants Permission to Grant More Power to Self."

Sure, many Americans ended up hating Bush for what he did with his authority, just as many Bulls fans hated Jordan for opting to end his career on the Washington Wizards. But many still want a Michael Jordan as president—a reality, by the way, that George W. Bush's successor has long understood and capitalized on.

For all his happy talk of "bottom-up" politics, movement building, and community organizing, Barack Obama's political genius has been understanding the Jordanized world he occupies. While his rivals have run scrappy electoral and legislative campaigns against him by appealing to voters and special-interest constituencies on the basis of ironclad issue positions, Obama (like Reagan before him) often pitches his personal intangibles (pragmatism, optimism, bipartisanship, etc.) as his unique selling proposition. Tellingly, he tends to eschew concrete positions when he can, not only because he's afraid to accidentally flip-flop or because he doesn't want to gum up fragile negotiations, but also because his fundamental sales pitch to the public has always been about how his individual talents—regardless of his positions—can best serve the nation.

Obama is not shy about this self-image. During the presidential campaign, he told aides that, "I'm a better speechwriter than my speechwriters, I know more about policies on any particular issue than my policy directors and I'll tell you right now that I'm gonna think I'm a better political director than my political director." When a staffer later sent him an email saying, "you are more clutch than Michael Jordan," Obama replied, "Just give me the ball."

It's back to Jordan's Archangel Offense: Give the legislative rock to Barack, and he alone will find a way to lead Team America to victory.

As much as this starstruck worldview subverts notions of grassroots people power, shared responsibility, and political accountability, it is precisely how Americans looked at Obama during his presidential run. His appeal wasn't about specific promises, position papers, or policies—it couldn't have been when so many of his senate votes on issues contradicted his presidential campaign promises and when so many of his position papers and policy statements conflicted with his major donors' agenda. Obamamania was instead about voters desperately wanting an idol—any idol. And when Obama bragged of being a Jordan-esque leader in a society that was "hungry for something new," he was (unconsciously) echoing the original Jordan himself. As the Bulls star said in 1998, his rise to deity status in the 1980s came about because "society was looking for something positive."

Newspeak is rarely so honest—or true.

In a perfect world of simple challenges, benevolent elites, meritorious celebrity, and discerning voters, the hyperindividualism created in the 1980s might have served us well. An Oceania ruled by John Galts might be great if life were as straightforward as a professional basketball season and we all made the Bulls roster as part of the "supporting cast." His Airness did win six championships, after all.

There're just three problems.

First, the real world is not perfect—and it is far more complex than running an NBA offense. The 1980s may have taught us that every obstacle can be overcome by emulating this or that Michael Jordan and by defeating this or that Jordan nemesis. But there's no way for one guy to instantaneously block the shot of, say, a 9 percent jobless rate.

Structural unemployment is not Bill Laimbeer, the Detroit Pistons center. It may be as persistently maddening and merciless as Bill Laimbeer, but it is not him. It's not even Detroit's entire twelve-man "Bad Boys" squad of 1989 that gave Michael Jordan so much trouble.

It's structural unemployment—a personal, community, and national problem, and therefore even the most skilled phenom can't just swat it into the backboard in a twenty-four-second possession. Same thing for international affairs. Bush and the neocons were clearly convinced that if they just went coast to coast and dunked on Saddam Hussein, the entire Middle East game would be won. But Middle East strife isn't Bill Laimbeer, either. Life is just more complex than that. Indeed, despite media portrayals to the contrary, our world is not as simple as a basketball game—and that goes even for the parts of life like foreign policy that can seem most like a game.

Second, most of the Michael Jordans we worship aren't Michael Jordan, they are more like the notorious Jordan wannabees of the 1980s, and we can be seriously disappointed when we build our personal franchises around them. Some such as CNBC's Jim Cramer are only Dominique Wilkins, possessing some skill and pizzazz, but not the kind of ability to bring you a financial championship. Others such as speculator Bernie Madoff are Orlando Woolridge—stars who put up huge numbers for a time, but whose ball-hogging selfishness ultimately wrecks their teams. And still others such as Senator John Edwards are Roy Tarpley—blockbuster talents whose stunning off-court recklessness nonetheless destroys both their career and the dreams of their fans.

Finally, even if some of the individuals we worship *are* Michael Jordans, a nation of Mars Blackmons will be doomed by the polarization of its own cultism.

Being a fan of Michael Jordan's in the 1980s was comforting because you always had someone awesome to root for, and always had opponents to root against and demonize. Same thing when we outsource basic cognition to the other Michael Jordans in our lives—and now especially the political ones.

More and more of us no longer study up on public issues. We trade in the responsibilities of democratic citizenship for the pleasure of a superfan's hysterical enthusiasm by simply backing whatever is being pushed by the political Michael Jordan we like, and opposing whatever his or her archenemy supports. We don't pay attention to local democracy, we don't pay attention to local issues. We flock to Obama rallies and cheer when he says "change." We mob Sarah Palin book signings because she "stands for what America is."

We are clashing mobs of rabid fan clubs boorishly following the feuding Jordans at the very top, without regard for what the competition is all about—and to dare challenge the Jordans' motives, rationales, or ideas is to commit a thoughtcrime.

Bulls fans barely questioned Jordan's gambling, conservative activists don't ask about Sarah Palin's flip-flopping, and libertarians don't wonder why Glenn Beck supported the massive bank bailout—they all just obediently worship. In the same manner, Obama volunteers don't question the president's broken campaign promises or demand he legislate any specific program. They are, as *The Washington Monthly* wrote, simply "united by their affection for the president—no matter what he chooses to do in office."

Organizing for America, the Democrats' grassroots outfit that emerged from the 2008 campaign, openly advertises this cult-of-personality thrust as its entire mission, saying that its "primary focus is to advance the president's agenda"—and as the last weeks of the 2010 health-care debate proved, millions of liberals obediently follow right along regardless of what that agenda actually is.

For months, polls showed that a substantial percentage of Americans who opposed the Democrats' health care proposal did so specifically because they believed it wasn't progressive enough. But the moment Obama put his imprimatur on the bill and insisted on its passage, polls showed a complete evaporation of that liberal opposition.

It was yet another reminder that in the Oceania created by the 1980s, mindless orthodoxy in support of our Jordans rules the day, and as Orwell said, "Orthodoxy means not thinking—not needing to think" because "orthodoxy is unconsciousness."

The result is a cloud of counterproductive confusion and contradiction increasingly divorcing us from what's actually going on in the real world. Many self-described "anti-war" Democrats now cheer on their Jordan president as he escalates militarism in the name of ending military conflicts, just as antigovernment Bush voters trumpeted their Jordan president as the Republican used state power to trample civil liberties in the name of democracy.

We've heard it since 1984—war is peace, freedom is slavery, and ignorance is strength.

Except that they're not.

JUST DO IT

What we need to convey is just go ahead, just fuck it.
—ADVERTISING EXECUTIVE DAN WEIDEN, 1987

There is no reason why [Wall Street speculators] shouldn't earn $1 million to $200 million a year. —DEMOCRATIC PARTY DONOR, 2009

Between Googling yourself, texting what you had for lunch, posting a description of your recent bathroom break to your Facebook page, and blogging your feelings about the latest episode of *The Hills,* it is possible you stumbled across a 2008 article noting that physicians now expect 6 percent of Americans to come down with Narcissistic Personality Disorder at some point during their lifetime.

It seems at first like a shocking number—one in every seventeen people will at some point be obsessed with himself and his own perceived mega-awesomeness to the point of debilitation. That's a bigger pandemic than the more famously glamorized mental illnesses like obsessive-compulsive disorder and bipolarity. And when we're talking about Narcissistic Personality Disorder, remember, we're not talking about the normal senior-year-of-college pomposity that gets routinely crushed in that demoralizing freshman year of the rest of your life. We're talking about clinically diagnosable arrogance: incessant public bragging, long evenings staring at giant mirrors, perhaps the obligatory sex tape posted on YouTube—in short, self-lust at medically hazardous Paris Hilton levels.

But are you *really* shocked?

If you look around the world—and even just your own little slice of the world—I'm betting you can pick out four examples of unadulterated narcissism without so much as lifting a finger. I'm sitting in a coffee shop on a Wednesday afternoon in a midsize, noncoastal American city, and within a few feet of my table there are at least that many. A fiftysomething screaming into his cellphone doesn't care that he's disturbing everyone around him; the woman sitting next to me is frantically blogging about her favorite new movie as if the world is waiting for her opinion—and she's blogging about *Julie and Julia,* itself a flick about the success of a narcissist and her blog; a pair of tweens just cut the checkout line; I just got a spam email for penis enlargement, perhaps the most narcissistic medical procedure ever devised; and the Amazon.com page I'm looking at suggests I buy either the hot new rerelease of *The Fountainhead* or order Karl Rove's *Courage and Consequence: My Life as a Conservative in the Fight.* No shit, an autobiography in which the author—not a reviewer, but the *author*—labels *himself* courageous on the cover.★

A lot of this is harmless, of course. There's no great damage done

---

★Two additional thoughts: (1) Full disclosure: I'm a politically progressive person and, therefore, I'll be the first to admit I'm—ahem—not a fan of Karl Rove. More full disclosure: I'm not citing Rove here because I dislike his conservative politics—I'm citing him here because this choice of book title is an intense example of raw narcissism. As *The Atlantic*'s Matt Cooper suggests, it may be unprecedented in modern publishing history. "Who uses *courage* in their own memoirs?" Cooper asked in a dispatch trying to honestly answer that question. "John F. Kennedy famously wrote—or had written for him—*Profiles in Courage,* about other people. John McCain called his memoir *Faith of My Fathers,* not *I'm So Brave.* Not really sure a direct-mail guy turned political consultant turned top White House adviser should call himself courageous." The closest Cooper could find was the autobiography of former senator Max Cleland, the Vietnam vet who lost three limbs in the war and was then rewarded with attack ads equating him to Osama bin Laden. But even that work only included a subtitle reference to the triple amputee's "finding the courage" to survive war, bodily injury, and a vicious campaign indicting his patriotism—hardly a narcissistic statement. (2) If Rove's book does well and this book doesn't, perhaps it's a lesson that I should have named this book "I'm Awesome: Why You Should Bow Down Before Me And My Amazing Courage."

when your buddy keeps spamming you with pictures of him getting lap-danced and shitfaced at a Vegas strip joint. The future of the republic is not (directly) threatened by a sharp increase in sales of Karl Rove's book, nor is it imperiled even by a rise in the number of assholes who drive over the median to cut in front of traffic at the freeway's clogged exit. And sure, the planet will survive—and maybe even thrive—in spite of the rise in cosmetic surgeries.

There is, however, potential for damage when the achievement of fame and kingly wealth becomes the central organizing objective of society. The future of the republic is threatened by a sharp increase in the number of people who care only about themselves; and the earth's ecosystem may not survive the scourge of smog-belching and gas-guzzling "me" culture that first spread in the late 1970s and 1980s.

This modern blast of narcissism all but defines America now, an ugly symptom of a deeper infection that predates the rise of the Internet.

That's an important point: The most common—and idiotic—way to explain contemporary narcissism is to do what *Time* did in 2006 when the company bought 7 million (!) pieces of reflective Mylar, taped them onto their magazine covers like a mirror, declared "You" the Person of the Year, and then exclusively blamed the Internet for the rise of epidemic vainglory.

Though *Time*'s cover was taking a momentary break from its ridiculous practice of naming one human out of the planet's 6 billion Person of the Year, it was only taking that break to celebrate narcissistic self-absorption—self-absorption that is the predictable product of stunts like a Person of the Year award.

The Jordanized deification of the individual and further suggestion that self-help can turn us into divinities ultimately gave rise to the virus in the machine. It is what created today's narcissistic symptoms we all know and (allegedly) hate—today's me-first, fuck-everyone-else reflex, kill-or-be-killed instinct, and belief that strangers will be interested in what our latest blog-posted daydream is about.

That's what modern narcissism really is—a pernicious mix of qualities defined by three words that start with *self: selfishness, self-absorption,* and *self-importance.* In contemporary parlance, it may be known as asshattery, douchebaggery, or dickwadishness, but it's all one or another spin-off of a virulent egomania spawned in the 1980s.

Sure, the Internet may amplify and publicize much of it. But the clicking, typing, and tweeting are just electronic expressions of a deeper everyone-for-himself ideology manufactured way before the rise of interconnected computers. Indeed, before Bay Area Apple geeks were perfecting early Macintosh prototypes and before suburban-Seattle Microsoft nerds were polishing off their first versions of Windows, Nike's industrial-strength hero factory right between them on Interstate 5 was already marketing a three-word operating system of twenty-first-century conceit.

Judging by the quasi-religious idolization of various late-twentieth-century superstars, the 1980s succeeded in grafting a feudal sensibility onto a country that had, for years, clung to a democratic dream. For sure, America has never *actually* been a functioning democracy. Since the country's founding, the rich have been buying elections and a permanent aristocracy has been exerting undue influence on the government. But up until the mid-1980s, many Americans clung to that civics-class ideal—that one-person-one-vote, up-by-the-bootstraps vision of a democratic society in which middle-class folks playing Monopoly over beer and pizza were (or, at minimum, could be) as important as that Mr. Peanut–looking guy in the top hat.

That changed in the 1980s when an explosion in economic inequality coincided with a strain of ad campaigns, political reporting, and entertainment products teaching us that, in reality, there are Kings such as Jordan, Reagan, Schwarzenegger, and Iacocca who possess mystifyingly great powers. Then there are the Rest of Us who can't possibly hope to be those sovereigns—the faceless serfs who supposedly have no value beyond our willingness to worship the Kings, whether via the ballot box, ticket booth, or television set.

None of this was said out loud. As both eighties class divisions and one strain of eighties pop culture implicitly reinforced ninth-century notions of stratification between The Venerables and The Vassals, another strain of equally powerful eighties propaganda offered a sliver of hope. There, in the midst of exploding economic injustice,

Reagan's Republican Party was still paying homage to American Dreams sculpted with commoner-makes-it-big tales and rags-to-riches hagiography.

During tough times America has always told itself these two stories: the more authentic one about gross inequality and ruling classes, then the feel-good fantasy about those wrongs being overcome by personal heroics. But eventually the mundane realities of systemic oppression evoke a pining for something different—something aspirational, something more concrete than myth, something full of (here's that political cliche) hope.

Then comes the inevitable reckoning.

In the Gilded Age, when a nation of faceless chattel finally got sick of Rockefellers and Carnegies and Horatio Alger dime novels, that meant pitchfork-and-picket populism—a revolt of farmers, miners, immigrants, and sweatshop workers calling bullshit on the industrial revolution, throwing out the old order, scaring the bejesus out of the moneyed establishment, and eventually bringing about the more communitarian progressive era and New Deal. By contrast, in the similarly stratified economy of the late 1980s, the same moneyed establishment was better equipped to thwart that kind of uprising when it looked ready to commence. Instead of early-twentieth-century-style compromise or class appeasement that might address real blue-collar grievances, the 1980s forcefully doubled down on the propaganda side of the equation and bet the house on an aphorism that could have been Horatio Alger's own: Just Do It.

The particular philosophy of Just Do It and its myriad spin-offs would bridge the gap between crushing economic realities and meritocratic American Dreams by harmonizing the 1980s Cult of the Individual with our old-fashioned populist fantasies of fairness, opportunity, and equality.

Athletics was the natural messenger. Newly commercialized but still infused with ancient folklore, professional sports in the 1980s was emerging from its economic doldrums and moving toward eventually becoming the tenth-largest industry in America. Many of its stars boasted rags-to-riches stories, and, more fundamentally, sport has always been "understood to be a meritocracy—the best man or woman plays and wins a contest," as NFL linebacker Dave Meggysey has written.

Nike capitalized on the moment with its 1987 "Revolution" ad, a prototype of the subsequent Just Do It invention. Instead of yet another comic-book-worthy campaign showing only sensational athletes and their dazzling skills, this spot mixed black-and-white clips of those superstars with shots of regular people of all ages participating in amateur sports. The image of a child shooting a layup became the image of Michael Jordan gliding toward the basket. Film of John McEnroe stressing out over a professional tennis match was interspersed with film of sweaty amateurs doing the same in their own contests.

Soon after the "Revolution" campaign was launched, Portland adman Dan Wieden convened a discussion with Nike executives about how to continue moving from heroizing individual stars and into the even more lucrative business of personal inspiration. "What we need to convey is just go ahead, just fuck it," he said.

The impulsive refrain embodied a sentiment already well on the way to epitomizing the 1980s—a bloody shirt of oversimplified conceit originally waved by 1983's *Risky Business* when Curtis Armstrong (later of *Revenge of the Nerds* fame) famously pressed Tom Cruise to "every now and then say, 'What the fuck.'"

From Booger to Wieden to Nike to the profanity censors—and on out to the planet as one of the most trenchant slogans of all time.

Just Do It—its brilliance was its balance. It stipulated that the Kings were worthy of worship—Jordan was still a god, Reagan still royalty, Oprah still an oracle, and the Great Man Theory of History still intact. At the same time, it also implied that lesser individuals toiling in obscurity could realistically hope to one day claim Great Man status for themselves.

Knowing that the most gripping marketing requires extreme caricatures, Nike wasn't content to just show regular people overcoming regular challenges, it emphasized superhuman achievement with the wild-eyed exuberance of a *Ripley's Believe It or Not* episode. The first Just Do It spot, for instance, featured Craig Blanchette excelling at basketball and racquetball—and then revealed that he's actually in a wheelchair. Another ad focused on a formerly obese smoker and drinker who won the New York City Marathon. Yet another spot starred Walt Stack, an octogenarian who runs seventeen miles a day.

Nike designed the spots as personal fantasy. Watching the ads, viewers both see the possibility of taller, thinner more muscular versions of themselves and glimpse the prospect of individual superstardom—as long as they Just Do It.

"Although at one level all we're really doing is selling sneakers, there's something about athletic shoes and clothes that can inspire," Wieden said in an interview as Just Do It ads first proliferated. "There's an honest-to-goodness belief that we're selling something that will help people. It's like an ancient call to a way of life."

Undergirding all of the Just Do It–infused campaigns would be a message telling the audience that the difference between success and failure is individual desire and willingness to persevere through impossible trauma. Sometimes this would be explicit, such as the Nike ad glorifying a runner vomiting at the end of a victorious race and a boxer absorbing a blood-splattering jab. Other times this would be implicit, such as Nike's Tiger Woods ad in the mid-1990s about how he had to work extrahard to break into a sport that still used "courses that I am not allowed to play."

But no matter the commercial, Nike was always saying that you could reach superstar status as long as you pledged to just do it.

In a 2009 CNBC interview, adman Dan Weiden correctly pointed out that the late-1980s idea of Just Do It "spread like a disease," and it did so because it sloganized a zeitgeist that was already metastasizing throughout the political and popular culture.

Since claiming victory in the 1980 election, Ronald Reagan's Republican Party had been banging the American Dream's drum about a country where there are supposedly no economic or racial barriers—a *Secret of My Success* nation where with a little hard work, anyone, even a short mailroom clerk named Brantley, can make it all the way into the boardroom and into Helen Slaters's pants. That set the stage not only for Nike's late-1980s explosion, but for a whole new self-centered, individualistic, and ultimately narcissistic theme in marketing.

For example, at the same time Nike was formulating its Just Do It ads, Reebok was launching its own "U.B.U." campaign. In 1989, *The New York Times* reported that Burger King was the latest to join "a raft of advertisers that are shifting their attention from products to attitudes and updating the countercultural anthem, 'do your own thing.'" Soon, E★TRADE, first founded in 1982, was dumping ad dollars into a "Fire Your Broker" campaign, a financial-industry equivalent of Just Do It that looked "to capture the sentiment of empowerment," as its CEO put it.

This focus on the possibility of individual ascendance was buttressed by the eighties' celebration of money as the ultimate morality. From the glorification of yuppies to the proliferation of get-rich-quick schemes, "The eighties were about acquiring—acquiring wealth, power, prestige," said Republican political strategist Lee Atwater, the Karl Rove of the 1980s.

Out of Hollywood came a slew of productions—from *Trading Places* to *Silver Spoons* to *Falcon Crest* to *Dallas* to *Dynasty*—that were celebrating extravagant wealth, and the subterfuge necessary to accumulate and preserve it. These were capped off by the aforementioned *Secret of My Success,* the movie *The New York Times* called "as frank a tribute to unbridled ambition as the movies have produced in years," especially in how it "regards business success as utterly glamorous, uncomplicated and in no way incompatible with standing up for the things one believes in."

"It was in the eighties that the American Dream began to take on hyperbolic connotations, to be conflated with extreme success: wealth, basically," wrote *Vanity Fair*'s David Kamp. "The representative TV families, whether benignly genteel (the Huxtables on *The Cosby Show*) or soap-opera bonkers (the Carringtons on *Dynasty*), were undeniably rich. 'Who says you can't have it all?' went the jingle in a ubiquitous beer commercial from the era, which only got more alarming as it went on to ask, 'Who says you can't have the world without losing your soul?'"

But maybe the best example of the intensifying trend came from the military. In 1981, with Vietnam having shaken the public's confidence in the armed forces, the army started its "Be All That YOU Can Be" campaign. Explicitly about individual self-empowerment, that motto eventually went on to be the even more self-focused "Army of One" slogan. The martial messaging was aided and abetted by Hollywood hits such as *An Officer and a Gentleman, Stripes,* and *Spies Like Us*—the former showing the navy summoning individual heroism from a common misfit, the latter two portraying pairs of jerk-off ne'er-do-wells pulling themselves up by their bootstraps, winning the Cold War for the United States, and—of course—becoming international celebrities. Indeed, even in depicting the regimented confines of absolutist institutions such as the army, the 1980s were insisting we could all be iconic superstars—as long as we Just Do It.

The pitch worked. You could see the returns in Reagan's popularity and in the military's significantly improved public-approval ratings. You could see it in reports that Nike was both selling lots of sneakers and receiving tens of thousands of letters and phone calls from citizens saying the motto had inspired them to leave abusive spouses, try harder at their jobs, and perform Good Samaritan heroics. And you could see it in the booming self-help industry—an industry whose very moniker, *self-help,* is a synonym of Just Do It.

Today this industry is so omnipresent that it's hard to imagine American culture ever existing without it. It's inside every bookstore that now has a self-help section, embedded in a television world that increasingly teems with personal-motivation programming, and woven throughout an Internet that often seems like a vast do-it-yourself guide. But the early- and mid-1980s are widely regarded as the big bang moment for this self-centric universe.

In 1982, Scott Peck's *The Road Less Traveled,* considered a foundational text in the modern self-help canon, first hit the bestseller list. A year later, sales of self-help monographs were accelerating so quickly that *The New York Times* created a separate bestseller list for "Advice Books." In one more year, the Federal Communications Commission would relax television advertising rules in a way that permitted the proliferation of infomercials, the high-octane fuel of the modern self-help machine.

Anthony Robbins's story tells it all. In 1986, Robbins penned his first bestseller, called *Unlimited Power,* and within the first five years of broadcasting infomercials, he reportedly sold $120 million worth of audiotapes. In recent years, he's been called the $80 Million Man, a reference to his annual salary.

Robbins is one pillar of an industry that today is estimated to be worth $10 billion in annual revenue. That industry at the end of the 1980s had somewhere between 12 and 15 million Americans actively involved in nonprofit self-help groups, and today those figures are even higher. Self-help is so sprawling that it now includes everything from the Oprah-style talk-show-as-support-group programs that started in the 1980s, to business books to life-coaching seminars to extreme-makeover reality TV.

"We are the new televangelists," Robbins's infomercial producer says.

In the obituary of one of the industry's founders, you can see how self-help was, and remains, fundamentally rooted in the Just Do It philosophy.

"We alone have the power within us to solve our problems, re-lieve our anxieties and pain, heal our illnesses, improve our golf game or get a promotion," *The New York Times* quoted the Reverend Eric Butterworth in his 2003 death notice. Butterworth, whom the *Times* called one of the early "leaders" of the self-empowerment move-ment, had offered that summary of the self-help idea in 1987, but he could have said it today because it's the same idea that still defines both the self-help industry and Americans' larger worldview.

Let's stipulate that even though the 1980s significantly intensified the Just Do It ethos, that ethos is far from an exclusively 1980s phenom-enon. It has been a part of the American lexicon in some form for the country's entire existence. Phrases such as *rugged individualism, anyone can grow up to be president,* and *land of opportunity* are all earlier presen-tations of the 1980s three-syllable endorsement of self-sufficiency. You get the sense that had he thought of it himself, Ben Franklin might have just as easily scrapped his Join, or Die refrain in favor of Just Do It's aspirational theology.

But in the last quarter of the twentieth century, this theology came to dominate in a way it never had, and not just because Nike came up with the perfect trio of words. The 1980s saw the theology uniquely amplified by the ahistorical rise of ostentatious celebrity, hero-worship culture, and the attendant promise of divine rewards that never before existed.

To Just Do It in the 1780s meant starting out as a junior bootblack or seamstress and after two decades of backbreaking work, getting rich as the owner of a tannery or tailor shop. That in turn meant a steady diet of grade-B mutton, perhaps a servant, and a spouse with (if you were really lucky) most of his/her teeth who bathed once a week—but still sweaty-ass, no-air-conditioning summers, freezing-cold winters, and zero indoor plumbing.

To Just Do It in the 1880s meant risking life and limb for years on the frontier, hitting the gold-rush jackpot, and maybe becoming well-known in a brand-new state. That might translate into a nice patch of land for you and your family, ownership in a mining corporation staffed by quasi-slaves—but also the constant threat of being killed or maimed by (A) your quasi-slaves, (B) cowboy bandits, or (C) the Indians you had to slaughter to obtain the gold in the first place.

By contrast, to Just Do It in the 1980s meant starting out as Bud Fox and over a few months of light office work becoming Gordon Gekko, which in turn held out the guarantee of five-star restaurants, your own entourage of personal staff and security, mansions, private jets, renown in the world's opulent capitals, and, of course, nightly sex with the dentally perfect and impossibly leggy Darryl Hannah.

Considering how the American Dream changed from one envisioning local notoriety, decent lamb meat, and a butler into one promising global fame and Robin Leach's "champagne wishes and caviar dreams," it's easy to see why America's age-old aspirational theology began transforming in the 1980s from a noble ethic of self-sacrifice into a justification for narcissistic self-absorption and selfishness. The promised rewards for Just Doing It became so great, and the multimedia exhortations/rationalizations to Just Do It so pervasive, we became obsessed with Just Doing It without regard for anything else.

With Nike ads playing on loop in the background, the self-help industry didn't only grow into a multi-billion-dollar industry,

Lifestyles of the Rich and Famous didn't just become *MTV Cribs,* Michael Jordan didn't merely get replaced by Tiger Woods, and Ronald Reagan didn't simply become George W. Bush. The entire country became exactly what Tom Wolfe and Christopher Lasch predicted in their works: a "me" nation dominated by an entire "culture of narcissism"—one with significant downsides.

As the 1980s became the present, personal debt skyrocketed both because of declining wages, and because of the added pressure to "keep up with the Joneses" in an ever-more-garish society. Meanwhile, participation in civic organizations dropped precipitously. Between 1980 and 1995, the number of Americans who said they attended even one public meeting (PTA event, town hall meeting, etc.) declined by 33 percent, and between 1985 and 1994, active participation in community organizations dropped by 45 percent.

Some of that can be explained away as the product of economic hardship (lower wages forced more people to sacrifice social time to work longer hours, unions were crushed by antilabor employers, etc.). But there's ample evidence that much of the change had to do with an attitudinal shift toward self-absorption.

For instance, at the same time participation in public and community-oriented institutions and causes started declining in the 1980s, participation in the self-help industry started skyrocketing. So it wasn't just a matter of time being lost, it was also a matter of time being diverted into more self-centric activities.

Same thing for the "we're all in it together" notions of solidarity. Princeton University researchers found that "virtually all" the decline in unionization during the 1980s "seems to be due to decline in *demand* for union representation," not decline in union opportunities (although that was happening too, thanks to corporate union-busting campaigns). Importantly, the decrease was not necessarily because workers started internalizing negative 1980s caricatures of unions as corrupt, but because in the 1980s workers increasingly abhorred the idea of interpersonal solidarity.

"The young worker thinks primarily of himself," wrote one leading labor economist at the beginning of the decade. "We are experiencing the cult of the individual, and labor is taking a beating."

In politics, this narcissism came to be expressed as support for more and more economically punitive politics. The social safety net, once the sign of a compassionate and civilized country, began being ridiculed by Republicans and nascent "New" Democrats as a wasteful handout, serving only to hold individuals back from achieving their dreams of millionaire-dom. Foreign aid to impoverished countries, a tiny fraction of the national budget, started being criticized as a handout to the undeserving. The poor, once viewed as unfortunate casualties of inequality, were attacked—by Democrats as lazy, and Republicans as selfish. And the politicians leading the charge, whether crusading Reaganites or end-welfare-as-we-know-it Clintonites, were (and are) rewarded with election victories for their stands.

Technology certainly played a role in this rise of selfishness and greed in the eighties, not only in the way that the Internet today gives us all our own platform, as *Time* asserted in 2006, but also in the way it started isolating us from each other. Those green screens and electronic ticker tapes and hulking RadioShack TRS-80 computers featured in *Wall Street* were the beginning of all the newfangled financial instruments that ended up distancing people from the human consequences of their greed.

Beginning in the 1980s, electronic trading detached the buyer from the seller, complex derivatives insulated the investor from the company, CDOs sequestered the lender from the borrower—in other words, the decade constructed a system that allowed us to rip each other off without fear of having to look at the ramifications of our actions. Safely sequestered behind antiseptic numbers, legal clauses, and information-age anonymity, individuals consequently started finding it far easier to rationalize a kind of unbridled avarice that they may previously have shied away from.

Taken together, the trends show a 1980s America deliberately replacing its we're-all-in-this-together activities and worldview with a Just Do It conceit that viewed any requirement for personal sacrifice as an obstacle to personal achievement and a roadblock on the way up Mt. Olympus.

For those who lived through the eighties, the decade's move away from a sense of community may have seemed less like a genuine social phenomenon than a matter of personal perception. As the 80s generation experienced the natural journey from idealistic youth to more jaded middle age, many probably concluded that the world wasn't changing—it was just more self-centered than they previously thought. However, the feelings of young people today suggest that the decade did indeed initiate a radical and enduring shift in societal attitudes.

Consider the landmark 2007 study of more than sixteen thousand college students over the last twenty-five years. Psychology researchers report that two-thirds of students notched above-average scores on the Narcissistic Personality Inventory in 2006, a whopping 30 percent more than in 1982. Students themselves are quite self-aware about this: As *USA Today* reported, a 2009 poll by the author of the book *The Narcissism Epidemic* found two-thirds of college students saying "their generation was more self-promoting, narcissistic, over-confident and attention-seeking than other generations."

The increase is reflected in the economic attitudes of young people: A Higher Education Research Institute report released in 2010 found that three-quarters of college freshmen said being "very well-off financially" was their top goal—a record high in the study's four-decade history, and a 22 percent jump since 1980. Additionally, in UCLA's 2007 report, more than two-thirds of students said they were attending college specifically "to be able to make more money"—a 27 percent increase from 1976.

Yes, Gordon Gekko ambitions and Just Do It narcissism have replaced Peace Corps dreams and Save the Children altruism, even for the "best and brightest" who were once renowned for their noblesse oblige. With brand-new *Atlas Shrugged* reprints undoubtedly stuffed in their briefcases, two in five Harvard seniors in 2008 said they had lined up jobs in consulting and finance. These kids aren't making such career choices in a vacuum. They are a product of a social ecosystem whose air is now vanity and whose water is now selfishness.

How does the resulting narcissism infect everything on a mass scale? In sports, it's LeBron James nicknaming himself King, holding an hour-long television special about his decision to leave the Cleveland Cavaliers, and then explaining his basketball philosophy by saying, "It's not about sharing, you know, it's about everybody having their own spotlight." In business, it's bankers who "feel there is no reason why they shouldn't earn $1 million to $200 million a year [and] don't want to be held responsible for the global financial meltdown," as one Wall Street fund-raiser told *The New York Times* in 2009. In the words of *Rolling Stone*'s Matt Taibbi, it's "pop culture priests filling the population with shame and nervous self-loathing to the point where (Americans see) anyone who isn't rich and famous, or trying to be, as a loser."

In politics, this manifests itself in myriad ways. It's a Republican president responding to 9/11 by telling everyone not to brace for collective sacrifice, but to instead go shopping. It's a Democratic president reacting to the biggest oil spill in history with a declaration that "Americans can help" not through collective forfeiture, but by going on vacation and "continuing to visit the communities and beaches of the Gulf Coast." It's populist rage directed at anything that reeks of altruism on the grounds that while individuals need to Just Do It for themselves, they shouldn't have to chip in to any kind of program that helps others Just Do It too.

In short, it's Glenn Beck.

Not surprisingly, this product of the 1980s brands himself as a Just Do It success story—the alcoholic-turned-teetotaler who revived himself via the 1980s-born self-help boom, the "rugged individualist" who has become the most prominent proselytizer of narcissism in contemporary history. "I feel like I need to keep saying that word so it stays in the front of your and everybody's mind—individual, individual, individual!" he wrote in a typical 2009 screed on Fox News' website.

Beck has been rewarded with a huge following and he, Rush Limbaugh, and the rest of the 1980s-molded icons who still dominate the radio dial have baked their 1980s narcissism into everything. They've gone beyond *Ghostbusters II*'s quintessentially 1980s refrain that "being miserable and treating other people like dirt is a God-given right"; like their idol Ayn Rand, the Becks cast selfishness as a moral responsibility.

"We're not all in this together," Beck says. "It's our independent spirit that has pulled us out of tougher jams than the one we're in now."

Beck is a symptom of a symptom. He's the itchy, pus-bloated pimple on a butt rash of cynicism—the same cynicism we see when major political candidates can't even be taken seriously when they dare float the notion of pitching in. Since Walter Mondale was thoroughly humiliated in 1984 for challenging Just Do It narcissism by demanding rich people pay a little more in taxes, the "ask not what your country can do for you" idea has become a mantra of electoral suicide—whether it was an independent-minded John McCain in 2000★ being crushed by voters for begging Americans to "serve a cause greater than themselves" or Howard Dean in 2004 being laughed off for saying the country needs "to make common sacrifice for the greater good."

But it's not just in the abstract realms dominated by faraway talk-radio hosts and politicians—narcissism is right in our boring daily lives.

It's the teenager who screams into his cellphone during the movie and the short guy enjoying the extra legroom of the exit row while nonetheless leaning his airplane seat back without regard for the tall guy right behind him. It's the perennial stories of people getting injured, or even killed, during Black Friday stampedes into toy stores. It's that Beverly Hills asshole speeding his luxury Hummer past a homeless vet during a $4-a-gallon gas crisis and that Upper West Side schmuck complaining about property taxes while New York City slashes social services to the indigent.

And, maybe most irritatingly of all, it's reality TV.

You can argue that this now preeminent genre was never meant to be a product of or tribute to the narcissism that first began in the 1980s; you can argue that it was the cost-cutting side effect of an unplanned late-eighties screenwriters' strike and the raw expression of innocuous voyeurism. You can argue this because one set of reality TV enthusiasts cite *Cops* as the first reality TV show. It debuted on Fox in early 1989 during a Hollywood writers' walkout and became an immediate sensation. From the stumbling-drunk dudes in their

---

★Please note that I draw a clear distinction between the "independent-minded John McCain" of 2000 and the lockstep-Republican-hack John McCain of 2008.

beer-stained wifebeaters, to the screaming old ladies in their voluminous polka-dot nightgowns being dragged out of their tenements, to the officers' mustaches and yellow sunglasses—audiences were uncontrollably drawn to the grotesquerie of unvarnished authenticity.

Then again, another faction of cultural archaeologists carbondate reality TV's two big bangs to pure Just Do It–ness—specifically, to Merv Griffin's 1979 creation of *Dance Fever* and Ed McMahon's 1983 launch of *Star Search*. Both shows' raison d'être was individual aspiration to fame and fortune. On the former, celebrity judges on a *Saturday Night Fever*–esque set rated amateur dance couples in dance-offs emceed by actors Deney Terrio and Adrian Zmed. On the latter, amateur singers, models, comedians, and dancers endured multiweek competitions and creepy, sometimes ogling interviews with a panting McMahon for a $100,000 prize and the chance to become—as the show's title says—a star.

Though the *Cops*–versus–*Dance Fever/Star Search* debate will continue among entertainment historians, it's clear both types of eighties reality shows made significant contributions to today's pedagogy of narcissism.

The voyeuristic legacy of eighties institutions like *Cops* can be found in today's most narcissistic clichés—in the grainy celebrity sex tapes that have become a standard Hollywood credential, and in the constellation of cable programs that film amateurs from the documentarian's fly-on-the-wall perspective. Most of these shows do not overtly push the Just Do It message (for instance, watching the Hulkster in *Hogan Knows Best* take his wife on a romantic weekend in a Hummer limousine in no way suggests you could one day be a ripped, three-hundred-pound monster). However, almost all of them revolve around blatant attention freaks, people so self-important, arrogant, and supercilious that they've invited cameras into their lives to film their every move.

Ultimately, the centrality of narcissists (*The Osbournes, The Girls Next Door,* etc.) and the preposterously contrived social settings to stress their narcissism (*Road Rules*) is what separates reality television from documentary. And because these narcissists gallivant around in a seemingly *Real World,* we are led to believe that such attention-starved arrogance is perfectly normal, acceptable, tolerable, and, in fact, desirable.

As for the contest shows that came out of the 1980s, they sow the aspirational seeds of narcissism. When *Dance Fever* became *So You Think You Can Dance* and when *Star Search* became *American Idol,* television was simply boosting the decibel level of a message telling Americans that in each of us there may be a Michael Jordan. These programs are even more powerful than Nike's personal-fantasy commercials. We don't have to fantasize through suggestive image juxtaposition anymore. Each week, we get to actually watch no-name nobodies just like us turn into famous celebrities right before our eyes—and it's mesmerizing.

When we watch Susan Boyle, the frumpy old maid with the cat, suddenly become a superstar singer, and when we see *Survivor's* Elisabeth Hasselbeck rewarded with a permanent commentator spot on ABC's *The View,* our mind's eye thinks it's gazing into a looking glass, one whose reflection says those "champagne wishes and caviar dreams" are right there for the taking, if only we too Just Do It.

"Dude, what's wrong with a little inspiration?" said a friend of mine when I told him about my ideas for this chapter. "Seriously, what the hell's wrong with society telling people they can get ahead if they put their heads down and do whatever it takes to succeed?"

It's true, we all need inspiration, and many of us outright pine for it—hence American office products (disproportionately advertised in airplane catalogs) emblazoned with "man in the arena" quotes and a whole line of cheesy motivational posters, like my favorite one, the one showing a guy rock climbing on some absurdly steep cliff, and the words underneath him screaming, "PERSEVERANCE: What the mind can conceive and believe, it can achieve."

But inspiration—even contrived Hallmark inspiration—is not blind faith. Being moved to work toward realistic goals is great. But just because you can "conceive and believe" doesn't mean you "can achieve," no matter how many times the culture tells you otherwise.

As we get older, most of us come to terms with life's limits. We learn that we're probably not going to make it as a professional basketball player, that we're probably not going to be president of the United States, and that trying to scale Himalayan rock faces without some serious training isn't "perseverance"—it's idiocy. In other words, we mature, and in the process we discover that the most cartoonish forms of Just Do It create "something that nobody can live up to," as even Nike CEO Phil Knight admits.

But by the time this happens, our brains and worldviews have already been rewired, and they continue to be rewired throughout adulthood. Sure, we don't believe we're going to be an NBA star, but many of us do believe we'll be *some* kind of star one day, as long as we muster Jordanesque work ethic and Barkley-esque toughness. Those oft-repeated dictums—"putting the nose to the grindstone," "whatever doesn't kill you makes you stronger," "if you will it, it is no dream," "what the mind can conceive and believe, it can achieve"—they're all telling us that in their own way. And they continue to morally rationalize selfishness the way Just Do It first did back in the 1980s.

This goes a long way toward answering some of society's most vexing questions involving those three *self* words that define narcissism, *selfishness, self-absorption,* and *self-importance.*

What's the matter with Kansas, you ask? Why do laid-off blue-collar workers in flyover country vote against politicians who want to raise millionaires' taxes? Why, since the 1980s, have these so-called Reagan Democrats started "voting against their own self-interest?" Because in their mind, it's not "against their own self-interest" at all. Regardless of the statistically slim possibilities, many look in pop culture's mirror and still see in themselves a future millionaire, just as they saw a millionaire when they first looked into that mirror back in the 1980s. And when they're a millionaire, they're not going to want to have to pay slightly higher taxes.

Why do so many Americans vehemently oppose campaigns to create a universal health care system? Why do so many get so angry about the federal budget's minuscule amount of social safety-net spending? Why do so many still channel Reagan and insist, as one conservative protester recently told *The New York Times,* that America is plagued by "a welfare class that lives for having children" and collecting a public handout? Because irrespective of the structural economic forces that have created crushing poverty, our culture of inspiration, aspiration, and self-help has been telling us that the only people who could possibly need that kind of community assistance are layabouts, loafers, and leeches who refuse to Just Do It.

Why aren't Americans more willing to deal with climate change or reduce consumption of natural resources? Because the most severe consequences of global warming and a depleted planet will be experienced first by foreigners whose poorer countries can't protect themselves from floods and droughts—and then by future generations after we're dead. Sure, Dick Cheney allows for the idea that "conservation may be a sign of personal virtue," a personal choice by some nice people. But he was quick to insist that "it is not a sufficient basis for a sound, comprehensive energy policy" because it would require collective sacrifice that might get in the way of our individual narcissism. And much of America agreed with him. Why give up the SUV and the McMansion? Why not Just Do It?

But, then, what does "doing it" now mean?

Even if you believe that America is a meritocracy—even if, as my friend asserted, everyone has the chance to "put their heads down and do whatever it takes to succeed"—the definition of "succeeding" has been laced with narcissism thanks to the eighties.

After Wall Street melted down and the government gave trillions of our tax dollars away to speculators to cover their losses, there were few mass protests—and none that made a damn's worth of difference. The bankers who had destroyed the economy soon went back to paying themselves billions in bonuses, only now financing them with public money. More telling, the superrich felt free to flaunt their narcissism without fear of a backlash. With one in four kids on food stamps and with unemployment at 10 percent, one Wall Streeter told *The New York Times* that Congress should oppose executive pay caps because "$500,000 is not a lot of money," while a major Democratic Party donor said, "The investment community feels very put-upon"—the same "investment community" that got $12 trillion in taxpayer-financed bailouts.

Far from railing on this kind of gluttony, the media joined in to promote it. In typical dispatches, *The New York Times* published an article insisting that half a million bucks a year "can go very fast," while *The Washington Post* headlined a piece "Squeaking By on

$300,000" and lamented the plight of those in the top 1 percent of income earners.

That economic bias is only the beginning. Inside the media, success no longer means solid reporting or creativity, it no longer means being the supertalented Michael Jordan of journalism. It means being a Deion Sanders, a far-less-talented, but far-more-self-centered spectacle. Morton Downey, Jr., Jerry Springer, Howard Stern, and their guests started teaching us that in the 1980s; Pamela Anderson and Tommy Lee then taught it to us in the 1990s; and now today's media teems with ever-more-ridiculous exhibitionism.

In a given year, our attention flits from an Ohio plumber named Joe pulling an on-camera stunt during a presidential campaign to a frantic police manhunt for a Balloon Boy to a days-long wall-to-wall television miniseries about two starfuckers who crashed a White House dinner party. In each case, the media, the narcissists, and the audience knows the controversies are completely synthetic—we know Joe the Plumber is just a glory-seeking egomaniac trolling for some notoriety; we know reality TV star Richard Heene set up a hoax so as to get his own show; and we know the Salahis broke into the White House specifically to hype their upcoming appearance on Bravo's *Real Housewives.* And yet, despite all that, we still reward these freaks with exactly what they want: attention.

Obviously, these icons—who increasingly dominate the media and become grassroots folk heroes—are motivated by narcissism and narcissism alone. They are not aiming to achieve celebrity status for the purpose of "serving a cause greater than themselves" or "sacrificing for the greater good," they're not ripping open their button-down shirt to reveal a STOP THE WAR message or stealthily unfurling a HEALTH CARE NOW banner. They're Just Doing It, and their goal is fame for fame's sake. Taking cues from their 1980s ancestors, they, like all of us see the public square as a field of play for an elbow-throwing game of King of the Hill. Narcissists compete with narcissists to see who can fleetingly hold the spotlight the longest.

Now, if that game were confined to entertainment media, then maybe there'd be nothing to worry about. But, as *The New York Times* notes, the vanity contest now dominates the highest echelons of our politics, creating "an upside-down dynamic in Washington (whereby) some politicians seem to seek office mostly for the purpose of land-ing on TV."

The once sterile and serious business of governing used to define success as passing legislation and fixing problems. Thanks to the eighties spirit, though, political success today is defined by politicians, reporters, and the public as making oneself a television star, not for any ideological cause, but for the cause of television stardom itself.

Take Mike Huckabee as an example. The former two-term Re-publican governor of Arkansas with the everyman style ran a spirited underdog campaign for the Republican presidential nomination in 2008 and ended up finishing a surprising second, which soon landed him a weekly show on Fox News. But when polls showed him the leading candidate for the Republican nomination in 2012, Huckabee admitted his major hesitation about running again was having to give up his television show. "This Fox gig I got right now," he said, "is really really wonderful."

At least his program is vaguely about political issues—that is, at least you can argue that he's not putting his television fame before po-tential public service *only* because he desires stardom and nothing more. You can't make that same argument about Sarah Palin, the em-bodiment of narcissism for its own sake.

A former half-term governor from one of the least populated states in the country, she is nonetheless one of the most famous polit-ical figures in America. Why? Not because she champions any partic-ular cause or passed any legislation. She is the ultimate Just Do It story in the biggest reality television show there is—infotainment. This *truly* average American wins the fame lottery, makes it big on the Re-publican presidential ticket in 2008, and now continues making it big by becoming a celebrity for celebrity's sake.

"Is Sarah Palin, at this point, a politician, or is she the star of some 'frontier family' reality show?" the *Times* wondered during her book tour. "In fact, she seems to realize that the changed environment al-lows her to be both at the same time."

These people and all the others like them are narcissists them-selves, but more important, they have figured out that our culture now *rewards* narcissism the more the narcissists are willing to flaunt their conceit, and further, that society often rewards narcissism more than we reward relevant experience or substantive skill. As Louisiana's Republican senator David Vitter said in promoting a Palin candidacy against President Obama, "I'll take a TV personality over a community organizer any day."

That refrain shows that since the 1980s we have realized the 1961 prediction of historian Daniel Boorstin: We are a society that confuses "celebrity-worship and hero-worship," a society that tends to idolize not those who become "famous because they are great," but those that "simply seem great because they are famous."

We are all complicit in this attitude, and we emulate its bizarre version of the Just Do It ideology in our own oxymoronic ways. It prompts some of us to proclaim our love of political leaders without knowing what those stand for. It compels some to know more about the characters on *Jersey Shore* than the folks in their own town. And it spurs others to tweet and blog and update their Facebook status in the name of "community"—all while railing against taxes, having no idea who their neighbors are, cutting people off on the highway, extending their seat backs on the cramped airplane, and buying silver BMWs on credit.

Whether Palin, Joe the Plumber, the Balloon Boy family, or any other professional spectacle in the headlines, the narcissists' "success" reflects what the 1980s did to us, and what the 1980s mentality makes us want to be.

OUTLAWS WITH MORALS

It's just been revoked. —SERGEANT ROGER MURTAUGH, INFORM-
ING AN AMBASSADOR HE JUST MURDERED THAT HE HAS UNILATERALLY RE-
SCINDED THE AMBASSADOR'S DIPLOMATIC STATUS, 1989

President Bush has quietly claimed the authority to disobey more than 750 laws enacted since he took office, asserting that he has the power to set aside any statute
passed by Congress. —BOSTON GLOBE, 2006

When it launched in 1988, the Just Do It campaign was an instant and groundbreaking success. Ayn Rand may previously have outlined the Objectivist rationale for individualism and narcissism, but Nike's slogan (and all the other rip-offs) mass-marketed that individualism and narcissism as aspirational theology.

And yet, for all of Just Do It's instant success, that 1980s campaign took five years to produce its most famous ad of all.

"I am not a role model," said Charles Barkley as he scowled at the camera in 1993. "I am not paid to be a role model. I am paid to wreak havoc on the basketball court. Parents should be role models. Just because I dunk a basketball doesn't mean I should raise your kids."

Then, as always, silence, and a black screen pierced by the white lettered words JUST DO IT.

The spot went beyond sports and way beyond product advertising (a sneaker wasn't even mentioned); it was definitive social commentary, and it made a huge splash. Pundits pontificated on its meaning, talk shows discussed its message, and *The New York Times* devoted an entire editorial to it, calling the spot "the most subversive sneaker commercial of all time."

At one level, the ferment reiterated how the 1980s zeitgeist had blurred the distinction between sports, media, pop culture, and politics. At another level, though, it showed that Nike executives realized their company had been one of the Dr. Frankensteins creating an out-of-control monster. The shoe corporation, which had spent millions of dollars a year both deifying superheroes and telling nonsuperheroes they could become superheroes, was pausing—if only for a short commercial break—to try to stop the madness.

I remember this ad vividly. I was seventeen years old and a big Barkley fan from his days as the "Round Mound of Rebound" on my hometown team, the Philadelphia 76ers. I hadn't swayed in my loyalty when Barkley put up the occasionally weak numbers, when he spit on a fan, when he made jokes about beating his wife. Why? Because I had been told in thousands of commercials that he was somebody to emulate—a guy who overcame his physical deficiencies (shortness, weight, unspectacular jumping ability, to name a few) by working extrahard, just as everyone else allegedly could, too.

Not a role model?

Since the mid-1980s, my bedroom in Philadelphia's suburbs was (and, by the way, still is) festooned with posters of this bald, roly-poly power forward from Alabama. My AOL handle, which I first signed up for in the late 1980s, had (and by the way, still has) the number 34 in it in honor of Sir Charles. Many hours of my day in high school were spent honing arguments about why, despite the statistics and win-loss records, Barkley was clearly—obviously!—the best player to ever play in the NBA.

Not a role model? What the hell was he talking about?

Barkley wasn't merely a role model, he was one of the 1980s most prominent archetypes constructed specifically for young people.

While Nike always had a few smiley all-Americans such as Michael Jordan and David Robinson, its image was also anchored in rule breakers. The first Nike endorser was University of Oregon track star Steve Prefontaine, an iconoclast who repeatedly tangled with sports governing bodies, "a rebel from a working-class background . . . full of cockiness and pride and guts," as Nike CEO Phil Knight said. Its next star was the Charles Barkley of tennis, John McEnroe; then, Barkley himself. After that it was Bo Jackson, the phenom who broke the "rule" that said no one can be a two-sport professional athlete. Then the long-haired Andre Agassi, whose commercials were all about "shak[ing] 'em up at the country club." Then Braves outfielder/Falcons wideout Deion Sanders—a glitzy mix of Bo Jackson, Barkley, and M.C. Hammer.

"I'm looking for a special attitude," said one of Nike's talent scouts, when asked about what makes the right endorser. "If I was pulling together a competitive basketball team instead of a Nike team, I might need a great center, a player like Brad Daugherty,★ somebody who'll get everybody involved and help you win. But when we go after somebody for Nike, that player has to represent something more."

That "something more" was a mix of brooding lonerism and righteous rebellion—not merely because the company wanted to differentiate its brand but because it wanted to appropriate the particular form of individualism that was already in ascendance. Its intuition finely tuned to the cultural moment, Nike understood that in teaching us to worship the individual Jump Man and see ourselves as potential superheroes, the 1980s was defining exactly what *kind* of superheroes the youngest generation should emulate—the self-sufficient renegades, the seething rebels, the "outlaws with morals," as one Nike executive called them.

For the older crowd, Ronald Reagan had long been seen as an

★Daugherty, the all-star center for the Cleveland Cavaliers, was the classic kind of player the NBA used to pride itself on—the lumbering big man like George Mikan, Wes Unseld, Willis Reed, Jeff Ruland, Jack Sikma, and Kareem Abdul-Jabbar, whose pitch-perfect fundamentals compensated for their inherent athletic weaknesses (lack of speed/body control, clumsiness, etc.). Daugherty, despite stellar play, achieved almost no notoriety as an NBA center in the 1980s and has largely been forgotten. He was Tim Duncan before Tim Duncan, and the fact that many casual sports enthusiasts have heard of Allen Iverson but not Tim Duncan proves the showboat factor remains the dominant paradigm in professional sports.

"outlaw with morals" thanks to his cowboy fashion and shoot-from-the-hip swagger. And in the 1980s, he was mainstreaming a Barkley-esque bluster that had previously sent Republicans down to crushing defeat. The same party that saw Barry Goldwater's 1964 dema-goguery ("extremism is no vice") and bellicose threats ("Let's lob a nuke into the men's room of the Kremlin") result in the largest land-slide loss of the twentieth century was riding high on Reagan yelling at the Soviets to "tear down this wall" and telling hostage-taking Is-lamic radicals that "after seeing *Rambo* last night, I know what to do the next time."

Reagan's salutes to movies was neither random nor only an ex-pression of his past career in Hollywood. They deliberately capitalized on the 1980s heyday of the Vigilante Film—those cartoonish fantasies whose protagonists must break social conventions, rules of etiquette, and concrete laws for the greater good. It was also the golden age of television action/adventure series positing that the hired gun—and definitely *not* the government—is the panacea for society's ills. And let's not forget the dramatized after-school specials and the sensation-alized "based on a true story" miniseries, a genre that typically por-trayed aggrieved "average Americans" struggling against "the system" to right society's wrongs.

These parables successfully turned the 1980s phenomena of hero worship and narcissism into a cogent political ideology that is at once authoritarian and antigovernment. Because so many of these stories were aimed at kids, they endure in a way that other eighties styles do not.

We, the children of the eighties, didn't just learn to bow down to cultural gods nor learn to see ourselves as future heroes as long as we Just Do It. We learned that Just Doing It means "taking matters into our own hands," "shooting first, asking questions later," and all the other one-liners that glorify the violating of rules, regulations, and conventions.

The modern manifestation of such ends-justify-the-means im-pulses can be summed up with contemporary clichés like "straight talk," "maverick," and "toughness." Those terms are part of an en-tire (and entirely overused) vocabulary that exalts today's outlaw with (alleged) morals. But don't think they were immaculately conceived.

They weren't. Their ancestors were Barkley, the Ghostbusters, and the original maverick himself—a naval aviator actually named Maverick.

It's easy to forget that America was once a country that largely embraced "big government" and its "everyone's in this together" rationale. And it's easy to forget how rapidly that changed. In just a single decade, we went from a nation that rewarded proponents of the New Deal and Great Society with massive electoral majorities to a country that, according to public opinion surveys, now despises government as much as it detests rapacious health insurance corporations.

This is a transpartisan, trans-ideological animus. Conservatives cheer when politicians sell off Eisenhower-era public infrastructure (highways, bridges, etc.) to foreign private firms. Liberals demand those same politicians "get the government out of our bedrooms." The rage is so white-hot it has driven some of our fellow countrymen to incoherence—for instance, the senior famously asking his congressman to "keep your government hands off my Medicare," or the retired air force officer and teacher, whose career and pension is being financed by the government, nonetheless telling *The New York Times* he's angry at those who dare "receive payment from the government" as a means of subsistence.

One oft-repeated theory claiming to explain this shift against government revolves exclusively around politics. In the post-Watergate, post-Vietnam 1980s—a decade that saw indictments of government officials spike by 150 percent—polls showed public confidence in government cratering. This was the moment of vigilante saviors such as the Guardian Angels and the folk-heroization of Bernie Goetz—outsiders (the myth went) doing the supposed good that the government itself was failing to do.★

Not surprisingly, Ronald Reagan was winning hearts and minds with quips like "The nine most terrifying words in the English lan-

---

★In Goetz's case, I stress the word *supposed*. I do not subscribe to the belief that his gunning down of four young men on the New York subway in 1984 was in any way "good."

guage are, 'I'm from the government and I'm here to help'"—
rhetoric presenting the government as the deceptive serial killer who
everyone says seemed like such a nice guy before he started eating
neighbors' livers with fava beans. And the Republican president was
waging this scorched-earth campaign just as free-market think
tankers, technocrats, and propagandists were applying their privatize-
everything theories to the world's economies.

When the go-go 1980s economic boom hit, it didn't seem to
matter that much of the boom was the result of good old-fashioned
Keynesian deficit spending by the government (think Reagan defense
budgets). All the electorate seemed to know (or care about) was that
the boom was happening at the same time our beloved cowboy president was vilifying government and venerating the titans of private industry as "heroes for the eighties." Hence, many voters made the
specious cause-and-effect leap, crediting Reagan's policy-fake but
rhetorically real antigovernment posture for turning on the bright
lights and reviving the big city.

Yet, while politics clearly played a role in stirring up anger at public institutions, crediting only politicians and their rhetoric for America's more visceral shift against government feels too oversimplified,
too reliant on the hackneyed pendulum theory that purports to explain every event and trend as the normal ideological oscillation of
American elections. This was anything but normal—this was not, say,
history's languorous fluctuation between isolationism and interna-
tionalism or between laissez-faire and economic interventionism.
This was also not just a modern expression of our Founders' rational-
but-not-paranoid distrust of state power. This was something deeper,
a shift at least partially rooted in all those 1980s television shows and
movies that are still replayed on cable TV.

These, as much as the elected officials, party platforms, and political ads, were beacons of two enduring messages: The government is
benignly ineffectual and the government is straight-up evil.

For adults, these themes were reiterated over and over by programming obsessed with the outside savior who swoops in to resolve
the issues the government cannot—or will not—solve itself.

The Fall Guy told the story of a Hollywood stuntman who doubles as a bounty hunter. *The Equalizer* revolved around a former

covert operative who does penance for his past government sins by offering protection to people in desperate situations. *Highway to Heaven*
featured an archangel being chauffeured around America by a scraggly
ex-cop, fixing American society along the way.★ *Hardcastle & McCormick* followed a former judge tracking down the criminals he failed to
put away—a renegade "whose respect for the U.S. Constitution
roughly equals Ronald Reagan's respect for the *Communist Manifesto*,"
as *People* magazine noted. And there was *Remington Steele, Riptide,
Simon & Simon, Spenser: For Hire, Magnum, P.I.,* and *Moonlighting*—
each about mercenary detectives and their crusades for the greater
good. Indeed, if you turned on the tube in the 1980s during prime
time, you were all but guaranteed to see a world whose challenges
were being solved—if at all—by some form of outside vigilante who
was filling the vacuum left by the government.

Had these themes been substantive, exclusively political, and only
focused on the 1980s adult audience, they might have been a fad with
little persuasive staying power—they might have aided the typical political pendulum swing, and nothing more. But they operated in an
entertainment arena that, unlike politics, appears on the surface to be
nonideological—an arena, thus, where an antigovernment ideology
can be far more subliminal and therefore especially potent. And the
most virulent expressions of this new ideology in the 1980s came via
cartoons aimed at the malleable minds of the children that are now
today's adults.

It started at the end of the 1970s with the original kids' version of
an "outlaw with morals": Han Solo.

★I really never understood the premise of this show, even as I was uncontrollably
drawn to it (don't ask). For instance, why does an archangel with the divine power
of God need to be driven around the country by car, much less in a run-down
Ford LTD? Can't he fly or kinda beam himself there? Also, what about Mark the
drifter-turned-deity-chauffeur—what exactly was his job before he became the
messenger of God's driver? I mean, was he a glorified Big Lebowski, just rolling
around with nothing to do? Oh, and was Mark specifically chosen for his new job
on purpose, or was it by chance? Because the opening of the program shows the
angel just walking down some nameless highway and being picked up by Mark.
Was this show therefore condoning the picking up of hitchhikers, in hopes that
hitchhikers might be the Almighty (or at least the spokesperson/aide/deputy of
the Almighty)? I assure you, these were seriously confusing questions for a nine-
year old.

To children, he was the vigilante messiah, the genre's Jesus Christ figure, all the way down to his carbon-freeze crucifixion and miraculous resurrection. In a cast of *Star Wars* characters with different archetypal appeals,★ this mercenary surnamed for his lonerism was designed for the prepubescent boy. He was a fast-talking, irreverent shoot-Greedo-from-the-hip hustler working—for profit—against the technologized autocrats in government (i.e., The Empire), but also wearing his big heart on his sleeve.†

As with any formula proven to generate ticket sales, Hollywood extrapolated particular mythologies and replicated them ad nauseam, giving us kiddies all sorts of Han Solo clones after *Star Wars* hit paydirt.

There was *Knight Rider,* probably the best example of the "benignly ineffectual" government story line. The show, with a weekly audience of 14 million households in its prime, suggested that people with serious problems can't count on officialdom for help, so they have to turn to the privately financed think tank called the Foundation for Law and Government (FLAG), a mysterious Trilateral Commission–like cabal operating out of the back of a speeding sixteen-wheeler.

Set up by millionaire industrialist Wilton Knight, FLAG helps an undercover cop named Michael Long convalesce after he's shot in the face. Wilton resurrects Michael Long as Michael Knight, putting the "young loner" in charge of his foundation's "crusade to champion the cause of the innocent, the helpless, the powerless in a world of criminals who operate above the law," as the show's introduction explains. He is aided by K.I.T.T.—FLAG's mesmerizing Trans-Am whose artificially intelligent brain is *2001*'s Hal, *War Games*'s Joshua, and GM's On Star service all in one pimped-out dashboard.

In *Knight Rider,* public institutions aren't necessarily evil, per se.

★Examples: Princess Leia—sex appeal; Lando Calrissian—*Star Wars*'s version of Shaft; Obi-Wan Kenobi—bone-throwing to the supergeek *Star Trek* crowd.

†Not coincidentally, the same actor went on to play Indiana Jones, a Han Solo similarly chasing "fortune and glory," only in a World War II setting and as an esteemed archaeologist saving the day against an evil empire (the Nazis) where his own government could not. He also later played Richard Kimble in *The Fugitive,* another Han Solo, this one fleeing the government as he tried to save the world from another evil empire called the drug industry.

They're just not all that helpful, and certainly not as effective as a technologized Heritage Foundation, a suave super-agent, and a talking muscle car boldly righting society's wrongs.

The Dukes of Hazzard, television's second-highest-rated program in 1980, took this model a half-step further, straddling the line between the Benignly Ineffectual Government and the Evil Government message. Bo and Luke were Hazzard County's good-natured vigilantes championing the same causes as Michael Knight, only in the flannel-and-jeans South, not in the shoulder-pad-and-feathered-hair jungle of *Knight Rider*'s cityscape. The key plot difference was that many times, the Duke boys' crusades put them in direct conflict with the county's corrupt political leader, Jefferson Davis "Boss" Hogg.

The aesthetic contrast between the citizen-saviors and the Boss delivered an antigovernment message that was hard to miss. It was two strapping, young do-gooders in an everyman Charger against a corpulent, three-piece-suited dwarf politician who gets driven around town in a triple white Cadillac DeVille convertible (with large bullhorns attached to the front grill). But the show prevented its antipolitician plot from becoming a full-on hate-the-government screed by carefully casting the nonpartisan police department (via the bumbling Sheriff Roscoe P. Coltrane and his deputy Enos Strate) as merely reluctant instruments of Boss Hogg's maniacal machinations.

The same cannot be said for *The A-Team,* whose government-hating combined the technological wizardry of FLAG with the hooligans-do-right attitude of the Dukes.

Airing in the 8:00 p.m. family hour, the program featuring headliners George Peppard and Mr. T immediately became the third-most-popular program on television, and it gathered a particularly "large following of teen-agers and children aged 6 to 11," wrote *The New York Times* during the show's 1983 debut. By *The A-Team*'s second season, *People* magazine estimated that 7 million "preteens" (ages two to eleven) were watching the "vigilante TV" program every week—dwarfed only by Mr. T's spin-off Saturday-morning cartoon and its audience of 14 million.

This was troubling to watchdog groups at the time because *The A-Team* was (at that point) the most violent show ever to air in prime time. But it should also have been disturbing because of the Ted Kaczynski level of government hatred *The A-Team*'s creators were preaching. Consider just the program's key themes, explained each week in its opening voiceover (intoned over grainy photos of Vietnam combat ops):

Theme #1: The government as misguided gestapo imprisoning our nation's innocent heroes for "a crime they didn't commit," a crime the government actually ordered. The initial line of the voiceover tells us *The A-Team* was imprisoned in the early 1970s for "a crime they didn't commit." In the show's first season, this backstory is fleshed out in more detail: A group of heroic soldiers serving in Vietnam were secretly ordered to rob the Bank of Hanoi to help end the war.★ After succeeding, however, the commander who gave them the order was killed, meaning there was no proof these military patriots were acting under orders and meaning their robbery of the bank looked like petty larceny. To prevent international outrage at the orders the U.S. government itself issued, the government immediately sent our brave heroes to rot in military pound-me-in-the-ass prison at Ft. Leavenworth.

Theme #2: The government as so totally inept it cannot even properly incarcerate convicted criminals. Our brave heroes didn't have to mount some elaborate *Shawshank Redemption* plan over many years, or even months, to escape government-sanctioned incarceration. They "*promptly* escaped to the Los Angeles underground" says the voiceover—because, ya know, it's just that easy when the government is both generally inept and already happily letting the likes of Willie Horton out onto the street through a revolving door. In fact, this incompetence is so assumed—so believable in the 1980s—that all the program's announcer has to say is that they "promptly escaped" and the audience accepts the storyline's plausibility without further explanation.

Theme #3: The government as permitting a flourishing criminal "underground." Though it's not precisely clear what "the Los Angeles underground" is (drug dealers? The Mafia? Gangs? All of the

---

★It's really not clear how robbing North Vietnam's central bank would help accomplish this task.

above?), it doesn't need to be clear. In the 1980s, we expect that the government knows of said "underground," and even knows its geographic location, but is entirely helpless to shut it down.

Theme #4: The government as unable to catch said military-trained fugitives. The A-Team, says the voiceover, is "still wanted by the government" but, of course, is still at large.

Theme #5: Military-trained fugitives thriving as solvers of societal problems that the government is too inept to solve. The A-Team, we are told, now make their way as "soldiers of fortune." Though this was once a derogatory way of referring to arms dealers, hit men, and other assorted mercenaries, in the 1980s, it became known as something honorable. In *The A-Team,* our heroes didn't decide to retire to some tropical haven never to be heard from again. They decided that with their own government so totally inept, they'd stay around solving society's problems on their own (for pay and at the barrels of machine guns, of course).

Theme #6: To help you with the problems the government refuses to solve, there's a good chance the average person can track down the A-Team, even through the government is completely incapable of tracking down the A-Team. Maybe the most insultingly antigovernment comment of all, the voiceover finishes by letting us know that the average person anywhere who "has a problem" (and inevitably won't be able to find any help from the government to solve that problem) has a decent chance of finding the A-Team and getting some help. This, even though the combined resources of Interpol, the FBI, the CIA, and an alphabet soup of military intelligence agencies has been unable to locate the A-Team within the Los Angeles city limits.

To know that all of these programs preyed on children is to simply look at their gimmicks. *Knight Rider*'s main character was a talking Trans-Am. *The Dukes of Hazzard*'s shiny centerpiece was an orange Dodge Charger called the General Lee, decked out in a Confederate flag and automatically tooting a "Dixie" jingle whenever it went Evel Knievel over a ravine. *The A-Team* ran a mobile command unit out of the back of a GMC van, and every show ended with the squad building some super-awesome contraption that every kid wished he could re-create in his basement. These were the hallmarks of synergistic, child-focused marketing, as each of these programs promulgated spin-offs—action figures, die-cast models, ColecoVision video games, even cereals and animated Saturday-morning series. And these shows were each, in their own way, a precursor to the three most culturally powerful and subversively camouflaged antigovernment productions in children's entertainment history: *E.T.*, *The Nightmare on Elm Street* franchise, and *The Ghostbusters* series.

Steven Spielberg's 1982 alien megahit, *E.T.: The Extra-Terrestrial,* was a successor to his 1977 *Close Encounters of the Third Kind,* but the change in tone and target audience between the two films was telling. *Close Encounters,* a thriller for adults, presents a benign and even enlightened (if a bit secretive) government cautiously but welcomingly reaching out to space visitors as they land at the Devils Tower in Wyoming.

E.T., by contrast, depicts the government as a faceless menace seeking to apprehend the innocent alien and his grade-school friend Elliott for waterboarding-like experimentation right in the heart of a sleepy bedroom community. For most of *E.T.,* scenes involving law enforcement and government scientists are filmed like a Levi's cotton Dockers commercial, showing only the lower halves of muscular male bodies as they angrily traipse over America's idyllic suburbia.*

When these thugs track E.T.'s whereabouts, they send black kidnapper vans through quiet neighborhoods with a roving Patriot Act–style surveillance operation. When they find his exact location, these same thugs refrain from knocking on Elliott's front door and instead use space-suit-clad zombies to violently break it down and turn the house into a sealed torture chamber.† When they start chasing the

---

*Some theorize that Spielberg chose this looking-up-from-the-ground perspective not as an antigovernment frame, but merely to show the audience what the pursuers looked like to Elliott and E.T. From their short perspective, all adults (and, really, all tall people)—whether from the government or not—look physically menacing. However, I don't buy this theory, because in *E.T.* many adults (for instance, Elliott's mom, his science teacher, and his older brother) are not shown from this perspective—only government employees are.

†I was seven years old when I saw *E.T.,* and for years this image freaked me out. But over the years, I began to think I had exaggerated this scene in my mind. So I went back and watched *E.T.* again in 2009, and, nope, I hadn't exaggerated it. When I mean zombie, I really mean zombie. These guys literally tear into the house lurching toward the children with their arms maniacally in front of them—a pants-shittingly scary *Night of the Living Dead* reprisal that was not only hysterically antigovernment in its portrayal, but really not appropriate for any kind of movie marketed to children.

children, two federal agents are actually aiming cartoonishly huge pump shotguns at the kids à la the Elian Gonzalez photo.*

As in other eighties films like *Splash, Starman,* and *Project X,* audiences applauded when the central characters of *E.T.* are able to escape, rather than seek refuge in, their own government. We cheered, in short, the triumph over the evil government.

Nineteen eighty-four's *Nightmare on Elm Street,* by contrast, avoided this government-is-evil idea in favor of the government-is-inept thesis, but took that to its own frightening extreme.

To children, Freddy Krueger was the single scariest villain of the 1980s, scarier than even Darth Vader or Jason because this mass murderer specifically targeted youngsters (and even more specifically, when the lights went off at bedtime—an already frightening time for kids). How did this lunatic with the burned face, fedora, and wolverine hand become such an unstoppable menace? It was the government's fault, of course.

Midway through the film, one mother tells us that before going immortal as a ghost haunting our dreams, Freddy was once "a filthy child murderer" that for years evaded government authorities.

"But it was even worse after they caught him," she tells us. "The lawyers got fat, and the judge got famous, but somebody forgot to sign the search warrant in the right place, and Krueger was free just like that." Naturally, then, the families of the dead decided to mete out the justice the inept government refused to mete out itself.

"A bunch of us parents tracked him down," she concludes. "We found him in an old, abandoned boiler room where he used to take his kids. We took gasoline, we poured it all around the place and made a trail of it out the door, then lit the whole thing up and watched it burn."

---

*Just to prove that the antigovernment themes of *E.T.* were overt and deliberate—and not just my personal conspiracy theory—consider that in the twentieth-anniversary rerelease of the film, Spielberg digitally altered this scene to remove the shotguns and replace them with walkie-talkies. Apparently, in the intervening twenty years, he realized just how aggressive and extreme an antigovernment message his film was sending and decided to try to shave off its sharpest edges (ya know, like federal agents pointing shotguns at kids).

So, in other words, the government belatedly catches a child murderer on par with Jeffrey Dahmer, but, like the A-Team, Freddy is permitted to "promptly escape" because the government couldn't fill out its own complex forms properly. This government's wrong was only righted by a violent mob of soccer moms and office-park dads. The moral of the story for kids: The only possible way the government can stop the Dahmer in your closet from killing you when the lights go out is by simply not prosecuting parents when they themselves break the law and burn him alive.★

Only in *The Ghostbusters* series of 1984 and 1989, however, do we see the government both unable to deal with a problem and then actually *creating* an even wider one.

New York, the largest city in America, is under increasingly violent assault by interdimensional terrorists. These ghouls and goblins periodically bust out of their sleeper cells to read library books, fry eggs on apartment counters, fly around hotel ballrooms, turn unsuspecting tax accountants into canine gargoyles, and kidnap helpless infants. This seems to be either (A) of only minimal concern to the police and the military or (B) of mild concern to them, but far beyond their capacity to handle.

Enter a for-profit corporation called The Ghostbusters, swaggering through Gotham with "positron colliders" and "unlicensed nuclear accelerators" on their backs. With their own Ray Parker, Jr., theme song, this merry band's motto is appropriately swashbuckling. As Peter Venkman says at one point, "Shit happens, someone has to deal with it, and who you gonna call?"

The Ghostbusters not only exhibit zero respect for laws or property, but are openly proud of their business model as hard-charging war profiteers. We learn this early on: Ecto-1, their ambulance-turned-rescue-vehicle, has a flashing sign on it that says FOR HIRE, and

---

★I guess it's true that you could interpret the *Nightmare on Elm Street* plot as, at some level, pro-government and anti-vigilante, because after Freddy is finally incinerated, he reaches ghostlike, Obi-Wan Kenobi–style immortality in an "if you strike me down, Darth, I will become more powerful than you can possibly imagine" kind of way. However, I think that's bullshit. The initial problem is that the government fails to expeditiously track him down and then later lets him off. All the subsequent Freddy-related problems (e.g., slaughtering, maiming, terrifying, etc.) emanate from that original government failure.

after the Ghostbusters trash multiple floors of a historic hotel to capture a bloblike apparition, audiences guffaw as the foursome threatens to release the terrorist back into the hotel unless their absurdly inflated bill is paid in full.

Initially left to do as they please and unencumbered by the rules and regulations that hamstring public institutions, the Ghostbusters become rich and famous as protectors of a society whose government has failed in even its most modest security charge. Real problems only arise when the big bad government tries to put them out of business.

Two-thirds of the way through the first Ghostbusters film, a mid-level Environmental Protection Agency official named Walter Peck, whom one Ghostbuster had previously insulted, reappears with a court order, an armed police officer, and a union hard hat to shut the Ghostbusters down. Peck isn't motivated by any public-policy concern. He's the bitter pencil-pushing Lilliputian unduly abusing his power (and it's no accident that he's from a tree-hugging liberal agency, ordering around a representative from organized labor and enforcing his will with the threat of police force). When he follows through with his effort to arrest the Ghostbusters and turn off their ghost incarceration machine—the equivalent of releasing all convicted terrorists into Times Square—a nuclear explosion ensues, the ghosts declare World War III, and a metaphysical ayatollah named Zuul triumphantly waltzes into Manhattan and imposes a paranormal caliphate under the sugary white thumb of a Stay Puft™ Marshmallow Man.

It's a similar story in *Ghostbusters II*. An obsequiously conniving bureaucrat in New York's municipal government has our heroes locked up in a psychiatric ward for trying to blow the whistle on the second coming of Zuul. This time it's a seventeenth-century Carpathian warlock called Vigo, who has come back from the dead after being "poisoned, stabbed, shot, hung, stretched, disembowled, drawn, and quartered."

In both blockbusters, when all hell inevitably breaks loose, who rides in to save the day? Not the city police force. Not the Pentagon. Not the Department of Homeland Security. Not the president or any politician.

The private corporation, of course. Told by his hysterical staff and pants-pissing law enforcement officials of ensuing chaos and imminent apocalypse, New York's mayor declares that the government is basically useless.

"We've got no choice," he says. "Call the Ghostbusters."

In the first movie, the Ghostbusters are let out of prison and subserviently escorted by a military entourage to Zuul's front door. In *Ghostbusters II,* the mercenaries are expeditiously released from their detention cells, then permitted to literally commandeer (and happily destroy) the most famous public symbol of the American government, the Statue of Liberty, driving it into downtown Manhattan for their final confrontation with Vigo.★

E.T., Ghostbusters, and *Ghostbusters II* were, respectively, the first, second, and seventh top-grossing films of their years. Meanwhile, *Nightmare on Elm Street* launched a quarter-century-old franchise that is still churning out new movies today. Combined, these four film series have made more than $1.7 billion. And that's just the movies themselves. Like *Knight Rider, The Dukes of Hazzard,* and *The A-Team* before them, these films went global through synergistic marketing. (As just one example, *Time* in 1988 reported that "a syndicated TV series, *Freddy's Nightmares,* debuts on more than 160 stations . . . The Freddy mask and hat outsold all other Halloween costumes . . . New Line reports brisk sales for two *Nightmare* books, five LPs, and a board game . . . You can buy Freddy dolls, the familiar sweater, and the signature glove . . . and Freddy's got his own fan club, MTV special and 900 chat line").

Through such aggressive cross-promotion, these characters, stories and themes reached Jordanesque cultural saturation in the 1980s.

★I've watched *Ghostbusters II* probably forty times (I'm not proud to admit), and it's increasingly unclear to me why Venkman and crew feel the need to pull this elaborate stunt to win their battle with Vigo. Yes, it's a neat special-effect idea, but it makes zero logistical sense within the parameters of the film's fantastical "science." (For instance, though we know the psychoactive slime shakes when it hears the music of Jackie Wilson, how does it then take coordinated directional orders via a Nintendo joystick? And even assuming it could take such directional control, how does the steel scaffold construction of the stationary Statue of Liberty suddenly have the flexibility to bend and walk?) How does marching the Statue of Liberty down Broadway in any way help thwart Vigo? Couldn't they have driven down the street, then used a wrecking ball or a tank shell to crush the Jell-O shield encasing his museum fortress?

I'd bet there's not a single American older than 15 and younger than 80 who hasn't heard of at least one of these movies or television shows, and I'd bet a plurality could give you a direct quote from them on command—an "E.T. phone home," an "I love it when a plan comes together" or a "Yes, it's true, this man has no dick."

This might explain why so many of these productions are being resurrected and remade now—and, more important, why their themes infuse our worldview, and why their story lines have made the jump from fiction to reality.

It's tempting to spend the next few pages showing you how all of these eighties classics have gone nonfiction by citing the surprisingly compelling reality lineups of boutique cable channels. After all, A&E's *Dog, The Bounty Hunter* has a similar mission to Michael Knight's, the crew from Discovery's *Motor City Motors* sometimes look as if they're trying to re-create the end of classic *A-Team* episodes, and SyFy's *Ghost Hunters* behave as if they think they are Peter Venkman, Ray Stanz, Egon Spengler, and Winston Zeddemore.

But those are just aesthetic changes in the map of television real estate—the same themes moving out across the cable dial and into different genre neighborhoods. While the 1980s plots' ability to continue drawing audience share is certainly impressive, the real story is how the eighties' antigovernment mnemonic now dominates every aspect of life, not just the ones shown on television.

What, for instance, to make of popular reticence when it comes to the wholesale outsourcing of public security services?

Halliburton, which broadcasts commercials about the services it has taken over from the government, has become a household name for its blatant profiteering in Iraq. Same thing for the private security firm Blackwater, the security contractor that routinely made headlines for alleged violent atrocities in America's war zones. Back home, state governments hire out more and more incarceration services to private prison firms, at ever more exorbitant prices.

This has been a radical and rapid change. If, in the 1980s, you said that at some point in the future hundreds of thousands of for-profit contractors would be fighting our foreign wars, that a large portion of

America's prisons would be run by corporations, that much of our municipal infrastructure would be owned by private companies, and that the government would even outsource parts of its disaster relief services, few would have believed you. .

As we now know, this *RoboCop* meets *Blade Runner* future, while certainly dystopian, wasn't so distant. It's the world we now live in. Even more unfathomable, it accelerates with little fanfare or outcry. As Bob Dole might say, "Where's the outrage?"

Whereas during the Gulf War, there was one contractor for every thirty soldiers, today it's a one-to-one ratio, as roughly half of all Americans stationed in Iraq and Afghanistan are contractors, and now, when the media publishes embarrassing stories about contractor abuse, the government hires contractors to investigate the contractors.

For all this, there's minimal public interest, much less backlash, and what little data exists suggests many Americans are just fine with what's going on. Consider the poll taken just three years after 9/11, a catastrophe laid, in part, at the feet of lax private airport-security screeners. When asked whether government or private security screeners should be responsible for protecting the aviation system, 41 percent of Americans said they either felt more safe with the private screeners or weren't sure.

This is hardly shocking. Kids who grew up being taught that an inept government is actively trying to stop the good deeds of the A-Team will naturally be less concerned about—and, in many cases, more likely to support—policies that let today's A-Teams handle security at our airports. Those same kids who were told that the government can't prevent Freddy Krueger from stalking our streets are probably going to be a little more sympathetic to letting private companies run our jails. Children who looked at movie and TV screens and saw the success of government's handing over municipal security responsibilities to the Ghostbusters will naturally be less surprised/outraged when, as adults, they look at the same screens and see the government handing over the same responsibilities to the Ghostbusters' terrorist-fighting colleagues at Blackwater.

The opposite is also true. In part because of what we learned three decades ago, eighties-kids-turned-twenty-first-century adults are more prone to accept or support passionate Tea Party, talk radio, and cable-news screeds against the very concept of government—screeds that, not coincidentally, evoke the questions and imagery still lingering from the 1980s.

When, for instance, we hear rants against federal bureaucrats "taking over" health care, against environmental regulations hammering business, and against social programs being used as siphons for corruption, many of us check the screeds against our primordial memories and come to predictable conclusions. Yeah, we think, why should we let those jackbooted federal sentries from *E.T.* make our health care decisions? Yeah, who wants a grudge-holding Walter Peck from the EPA using a court order to shut down our small business? And damn right, how can anyone believe social programs aren't just a way for Boss Hogg to steal Uncle Jesse's hard-earned tax money and give it to Hazzard County political cronies?*

I'm not saying that being a fan of *E.T.* or the Duke boys or Hannibal or Peter Venkman (as I surely am) means you automatically hated the concept of government (which I do not). The human mind is not a vapid DOS prompt waiting to be programmed by pop culture. It is more like a boulder in the middle of a river, anchored but also slowly sculpted over time by a persistent current. In that sense, our expectations of "normal" were shaped by what our broader culture was teaching us, so that by the time all those private military contractors and for-profit prisons and secret Blackwater teams and privatization schemes became real public policy, many of us didn't even flinch.

That's not some crazy conspiracy theory, it's the common sense that most of us already appreciate in our basic comprehension of parenting. To believe that a mom's or dad's tutelage can shape the future thought processes of young children is to realize that entertainment media can have a similar impact. After all, children were being par-

---

*It's not just conservatives who employ this mnemonic. Have you ever seen the typical ad for a plaintiffs' attorney? You know, the ones all over daytime and late-night TV, the ones where the snarling lawyer promises to take up your cause when the government refuses, hunt down the corporate bastard who did you wrong, punch him in the throat, and finally make sure justice is served? Replace him with David Hasselhoff, and you're looking at *Knight Rider* pledging to stand up to "a world of criminals who operate above the law."

ented more and more by TV and movies in the 1980s, both because declining wages forced more families to become two-income, latchkey-kid households and because there was (as shown) more programming aimed at youths. PBS enthusiasts love to credit *Sesame Street, Electric Company,* and *3-2-1 Contact* for using this vacuum to teach kids behaviors and social norms, but, as shown, those weren't the only shows kids were watching—and learning from.

Government bashing, as Reagan, Hollywood, and today's Tea Party movement prove, is a compelling and abiding lowest common denominator. Everyone can relate to it in some way. Hating taxes, abhorring the DMV, despising prevaricating politicians, you name it—all of us can identify with the typical grievances aired in antigovernment advertisements, television shows, movies, and political speeches.

That said, government bashing can't, alone, survive as a cogent worldview because government quite often does the kind of Mom and Apple Pie stuff everyone also loves. Government—regardless of the Freddy Krueger parables—does actually manage to track down murderers, properly prosecute them, and keep them behind bars. Government also regularly puts out fires and rescues kids who fall in wells and mitigates major municipal emergencies. And for the most part, government does all this stuff pretty well.

Even at the peak of the Reagan hoopla, an antigovernment ideology required something more to explain the persistent reality of an oft-successful government—some idea that would make the discrepancy between antigovernment rhetoric and reality seem entirely consistent.

Meet San Francisco police inspector Harry Callahan.

Known to most of us as Clint Eastwood's Dirty Harry, his movie series spanned the 1970s and 1980s and made the rogue the ultimate American luminary, one that is both of the government but also heroically defying it.

Rogues, mind you, differ from vigilantes and righteous fugitives, and they do so in the same way Eastwood's rule-breaking police detective differed from the lawless cowboys of his spaghetti-western days. The key distinction between the archetypes is their position: The vigilante and the fugitive operate outside the system, the rogue from within established institutions.

Dirty Harry, who broke protocol inside the San Francisco police department, was an instant icon* who represented a pure form of rogue. His very nickname—Dirty—referenced his willingness to break laws in the name of justice. In the 1980s, he spawned a family of rogue offspring in every conceivable setting and genre.

He gave us crime-fighting television shows that, "despite a conservative, law-and-order frame of mind" made sure that "virtually every hero is either a private detective . . . a fiercely independent cop at odds with [the] by-the-book boss" or a protagonist "profoundly skeptical of the law-enforcement establishment," as *Time* reported in 1984. He gave us the rogue school administrator in 1989's *Lean on Me,* a bat-wielding high school principal who goes to war with the municipal education establishment. He gave us rogue spooks such as Emmett Fitz-Hume and Austin Millbarge in 1985's *Spies Like Us*. He gave us rogue space warriors like the *Star Trek* movies' James Tiberius Kirk, who saves the world but is demoted from admiral to captain for insubordination against his starfleet commanders. And he gave us all the police and military rogues—the soloists such as Axel Foley, John Rambo, Marion Cobretti, and John McClane; and the ampersand duos such as Crockett & Tubbs, Murtaugh & Riggs, Tango & Cash,

---

*One of the many reasons Dirty Harry became an archetype so rife with political and cultural meaning was because of what was going on in America at the time. The film was based on the unsolved Zodiac murders in San Francisco (and the Dirty Harry character is allegedly based on one of the case's investigators). When the first installment was released in 1971, it was just a few years after the Supreme Court's 1966 *Miranda* decision, which overturned a conviction of a Latino rapist because police had violated his rights at the time of arrest. The ruling compelled police to read suspects their basic rights. Many "law and order" conservatives presented such rights as yet another example of government getting in the way of justice, and Harry Callahan, who, um, didn't read suspects Miranda rights, was the screen representation of that grievance. When the movie came out, it became a flashpoint of controversy, with some prominent voices calling it "fascist." In a 2000 interview with *The Washington Times*, Clint Eastwood noted, "There was an enormous amount of liberal dither over Miranda rights at the time [and] there was also a sense that was interfering with the course of true justice." He added, "Dirty Harry spoke to that. People said, 'I wouldn't mind having Dirty Harry on the beat.'"

Maverick & Goose, Turner & Hooch, Hunter & McCall, and Dooley & Kane (alias Pinkus & McCarthy).*

Presented in ever-more-caricatured forms,† these one-liner-
spewing protagonists were heroes not despite violating rules, regulations, laws, and direct orders, but *because* of those violations. As three
of the 1980s most successful action films show, that message wasn't
subtle.

In *Lethal Weapon II,* Sergeant Roger Murtaugh corners a South
African ambassador who has been allowed to establish an organized-
crime syndicate in Los Angeles under the aegis of the U.S. government (of course). When, after gunning down a cop, the ambassador
pulls out his passport and cites "diplomatic immunity," he gets a bul-
let to the head and a declaration from Murtaugh that the immunity
has "just been revoked" (apparently police sergeants have the unilateral authority to override federal and international statutes).

---

*Bonus points if you can name all the movies and TV shows that go with these
heroes. Answers: Axel Foley—Eddie Murphy in *Beverly Hills Cop;* John Rambo—
Sylvester Stallone in the *Rambo* series; Marion Cobretti—Stallone in *Cobra;* John
McClane—Bruce Willis in *Die Hard*; Detective James "Sonny" Crockett & De-
tective Ricardo Tubbs—Don Johnson and Philip Michael Thomas in *Miami Vice*;
Sergeant Roger Murtaugh & Sergeant Martin Riggs—Danny Glover and Mel Gib-
son in *Lethal Weapon;* Lieutenant Raymond Tango & Lieutenant Gabriel Cash—
Stallone and Kurt Russell in *Tango & Cash;* Lieutenant Pete "Maverick" Mitchell
& Lieutenant Nick "Goose" Bradshaw—Tom Cruise and Anthony Edwards in
Top Gun; Detective Scott Turner and his dog, Hooch—Tom Hanks and Beasley
the Dog, Turner & Hooch; Detective Sergeant Rick Hunter & Detective Sergeant
Dee Dee McCall—Fred Dreyer and Stepfanie Kramer in *Hunter;* Security Guard
Frank Dooley & Security Guard Norman Kane (who go undercover as Pinkus &
McCarthy)—John Candy and Eugene Levy in *Armed and Dangerous.*
†The professional screenwriters and amateur film enthusiasts that I know often cite
the first fifteen minutes of 1986's *Cobra* as the most cartoonish rendering of the
rogue cop ever to grace the silver screen. Stallone, driving a ZZ Top–style sports
car, replete with a California license plate marked AWSOM 50, screeches to a halt at
a supermarket paralyzed by a hostage-taking terrorist. Stallone ignores the plead-
ings of his superiors not to escalate the situation, waltzes in, chugs a beer, taunts
the assailant on the supermarket's public speaker system, and finally knifes him
while saying, "You're the disease, I'm the cure." It took five more years of count-
less *Cobra* replicas for Hollywood to finally produce 1991's *The Hard Way,* in
which Michael J. Fox plays fictional Hollywood megastar Nick Lang as Lang studies fictional New York police detective John Moss (played by James Woods) for a
part in an upcoming film. The interplay results in a scathing satire of Hollywood's
caricaturing of police rogues.

Similarly, after *Die Hard*'s police officer John McClane success-fully bombs a group of terrorists that the police force has so far been too ineffectual to stop, a commanding officer screams at him, "You've just destroyed a building! . . . I've got a hundred people down here covered with glass!" A bloodied McClane then yells at him for com-plaining about a few bits of glass and asserts that the regular police force—the government—is "part of the problem."

All of that rogue triumphalism was echoed by *Top Gun,* what with Maverick's "circus-stunt flybys," his order-defying rescue of Cougar, and his insubordinate violation of the hard-deck. But that 1986 blockbuster also added in a 200-proof shot of Ayn Rand.

"What does [Maverick] learn, really? That he's too bullheaded? That he needs to learn to follow orders sometimes? That he has a re-sponsibility to the American people that supersedes his cockiness?" wrote *The A. V. Club*'s reviewer Noel Murray. "No, the lesson of the movie is that [his] selfish instincts have been right all along, and are what he should pass on to the next generation when he becomes a Top Gun instructor himself."

The brilliance of this kind of eighties rogue mythology was how it individualized the concept of government and avoided explicitly radical attacks on beloved institutions—all while simultaneously as-cribing those institutions' failures to faceless bureaucratic intransi-gence and their successes to Jordanesque icons. Roger Murtaugh's and John McClane's heroism doesn't argue for disbanding the police force, nor do Rambo's and Pete "Maverick" Mitchell's accomplish-ments make the case for shutting down the beloved armed forces. Their actions suggest that government can succeed only when rogues are unleashed to do whatever they want, irrespective of collateral damage.

In the middle of Reagan's second term, the president and his followers—both by choice and by necessity—converted this ends-justify-the-means spirit of the fictional rogue into a marketable plat-form in the political world.

Nineteen eighty-six was only a little more than a decade after America collectively dry-heaved upon hearing Richard Nixon tell interviewer David Frost that "when the president does [something], that means that it is not illegal." Yet, there was Reagan explaining his decision to circumvent Congress and send troops on covert missions in Latin America with the exact same theory of the rogue presidency.

"Anything [administration officials] do is in our national interest," he said, insisting he needed no formal approval from Congress, despite statutes to the contrary. From the president's lips to his aides' ears. The Dirty Harrys working for Reagan took this refrain literally, most famously orchestrating the extralegal Iran-contra arms-for-hostages deals from inside the administration. This scheme was not your typical operating-in-a-gray-area, maybe-going-a-little-too-close-to-the-line scandal. Conceptually and specifically, it was blatantly, undeniably illegal. In general, federal law does not permit the executive branch to sell arms and use the profits to fund rebel death squads, unless the executive branch at least tells Congress. In specific, statutes known as the Boland Amendments, passed in the early 1980s, expressly prohibited the use of any federal money to fund the very Nicaraguan death squads Reagan's administration was secretly underwriting.

Yet when it all spilled out in public view in 1987, Oliver North, the colonel who orchestrated the enterprise from his perch at the National Security Council, bet his future on American culture's new embrace of the rogue. In nationally televised testimony before a joint congressional committee, North articulated the Dirty Harry ethic perfectly. While making sure to express his respect for government and democracy in general ("I am in awe of this great institution just as I am in awe of the presidency"), he attacked the same government for its "fickle, vacillating, unpredictable, on-again, off-again policy" that tried to prevent him from his work "carried out in the best interests of our country."

"The Boland Amendments and the frequent policy changes were unwise," North said. "Your restrictions should not have been imposed on the executive branch . . . the administration acted properly by trying to sustain the freedom fighters in Nicaragua when they were abandoned . . . [You should] commend the president of the United States, who tried valiantly to recover our citizens and achieve an opening (that is) strategically vital."

Tellingly, North didn't deny the charges against him or make much of an effort to say that what he did was legal. Instead, he gambled that if he morally justified his illegal actions as the internal triumph of "the best interests of our country" over governmental incompetence, he'd be celebrated as an "outlaw with morals" and find the same demoted-but-heroized fate as Captain Kirk in *Star Trek IV* (the hit movie that was dominating theaters just months before North testified).

And guess what? North gambled correctly.

North's rogue message was incessantly repeated in ends-justify-the-means terms. *The New York Times* gushed that North "put on a bravura performance rooted in the American tradition: Underdog, true believer, one man against the crowd." Pat Buchanan insisted, "If Colonel North ripped off the Ayatollah for $30 million and sent the money down to help the Freedom Fighters, then God Bless Colonel North."

The public response was overwhelming. North's testimony generated "Olliemania"—T-shirts, buttons, letters, and phone calls of support to Washington lawmakers—"perhaps the largest spontaneous popular response to a congressional activity in American legislative history," according to historian David Thelen.

America consciously embraced the rogue. In the same 1987 *Time* magazine poll that showed 58 percent of citizens believed North "acted illegally," even more than that, 67 percent, labeled him a "true patriot."

North was the political rogue's version of Freddy Krueger, belatedly indicted for his crimes only to see his conviction eventually overturned on legal technicalities. Unlike his *Elm Street* counterpart, though, North wasn't burned alive and he didn't reach immortality in mere dreamscapes. He was celebrated and then immortalized in the real world, first raising $20 million and coming within 4 percentage points of winning a U.S. Senate seat in Virginia, then getting himself a nationally syndicated radio show and newspaper column, and now serving as a regular cable-news commentator who makes cameo appearances on prime-time television dramas.

For this, North will be remembered as one of the rogue ethos's most important intergenerational connectors. If a 1990s Jack Ryan was Hollywood's bridge from a 1970s/80s Dirty Harry to today's Jack Bauer and Dexter Morgan,* North was Washington's bridge from Nixonism to the Bush/Cheney "bring it on" principle, the McCain/Palin "maverick" phenomenon, and the Obama administration's extra-constitutional power grabs. Put another way, North helped popularize the rogue as a legitimate brand of politics and governance.

With both Hollywood and politics beginning to fetishize this renegade ethos in the 1980s, the cumulative effect over the years has been profound—especially in the post-9/11 era. In a society that came to see itself as the underdog hero in a never-ending reprise of *Die Hard,* 9/11 made it simple to sell almost any action with ends-justify-the-means, stand-on-principle rogueness. Where Dirty Harry didn't read suspects their Miranda rights, the Bush administration stopped respecting their Geneva Convention, habeas corpus, and due-process protections through a system of torture and indefinite detention. Where cops from eighties television beat information out of defendants, the Bush administration used the threat of another 9/11 as justification for going rogue against the constitutional doctrine of due process. Where Roger Murtaugh unilaterally revokes diplomatic statutes, the administration unilaterally revoked diplomatic relations with allies in the lead-up to the Iraq War. And where Oliver North had glorified extralegal operations, 9/11's booster shot to 1980s rogue-ism allowed President Bush to "claim the authority to disobey more than 750 laws enacted since he took office, asserting that he has the power to set aside any statute passed by Congress," as *The Boston Globe* reported.

The administration was reaching all the way back to Reagan's

---

*The resemblance of *Dexter,* the current Showtime hit based on Jeff Lindsay's recent books, to *The Star Chamber* (1983) and *Nightmare on Elm Street* (1984) is downright eerie (or, perhaps, plagiaristic). The latter, of course, is about the deranged serial killer Freddy Krueger. The former, starring Michael Douglas, was one of the many *Dirty Harry*–esque Hollywood rehashings of the conservative complaint about Miranda rights. It's plot was all about California judges who, frustrated with having to let criminals go free because of liberal privacy/civil liberties laws, hire hit men to extralegally execute those criminals after their acquittals. *Dexter* combines the two themes—he is Freddy Krueger, but one who only hunts down and murders obviously guilty criminals who are nonetheless circumventing, evading, or being let off by the weak, pathetic, or otherwise inept justice system.

"anything we do is in our national interest," and that rogue attitude from the 1980s was, for the most part, accepted by the 21st century public.

This is a key point. When (at least initially) selling these moves to the American people, Bush and Cheney weren't going rogue against public opinion. Like Oliver North and Dirty Harry before them, they were applauded as outlaws with morals by millions of Americans.

Polls showed that the Iraq War, while controversial, was initially backed by a majority of the country. More important, a Fox News poll a few months after the invasion found that almost half of Americans thought the administration was "intentionally misleading" about the rationale for war—but more than two thirds of Americans still backed the administration's decision to go to war. That suggests a sizable chunk of the population both believed the administrtion lied—and believed such deception was A-OK. For America's rogue sensibilities, the ends (i.e., taking out Saddam Hussein) justified the means (i.e., lying about WMD, shredding international relationships, etc.).

Much the same, when details of the administration's extralegal wiretapping program emerged in 2006, a Gallup poll found 55 percent of Americans said the Bush administration was right to listen in on phone conversations without obtaining a warrant. By 2009, two separate polls showed that by a 19-percentage-point gap, the majority of Americans supported "harsh interrogation techniques for terrorism suspects," even as the FBI and top military officials were questioning the value of the intelligence gleaned from such tactics. At the same time, a 2009 CBS News/New York Times poll found a stunning 62 percent saying there was no need for Congress to even investigate whether the government's "treatment of detainees, use of wiretaps and other Justice Department practices broke the law."

By the time the 2008 presidential primary was in full swing, Americans viewed the rogue as such a positive archetype that both political parties saw their respective rogues nominated for the highest office in the land, and these candidates won those nominations by juxtaposing themselves against the perfect examples of what to go rogue against.

On the Democratic side, Barack Obama framed the presidential primary as a David-and-Goliath battle between himself, an (allegedly) unconventional legislator with postpartisan politics, and Hillary Clinton, the epitome of outdated convention and ultrapartisan polarization. On the Republican side, the rogue triumphalism was even more intense: Both John McCain and former Arkansas governor Mike Huckabee tarred and feathered businessman and former Massachusetts governor Mitt Romney as the walking personification of the out-of-touch country-club Establishment.

The general election proceeded in much the same way. McCain, who had been fetishizing the rogue spirit since his 2000 presidential run, nominated half-term Alaska governor Sarah Palin as his running mate. Together, they turned the word *maverick* into 2008's equivalent of *lockbox* and attacked Obama as lacking in maverick credentials—a corrupt hack "born of the corrupt Chicago political machine," as their attack ads said.

America ended up flocking to Obama as the safer alternative—a rogue savior, but a nonthreatening rogue like the Reaganesque 1980s rogue Obama told voters he aspired to be. "Reagan changed the trajectory of America" by "put[ting] us on a fundamentally different path," Obama said.

The catch-22, however, is that Obama's promise, and the eighties culture it channeled, now limits his opportunities to bring about the generational change he promised.

By emphasizing the supremacy of the rogue, and now going rogue himself by preserving/expanding many of the rogue national security policies of his predecessor, Barack Obama has added bipartisan legitimacy to the antigovernment ideology from the 1980s. Public institutions, says this school of thought, can never work in a mundane and systemic way. They only achieve occasional success when the rare cowboy inside them such as Dirty Harry Callahan or John McClane scream "Make my day!" or "Yippee ki-yay, motherfucker!" while breaking all the rules.

That makes for an audience-pleasing film plot, but "going rogue" is not a blueprint for designing, say, a new health care apparatus, an effective job-creation policy, or a much needed financial regulatory regime. As a political and public-policy philosophy, it is quite the opposite: It is the same antigovernment rallying cry that Obama opponents are so effectively using to weaken and obstruct most of his farthest-reaching proposals, the same antigovernment rallying cry that led us into a financial crisis and then a recession.

In the lead-up to that meltdown, a clique of government-hating financial elites had been inflating a bubble of deregulation and shady investments. Everyone knew it. And like Patrick Dempsey and his high school friends in *Can't Buy Me Love,* these cool kids finally—happily—shit on our house.

In response, rather than considering any kind of serious regulatory intervention, Democrats and Republicans suffused with the 1980s antigovernment spirit settled on a bailout that simply handed trillions of dollars to the private banks. In that way, they outsourced the economic recovery to profiteering Ghostbusters, asking them to exorcise the demons because the government supposedly couldn't be trusted.★ What little direct government involvement that would be permitted would be solely vested in the secretary of the treasury (himself the immediate past CEO of one of the financial culprits, Goldman Sachs). The legislation gave him unilateral power to go Dirty Harry on any other federal agency that might get in the way of the vigilante strategy.

Perhaps most predictable of all was the public explanation, as President Bush told America, "The greater threat to economic prosperity is not too little government involvement in the market, it is too much government involvement in the market."

In a different time, the line would have generated shrieks of outrage and protest. Instead, both Pew and CNN polls showed a solid majority initially supported the no-strings-attached nature of the bailouts, a sign that for all the talk of advancement and progress, we

---

★This is being generous. To be completely accurate, handing money over to banks that had manufactured the crisis was like outsourcing an exorcism to the Ghostbusters only if Walter Peck had been correct in his allegations that the Ghostbusters themselves had originally created the ghosts.

are still living in the 1980s, the decade that originally commenced with Ronald Reagan telling us at his first inauguration, "Government is not the solution to our problem, government is the problem."

It has become an impervious notion, an axiom in the truest sense of the word. Regardless of events, this 1980s hatred of government prevails, even in reaction to the failure of antigovernment policies themselves.

In 2010, for example, Joseph Stack flew a plane into an IRS building as an antigovernment protest against the very financial bailouts that outsource economic policy to private corporations. This assault, which punctuated a wave of similar antigovernment terrorist attacks, came only weeks after NBC's national poll found that the antigovernment Tea Party movement was more popular among voters than either of the two major—and fundamentally antigovernment—political parties.

By the fall elections, we had, indeed, become the country imagined in 1985's *Brewster's Millions,* a nation craving a campaign like Montgomery Brewster's.

Looking to waste as much money as quickly as possible in order to win a massive inheritance, this forefather of the modern Tea Party discovers the best way to do that is to run for office in a nakedly corrupt election system, and to go rogue against the entire legitimacy of government as an institution.

"You know how it is around election time and you decide not to vote because the two candidates are so repulsive," he says in his campaign ad as he downs a beer. "*Repulsive*'s not the word—we're all full of shit. . . . Write in 'none of the above' on your ballot. Don't vote for any of us—we're assholes."

A quarter century ago when the antigovernment theology was only first being written, this was comedy. We laughed at Richard Pryor's fictional rendering of the political outlaw with morals. Today, though, his 1980s message is so pedestrian, so assumed, in our nonfiction world, we get angry only when someone dares to challenge it.

PART III

WHY WE (CONTINUE TO) FIGHT

Colorado Springs is a weird place—weird as in you can sense it's not what it seems to be.

On the occasions that I drive through the city of 360,000, I inevitably end up thinking of *V,* the NBC program about intergalactic aliens that gave me my first burst of nightmare-prompted panic attacks at age eight.

At first glance, the Springs (as we call it out here) looks like an antigovernment tattoo emblazoned on Colorado's politically purple midsection. Though its residents don't wear crimson uniforms like the Visitors, their conservatism leads them to vote Republican red at the ballot box and oppose almost every tax measure that might raise revenue for basic municipal services. When, in 2010, the city was forced to slash its police force, shut off streetlights, stop paving roads, and halt park maintenance because its meager public revenues dried up, one councilman presented the decisions as a Reaganite vision—and a Tea Party goer's wettest dream. The community, he alleged, was "actually putting America's limited-government ideals into practice."

It is the Springs as the 1980s vision of a shining, government-loathing city on a hill, and the image seems as convincing as the Visitors' cream-colored makeup (which, as sci-fi fans surely recall, was quite convincing).

Yet, just like the Visitors, when you scratch through the chalky veneer, you uncover a huge green monster.

See, for all the talk of "limited government," one-third of the Springs' entire economy relies on the biggest of Big Government—that gargantuan camo-colored behemoth called the U.S. military. As the flag-waving home of Fort Carson, the Air Force Academy, and NORAD (among others), the city is as close to a ward of the state as exists in America. If its Republicans got their wish and the government suddenly disappeared entirely, Colorado Springs wouldn't become Detroit, it would become the moon.

Simultaneous hatred of "government" and fervent fealty to the military—the Colorado Springs mind-set is, of course, the national mentality, as generically "real America" as Applebee's, Sarah Palin, and every other pervasive prefabrication that first came of age in the 1980s. The ideological oxymoron might not be as tasty as corporate food or as counterfeit as a shrink-wrapped politician, but it most certainly is just as artificial and blister-packaged for mass consumption.

Recall that only three decades ago trust in the armed forces hit an all-time low in Gallup's polling. Following the loss in Vietnam and a botched hostage-rescue mission in Iran, just 50 percent of the country said it had confidence in the military in 1981.

After ten years of hypermilitarist agitprop, though, Gallup's survey found 85 percent of Americans expressing "a great deal" or "quite a lot" of confidence in the same institution. That's more than one out of every three Americans radically changing their views, a previously unheard of statistical swing in mass opinion in such a short time.

Swing, though, is a misnomer, for *swing* implies oscillation, and there is no longer any metronomic back-and-forth. Despite the quagmires in Iraq and Afghanistan and despite perpetually bloated Pentagon budgets rife with headline-grabbing waste, the military has remained the single most trusted institution in America since the end of the 1980s—more trusted than schools, small business, and even organized religion.

As a result, a Constitution that vests civilian leaders with power over the armed forces is now increasingly at odds with a country whose democratic spirit has been replaced by authoritarian militarism. A nation that once believed Georges Clemenceau's adage that "war is too serious a matter to entrust to military men" now frames military questions as debates over the most irritatingly simplistic bromides of junta culture. All we seem to want to know is whether our fellow countrymen are displaying enough reflexive deference to "commanders on the ground"; why antiwar activists insist on giving "aid and comfort to the enemy"; and when those traitorous liberals/ hippies/America-haters will just "support our troops" and reflexively back war as a "just/noble cause."*

Abrupt as this attitudinal change has been over the last thirty years, it is rooted in the little-examined but long-standing relationship between the armed forces and the instruments of mass culture.

During World War II the government hired director Frank Capra to make seven films called *Why We Fight* to explain that conflict's rationale to a public skeptical of militarism after World War I. Forty years later, with a public similarly skeptical of militarism after Vietnam, the 1980s took Capra's model to the extreme as a colossal new military-entertainment complex taught us to never ever ask why we continue to fight—needlessly, endlessly, and indefinitely.

That this shift occurred during the same 1980s that saw Americans sour on the whole concept of government suggests we have embraced something grander than hawkishness. It shows we have specifically adopted the 1980s worldview of film director John Milius, who imagines the state's armed forces and the state itself as wholly distinct entities.

"I'm never skeptical of the military," he said at the end of the Reagan era. "But I'm always skeptical of government."

The architect of 1984's *Red Dawn* and the author of some of Hollywood's best-known battle cries, Milius was among militarism's most prolific auteurs in that formative decade after Vietnam.† While writing lines telling America to "love the smell of napalm in the morning," he helped the entertainment industry mold a dominant paradigm that is about more than mere differentiation, more than the nuance of supporting one branch of the state and opposing another. Since the eighties, we've learned to see the government as separate from the military. We criticize one and never dare question the other.

---

*For the rest of this chapter, I'm going to put these phrases and their iterations in italics when they are used in primary sources, just to give you a taste of how successful the 1980s was in embedding militarism's lexicon into the modern vernacular.

†He's also reportedly the real-life inspiration for John Goodman's character, Walter Sobchak, in *The Big Lebowski,* which, considering his films, isn't hard to believe.

Constructing that kind of oxymoronic thinking in service of militarism was no easy task after Vietnam, even with the help of Ivan Drago levels of anticommunist hysteria. It required a two-front assault.

The first would be aimed at adults and fought with dark retrospective films, tilted journalism, overheated political rhetoric, and at times the armed forces itself. The ideological objective was to reimagine, reexplain, and physically refight the Vietnam War in the 1980s so as to turn what might have become a cautionary tale about the dangers of adventurism (Hmm . . . maybe invading Iraq's a bad idea . . . ?) into a fearmongering justification for permanent military hubris ("We will be greeted as liberators!").

The second offensive was a more surgical and preemptive strike designed to shape children's future views of both combat and the military's broader role in a post–Cold War society. This couldn't be fought with presidents, anchormen, docudramas, anachronistic red-baiting, or any other conventional political weapons that young people typically ignore. Instead, it required asymmetrical ordnance such as after-school cartoons, comic books, video games, professional wrestling, trading cards, action figures, and, most obviously, over-the-top action/adventure films.

To be sure, conspiracy theorists tend to see the national security state's black helicopters in everything. But in the case of militarism's sales pitch to kids, the theories are largely true, as the Pentagon in the 1980s began discovering the clout of culture and the coercion of cool. Forget the hard sells of World War II newsreels and snarling Uncle Sam posters. During the Reagan era, the military forged shadowy relationships with mass-marketing mavens and imperceptibly embedded itself into seemingly apolitical content. When army brass weren't editing Hollywood scripts into aggrandized recruitment ads, they were conniving with baseball-card designers and video-game programmers to superheroize generals and simulate their wars in eight-bit pixelated glory.

To know the success of this two-pronged, thirty-year campaign is to observe today's debate—or lack thereof—over the moment's Vietnam-like quagmires. It is to watch antiwar protest become as evanescent as the media's scrutiny of the Pentagon. It is to hear the same 1980s revisionism about allegedly spit-on veterans and weak-willed politicians as the reason for past military defeats, and to see even critics of militarism repeat those shibboleths.

It is, in short, to behold a country of Colorado Springsians and John Miliuses at once railing on government and idolizing the military—exactly as the 1980s planned.

KICKING THE VIETNAM
SYNDROME

Left to their own devices, the Pentagon would have developed a winning strategy [in Vietnam]. . . . Too much authority was put in civilian hands. Hopefully in future wars, the commanders in the field will be given those responsibilities. —GEN. WILLIAM PEERS, 1983

Troop levels will be decided by our commanders on the ground, not by political figures in Washington, D.C. —PRESIDENT GEORGE W. BUSH, 2007

On August 18, 1980, Ronald Reagan lit the fuse of a political bomb when in a speech to a veterans' group, he came to the passionate defense of the military's conduct and objectives in Vietnam.

"It is time we recognized that ours was, in truth, a *noble cause*," Reagan said. "We dishonor the memory of fifty thousand young Americans who died in that cause when we give way to feelings of guilt as if we were doing something shameful."

The Republican candidate for president was immediately fragged by all sides. *The Washington Post*'s Haynes Johnson cited the statement as evidence of Reagan's reckless pugilism. Conservative Malcolm Forbes called Reagan "stupid" for glorifying "that most bitter and divisive conflict." The political-chatter machine was abuzz over whether it was a harmless gaffe or something far more menacing.

As the backlash intensified, Reagan was forced to hold an impromptu press conference on his campaign plane to try to snuff out the controversy. But the old Cold Warrior ended up only reiterating his statement and fanning the conflagration, prompting his own campaign aides to chide him for tone deafness. One told *The New York Times* that the former California governor simply "can't see the bad impact [the statement] will have."

Though Reagan would temporarily tamp down his belligerence and go on to win the White House, the week of the now famous "noble cause" speech was a political setback for the Republican standard-bearer, casting him as out of touch with a Vietnam-weary country that had understandably soured on militarism.

Fast-forward to 1988. Preparing to leave office, Reagan repeated the same coded statement almost word for word, telling mourners at the Vietnam Veterans Memorial that the armed forces were "champions of a *noble cause*" in Southeast Asia. So certain was the president of America's newly bellicose attitudes about war and militarism that he asked, "Who can doubt that the cause for which our men fought was *just?*"

The question was rhetorical, the lack of response by then expected—and illustrative. Save for a column in *The Washington Post's* style section and on PBS, Reagan's declaration—the same one that evoked a frenzy of criticism in 1980 and almost derailed his candidacy—elicited almost zero public outcry. His thesis had become such a point of consensus it was considered only minimally newsworthy.

That newfound silence represented the triumph of 1980s militarism. In just eight years, the once polarizing battle shriek of hardcore hawks had come to be seen as wholly uncontroversial. This was something more than manufactured consent—it was manufactured consensus, a truly amazing achievement of retrospective revision that preyed on a generation's desire to avoid agonizing emotions such as regret, guilt, self-doubt, and humiliation about the Vietnam War.

Though Reagan's VFW speech in 1980 drew headlines for passing judgment on that conflict's value, its broader, and far more lasting, intent was to begin modernizing the idea that defeat on the battlefield has nothing to do with the inherent problems of imperial arrogance and everything to do with the military's being "stabbed in the back" by internal dissent.

Kevin Baker of *Harper's* has called such betrayal imagery the post-Vietnam era's "sustaining myth" of nationalistic scapegoating: "Advocate some momentarily popular but reckless policy. Deny culpability when that policy is exposed as disastrous. Blame the disaster on internal enemies who hate America. Repeat, always making sure to increase the number of internal enemies."

In the 1980s, Reagan's specific "stab in the back" apologues about Vietnam had an express objective: "It was always understood that you were trying to rehabilitate the American attitudes toward defense [and] the armed forces," said Reagan speechwriter Aram Bakshian.

The first way to do this was to construct what author Jerry Lembcke calls the Legend of the Spat upon Veteran—the honest citizen-soldier "who has known at first hand the ugliness and agony of war" and yet is "so often blamed for war by those who parade for peace," as Reagan lamented in that fateful 1980 address.

This apocrypha has been around—and exploited—for most of modern history. To whip up popular rage, the ascendant Nazi Party bewailed how, following Germany's defeat in World War I, "degenerate deserters and prostitutes tore the insignia off our best frontline solders and spat on their field gray uniforms," as the infamous Hermann Göring said.

Same thing for the French. When their soldiers returned home from losses in Indochina in the 1950s, conservative parties in Paris constructed the same legend. And same thing for Reagan's Republican predecessors, Richard Nixon and Spiro Agnew, whose partisans spent the 1970s issuing increasingly brash to-camera screeds against Vietnam War critics for allegedly mistreating troops at peace protests, propping up the enemy, and demoralizing the war effort.

The motive of the Nixon/Agnew-led Republican Party in those years before the 1980s was entirely self-interest: They were desperate to deflect attention from the hideous failure of their bomb-the-hell-out-of-everything military policy. Reagan, always a loyal hippie-hater, had been an integral part of this GOP onslaught. In a televised 1967 debate with Robert F. Kennedy, he said antiwar "demonstrations are prolonging the war in that they're giving the enemy . . . encouragement to continue."

Days after Vice President Agnew's 1969 jeremiad labeling war protesters "an effete corps of impudent snobs" who disrespected veterans and made common cause with the North Vietnamese, Reagan went even further. Having already aired a nationally televised attack on war critics for *"lending comfort and aid"* to the enemy, he declared, "Americans will die tonight because of the [antiwar] activity in our streets."

Reagan's 1980 encomium eulogizing the Spat upon Veteran, then, just built on his own legacy, and with no regard for the fact that the legend had little basis in reality.

In his exhaustive book-length exegesis on the Legend of the Spat upon Veteran, Lembcke found not a single verifiable example that the fable is actually true. He certainly encountered Vietnam veterans who claimed they were spat on by antiwar activists, but he could find no physical evidence (photographs, news reports, etc.) that these memories actually occurred in real life, and his research was buttressed by extensive surveys of veterans at the time they were originally coming home.

A Harris Poll in 1971, for example, found 94 percent of Vietnam vets describing their stateside reception as friendly, and 75 percent of veterans disagreeing that "people at home who opposed the war often blame veterans for our involvement there." Additionally, most Americans who fought in Southeast Asia probably didn't hate protesters nearly as much as the Legend of the Spat upon Veteran would have us believe. One study in the early 1970s found that 75 percent of returning soldiers were actually opposed to the war and another found that it was "difficult if not impossible to find a 'hawk' among the Vietnam veterans."

But as Reagan and his fellow public-opinion sculptors in the 1980s knew, memory can be a tricky thing in the multimedia age, often shaped more by televisual historiography than actual events. Screams of "baby killer" at President Johnson; scuffles between long-haired protesters and billy-club-wielding national guardsmen; pro-war epithets aimed at antiwar vets—through years of inadvertent editing-room cuts and tendentious mythmaking, such images can easily turn into fantastical reminiscences of mistreated troops, especially in a pop culture cauldron as ideologically superheated as the 1980s.

With Vietnam War revisionism seeping into Reagan-era politics, films such as *Tracks* (1977), *Coming Home* (1978), and *First Blood* (1982) picked up the Legend of the Spat upon Veteran as a way of providing a reductive account of the U.S. military's multifaceted and depressing defeat. The war wasn't flawed, said Hollywood, America's commitment to the troops was simply too weak.

Hamburger Hill (1987) provides an especially poignant example. At various points in the film, demoralized soldiers preparing to march face-first into Vietcong machine-gun fire tell of girlfriends who break up with them, citizens who discriminate against them, and hippies who throw dog shit at them—all because of their venerable service to their country. We heard this story a zillion times in the 1980s—hell, even *G. I. Joe* comic strips showed vets literally getting spit on by hippies, then featured a peacenik character deferentially apologizing to military officials for "presuming so many horrible things about you and the Army."

Toward the mid-1980s, this melancholy became the more punitive wave of save-the-POW/MIA fantasies—*Uncommon Valor* (1983), *Rambo: First Blood Part II* (1985), *P.O.W. The Escape* (1986), and the *Missing in Action* series (1984–88), to name a few. They featured muscle-bound toughs heading back to Vietnam to kick ass, take names, and rescue their band of brothers who faced a fate worse than even saliva: Their country, so ravaged by the antiwar spitters, had simply left them behind to die.

In the more serious news media, contemplative retrospectives picked up where Hollywood left off. Bob Greene, one of the preeminent national newspaper columnists in the 1980s, devoted a four-part series and then his bestselling book *Homecoming,* in part, to promoting the legend. His colleagues in journalism, whether on editorial pages or in annual local news broadcasts of Veterans Day ceremonies, constantly depicted past protest of the war as protest of veterans themselves, largely omitting that (A) Vietnam vets were among the most important part of the antiwar effort, and (B) the few loogies that did fly tended to be hocked by militant pro-war veterans of earlier conflicts at their younger brethren who were opposing the Vietnam conflict.

As the Legend of the Spat upon Veteran gained traction, it complimented the 1980s' other parable of Vietnam revision—the Hands Tied Behind Their Backs Myth. This is the second part of the argument that claims internal dissent sows military weakness, and the assertion drawing militarism's key psychological distinction between the armed forces and the government.

In this specific iteration of the 1980s cant, the loss in Vietnam was portrayed as the result of honorable commanders on the ground being asked to fight "a war with one arm tied behind their backs by their own government," as Reagan said in a 1980 primary debate.

"We maybe owe [the military] an apology for the way that they've been treated and maybe we owe them a promise," Reagan continued. "A promise that never again will we commit the immorality of asking young men to fight and die in a war our government is *afraid to let them win.*"★

Such criticism originated in the 1970s with attacks on senator (and World War II bombardier) George McGovern and other congressional sponsors of legislation to end the Vietman war, but its volume was turned up to eleven in the 1980s by Reagan and the military's spokespeople.

"Left to their own devices, the Pentagon would have developed a winning strategy," said retired General William Peers in a 1983 *Christian Science Monitor* article headlined "Vietnam Revisited" that was typical of the chest-thumping. "[Vietnam generals] had at least one hand tied behind [their] back. . . . Too much authority was put in civilian hands. Hopefully in future wars, the *commanders in the field* will be given those responsibilities."

The propaganda equivalent of a Rube Goldberg machine built with shoddy pinball-machine parts, this line of thinking relies on a series of shaky assertions. You have to assume military hands were actually tied during Vietnam, despite both parties' leaders rubber-

★Reagan would not end this over-the-top campaign rhetoric as president. On the contrary, in a 1981 speech, he said Vietnam soldiers "came home without a victory not because they'd been defeated, but because they'd been denied permission to win." Likewise, in a letter to a Vietnam vet, Reagan wrote, "You fought as bravely and as well as any American in our history, and literally with one arm tied behind you—sometimes two."

stamping nearly every troop increase request from the generals and despite those generals', shall we say, unconstrained tactics (napalm anyone?). You also have to further assume that Vietnam would have been won had the military simply been "freed" from politicians, and you would have to ignore "commanders on the ground" in Vietnam such as General Frederick Weyand, who admitted at the time, "The war is unwinnable."

But that's precisely *why* the Hands Tied Behind Their Backs Myth worked so well in the 1980s and why it still endures as a justification for unending militarism.

Unlike the Legend of the Spat upon Veteran, which can at least be empirically challenged, this myth's supposition of victory can't be disproven because it's totally hypothetical, a quality lending itself to the very kind of fantastical conjecture that *Rambo* and other Hollywood commodities were taking to the masses in the 1980s.

Remember that in his first silver-screen appearance, Rambo was the saliva-stained Vietnam vet criticizing politicians who "wouldn't let us win" and lamenting antiwar activists "protesting me, spitting, calling me baby killer." In *Rambo: First Blood Part II,* the second-highest-grossing film of 1985, our persecuted veteran-hero is released from prison after thwarting an entire municipal police force and sent back to Southeast Asia for a grudge match against Vietcong still holding American POWs. Somehow, though, the new Rambo is weighed down by a bizarre weakness: This militarized version of Superman is suddenly paralyzed by a withering fear of internal dissent and its kryptonite-like effect on his powers of annihilation.

"Sir, do we get to win this time?" Rambo asks meekly, ripping off Reagan's "afraid to let them win" line almost word for word.

"This time," replies his commander, "it's up to you"—as if the last time, it was up to smarmy politicians holding Rambo back.

That's the entire theme of the movie. When Rambo arrives at his Southeast Asian staging base, he is greeted by Marshall Murdock, a whiny politician-bureaucrat in country-club garb who complains about the jungle heat and orders grunt soldiers to get him cold beverages. This same politician ties Rambo's hands by instructing him only to take photographs of POWs he finds—but not to rescue them. When Rambo goes rogue and risks life and limb to save them anyway, Murdock aborts the mission, leaving them all to die for fear of bad publicity. One of Rambo's military comrades, summing up the larger theory behind the Hands Tied Behind Their Backs Myth, protests, "He never had a chance, did he?"

Left for dead, Rambo then plots revenge on the hand-tiers. Recounting his life back home to an ally in the jungle, he fumes about "a quiet war against all the soldiers returning [from Vietnam]—the kind of war you don't win." When he radios back to headquarters, he promises vengeance on behalf of all the aggrieved vets, telling Murdock, "I'm coming to get *you*."

When Rambo does finally return victorious in spite of his own government that left him for dead, he sums up all the 1980s Vietnam revisionism about spat-upon vets and handcuffed soldiers in one final line: "I want what every other guy who came over here and spilled his guts and gave everything he had wants," he says. "For our country to love us as much as we love it."

In its 1987 story about Rambo being so quickly "installed in the pantheon of popular culture," *The New York Times* recounted how this Stallone archetype was infinitely amplified through a "ripple effect" of Halloween costumes, practical-joke telegrams (Rambograms), academic studies, and secondary references in other entertainment media. And as Hollywood's Rambo doppelgängers were soon shown victorious over peaceniks, weak-kneed congressmen, constitutional protections, and basic principles of human rights, Ronbo was replicating the fantasies in an attempt to prove the flip side of the Hands Tied Behind Their Back Myth.

From the White House, Reagan aimed to overcome the public's fear of repeating Vietnam (the so-called Vietnam Syndrome) by showing that decisive and casualty-minimizing victories in future Vietnams could be achieved, but only without dissenting vet-spitters, hand-tiers, and other assorted backstabbers. He swept aside congressional ambivalence and launched militarily successful proxy wars in Central America that limited U.S. body bags and allegedly halted communist creep in the southern hemisphere. He "defeated" Libya through a bombing campaign that involved no U.S. ground troops. Shutting down the media access that conservatives and military leaders said sowed Vietnam-era dissent, he then scored a speedy win in

Grenada, "so quickly that television had no time to bring the carnage into the house," as *Time* magazine noted.⋆

At least on the entertainment side, television didn't really care—it was too busy generating huge ratings for adult shows such as *Magnum, P.I. Knight Rider,* and *Simon & Simon,* whose central characters were rogue Vietnam vets winning the day, thanks to their open defiance of a civilian government that was so "afraid to let them win."†
Same for movies: The Vietnam-hardened commanders featured in *Top Gun* and *Heartbreak Ridge* were shown finally being allowed to mount the same kind of lightning-fast, strafe-the-shit-out-of-'em strikes on the third world that Reagan was executing in real life.

A look at *The Miami Herald,* which extensively covered American intervention·in Latin America, illustrates how fast the Hands Tied Behind Their Backs Myth took hold. In 1986, the paper ran a syndicated column by Lars-Erik Nelson correctly noting that if you "ask Americans what is wrong with the U.S. involvement in Vietnam, most will tell you that we tried to fight for our national interests with one hand tied behind our back."

⋆The military Establishment's anger in the 1980s at the media for supposedly losing the Vietnam War was particularly intense, as described in Lieutenant Colonel Gregory Sieminski's brutally frank 1995 report for the Army War College. He noted that "many in the military blamed the loss of the Vietnam War on the media's critical reporting, which, it was argued, soured the American public's will to continue the fight." He went on, "Nowhere is this attitude toward the media more evident than in [the Grenada conflict], where Vice Admiral Metcalf initially refused to allow the media access to the combat zone. The motive for this restriction was transparent." He quotes Metcalf stating unequivocally, "Shutting the press out of Grenada was . . . based on a fear that an unrestrained press might muck things up again as many senior leaders believed they had done in Vietnam. If the press [was] not present, then there [was] no need to be concerned about . . . media spin."
†The lead characters' connection to Vietnam was not some barely mentioned résumé point—it was definitional, and deliberately so. Thomas Magnum was a Vietnam-era intelligence officer who, along with two Vietnam buddies T.C. and Rick, saves Honolulu from what *The New York Times* in 1987 called "the staples of the television cop genre: drug lords, rapacious playboys, con artists, Arab gold dealers, hookers and treacherous police officers." Michael Knight was an intelligence officer in Vietnam who became a cop and then a privately funded vigilante. Rick Simon was a former marine in Vietnam, whose experience gave his private detective agency much needed street sense and grit. In stressing protagonists' connection to the war and showing them succeeding in their private paramilitary work—often against government—these programs brought the Hands Tied behind Their Backs Myth out of the history books and into the present.

Two years later, following Jane Fonda's apology for her dissent against militarism during the 1960s, the *Herald*'s publisher penned an essay capturing the newly minted consensus.

"We've learned some lessons from the Vietnam War," he wrote. "First, we can't go to war without strong support from Congress and the American people. Second, when we go to war, we must fight to win. It's impossible to wage war with one hand tied behind our backs."

Another few months later, Reagan would echo that language in the 1988 reprise of his controversial 1980 VFW speech.

"We can all agree that we've learned one lesson," he said. "Young Americans must never again be sent to fight and die unless we are prepared to win."

In the one newspaper article that bothered to cover that speech, *Washington Post* columnist Colman McCarthy disappointingly noted this "old Reagan refrain" had become a matter of faith over the 1980s, shared by almost everyone in the newly "military-minded" nation.

"[We] believe that if only America sprayed more Agent Orange on Vietnam, spent more billions of dollars on the war effort and dropped more bombs, the troops, alive or dead, would have come home winners," he wrote, adding that it was all part of a broader effort to "sanitize the last cause as *'just'*" as "a way of cleaning up preparations for the next one."

Little did we know how right McCarthy would be.

As the 1980s progressed, a kind of logical proof came to define America's lurch toward militarism. It went roughly like this:

1. The Military = Unquestionably Awesome

2. The Military = America

   Thus

3. Questioning the Military = Questioning America = Unquestionably Not Awesome/Unpatriotic/Unacceptable

The first component of the equation was achieved by transferring the blame for the Vietnam defeat onto internal dissent and by separating the bad government from the good military in the minds of Americans—that is, by spreading the Legend of the Spat upon Veteran and the Hands Tied Behind Their Backs Myth. But the equation's second precept—making the military as important a symbol of Americanness as the flag itself—would require a more sophisticated campaign.

As outlined in earlier chapters, Reaganites were, at heart, revivalists, and one of the specific emotions they aimed to rekindle from bygone ages was the ticker-tape-parade euphoria associated with the victorious post–World War II, pre–Vietnam military, and they wanted to merge that feeling with the broader idea of patriotism. Reagan himself initiated that effort by employing martial stagecraft in his daily activities, constantly surrounding himself with uniformed officers at public events and, more brazenly, initiating the now mundane tradition of presidential saluting.

Before Reagan, "even presidents who had once been generals employed civilian manners," wrote historian John Lukacs. "They chose not to emphasize their military achievements during their presidential tenure—in accord with the American tradition of the primacy of civilian over military rule." But when Reagan assumed the presidency, Lukacs says, "the militarization of the image of the presidency began."

White House aides, and soon everyone, started referring to the president as the "commander in chief." This "exaggerated vesting of the president with his supreme role as commander in chief," Lukacs wrote, "is a new element in our national history"—and one with a motive, says his fellow historian Garry Wills: to legitimize and "reflect the increasing militarization of our politics."★ Yet, it wasn't until the

---

★Though never noted in the media at the time, what's (slightly) funny (but mostly sad) is that Reagan's saluting was actually a sign of his ignorance of and/or hostility to military protocol—not his cognizance of or respect for it. Lukacs notes that Reagan "had no record of [combat] service" and spent World War II "in the motion picture unit of the Army Air Corps." Hence, he didn't know, as Wills reports, what "Dwight Eisenhower, a real general, knew"—namely, "that the salute is for the uniform, and as president he was not wearing one. [Therefore] an exchange of salutes was out of order." Indeed, before Reagan broke it, that tradition

small-bore military campaigns of the 1980s came along that militarism and patriotism really became the synonyms they are today.

It started with Grenada in 1983. Rather than presenting the conflict for what it was—little more than a police action on a tiny island nation the size of Boise, Idaho—the White House hyped the invasion as a World War II–level mobilization, calling it Operation Urgent Fury. When the strike ended, Reagan presented the victory as proof of America's renewed global strength after Vietnam.

"Our days of weakness are over," he said. "Our military forces are back on their feet and standing tall."

It was the beginning of a larger tonal shift away from humility and toward the shock and awe of fist pumping, muscle flexing, and penis measuring that has come to define modern militarism.

In journalism, the turn was dramatic and overt. Establishment magazines such as *Newsweek* fronted covers with celebratory headlines like "Gunboat Diplomacy," "Americans at War," "The CIA Is Back in Business," and "Grenada: One We Won." Top political reporters such as Bruce Morton openly boasted that Reagan's militarism is "clearly reflected in the news coverage—as it should be." Most blatant of all, CBS started repitching its evening news broadcast with its version of a stadium-ready "U-S-A! U-S-A!" chant: "We Keep America on Top of the World," said the network's new double-entendre motto in the mid-1980s.★

Madison Avenue simultaneously went with what one ad executive called "the Springsteen heartland of America approach" as flag-draped beer commercials, and car ads such as Plymouth's "The Pride

---

of presidents deliberately avoiding military trappings dated back to the founding of the country. It was "a principle that George Washington embraced when he avoided military symbols at Mount Vernon," says Wills. But if any decade was going to break a two-hundred-year-old tradition in the name of promoting militaristic imagery, it was bound to be the 1980s.

★The sloganeering was only slightly less saber-rattling than the overtly militaristic propaganda that was exploding in the alternative press. Samizdat such as *Gung Ho, International Combat Arms,* and *Soldier of Fortune* were suddenly claiming almost a half million paid subscribers, an enthusiastic customer base for rags that bragged about being willing to tell the Hands Tied Behind Their Backs Myth of "good soldiers and gutless politicians."

Is Back" campaign channeled an audacious Stars and Stripes revivalism.*

As expected, the cacophony ended up popularizing and hipifying the armed forces for a nation no longer compelled into service by conscription.

"No better evidence of the changed climate [toward the military] exists than the torrent of applications flooding the nation's Army, Navy and Air Force academies," wrote *U.S. News & World Report* in 1985.

However, it would take more than pop culture for the country to make the jump from the equation's first precept (The Military = Unquestionably Awesome) to its second one (The Military = America). To become a reality, the formula needed the paramount exaggeration of 1980s-grade militarism and nationalism: the Gulf War.

Because it arrived without a shot being fired, the fall of the Berlin Wall in 1989, which marked the official End of the Cold War, didn't comport with militarism's triumphalist story line in the 1980s. In fact, it fit much more neatly into the diplomatic/strategic-containment narrative of the pre-1980s—an anti-militarist narrative that threatened to leave the Pentagon lacking a Red-menace justification for continued spending and buildups.

President and World War II war hero George H. W. Bush, well aware of the PR problems this would create for his own brand of Reaganism, quickly tried to hype the 1989 police action in Panama in precisely the same way his predecessor had hyped Grenada. Deem-

---

*Note to Boss fans: The effort to appropriate Springsteen for any and all causes knew no bounds in the mid-1980s. In 1984, archconservative columnist George Will—apparently unaware of both Springsteen's progressive politics and the antiwar lyrics of his song—praised "Born in the U.S.A." as an ode to Reaganism. A few days later, Reagan himself touted Springsteen in a speech, calling the song a "message of hope"—again, having apparently not listened to the decidedly despondent lyrics. Springsteen responded by telling *Rolling Stone,* "I think people have a need to feel good about the country they live in, but what's happening, I think, is that that need—which is a good thing—is getting manipulated and exploited. You see in the Reagan election ads on TV, you know, 'It's morning in America,' and you say, 'Well, it's not morning in Pittsburgh.'" Two years after the Reagan episode, Chrysler reportedly bid $12 million for the right to use "Born in the USA" in a commercial; Springsteen said no.

ing the operation against Manuel Noriega Operation *Just Cause,*★ the
White House would try to cite the victory as proof that the Pentagon's dick was still breathtakingly elephantine—and then argue that if
America wanted to preserve its virility, we'd have to strengthen the
new militarism of the 1980s.

But this wouldn't cut it for long. Nineteen eighties Cold War
hype was like an extra dose of supercharged Viagra exciting us into a
throbbing priapism whenever the Pentagon initiated yet another
post-Vietnam adventure. Without that Cold War, though, operations
in defenseless banana republics were like handing the same nation a
few shards of a useless herbal knockoff. It just wasn't going to cue the
same hard-on for militarism, and the Reaganites knew it the moment
they saw a 1989 Washington Post/ABC poll finding that nearly half
of all Americans said the "thaw in East-West relations means the
United States can now make major cuts in defense spending without
endangering national security."

So when America's former ally and proxy Saddam Hussein in-
vaded Kuwait in August of 1990, Bush seized the moment to, as he
would say, "kick the Vietnam Syndrome," and thus solidify 1980s
militarism for good.

★The very naming of the Panama conflict—Operation Just Cause—was a landmark for 1980s militarism. After Vietnam, the Joint Chiefs of Staff had computerized and automated the naming of military missions, and according to Lieutenant
Colonel Gregory Sieminski's Army War College report, from 1975 to 1988
"there was little attempt to exploit the power of nicknaming to improve either
troop morale or public and international relations." But as over-the-top military
propaganda had become a hallmark of the 1980s, no boundary was left unbroken,
and the computerized system was discarded. "Just Cause was the first U.S. combat
operation since the Korean War whose nickname was designed to shape domestic
and international perceptions about the mission it designated," wrote Sieminski,
noting that the specific name came from a lieutenant whose background in journalism and public relations "equipped him to appreciate what others could not:
that naming an operation is tantamount to seizing the high ground in waging a
public relations campaign." Bush officials—and soon network news—repeatedly
referred to the Panama invasion by its operation name, and the PR success for militarism "ushered in a new era in the nicknaming of U.S. military operations, one
in which operations are given names carefully selected to shape perceptions about
them." So remember: Every time you hear a pundit or reporter or government
spokesman referring to the politicized or sugarcoated name of a military mission,
that's 1980s militarism talking to you.

In the lead-up to Desert Storm, Bush made constant reference to 1980s Vietnam revisionism, saying on the eve of the war, "I've told the American people before that this will not be another Vietnam, and I repeat this here tonight: *Our troops will have the best possible support* in the entire world and they will not be asked to fight with one hand tied behind their back."

After a decade of 1980s propaganda, the pitch found a receptive audience in Congress as both parties' leaders—and especially those who were Vietnam veterans—pushed the legislative branch to simply get out of the way and give soldiers the chance "to win this time." Chief among these militarists was Arizona Republican representative John J. Rhodes, formerly a U.S. intelligence adviser to South Vietnamese troops. He told *The New York Times'* R. W. Apple in 1991 that when it came to a major decision about war, civilian-elected officials "ought to turn it over to the *military commanders.*"

At the same time, Bush seized on chances to vilify war critics as demoralizing the troops in the theater. A classic example was his intervention in a Chicago-area elementary school that had asked all students to wear a yellow ribbon "to *support the service personnel* currently engaged in the conflict in the Persian Gulf."

Operation Yellow Ribbon,★ the activist group which spearheaded the campaign, was backed by the armed forces and its mission was quite explicit: to combat those who would dare spit on troops by expressing opposition to Pentagon policy.

★Recall that before it was a symbol of militarism in the Gulf War, the yellow ribbon was a symbol of solidarity with Americans taken hostage in Iran. The semiotic change was no accident. Turning expressions of freedom for the oppressed/ incarcerated into a symbol of support for the largest and most powerful military on the planet was one way to reclaim the Revolutionary War brand of underdog insurgency that we had so explicitly juxtaposed ourselves *against* during Vietnam—a war explicitly waged on underdog insurgents. Such rebranding of America as an underdog was ubiquitous. We weren't the empire coming to claim Mideast oil, the yellow ribbon said our troops were victims of antiwar voices who wanted to hold them hostage by opposing the invasion. We weren't helping autocratic corporatist authoritarians in Central America or al-Qaeda predecessors in Afghanistan against the Soviets—Reaganites told us we were helping "freedom fighters." We weren't the biggest, baddest military on the planet looking for geopolitical power or oil—we were *Red Dawn*'s Wolverines, God-fearing survivalist teenagers on the brink of being pummeled by Soviet invaders or Saddam's Republican Guard or cave dwellers in Afghanistan or insurgents in Iraq . . .

The yellow ribbon campaign in the schools was just one of many such efforts to bleed militarism into society and polarize any discussion of defense policy on "support our troops" terms. And when a few Chicago parents raised innocent questions about the appropriateness of teachers telling grade-schoolers to publicly demonstrate their support for war, Bush saw the chance for a media spectacle that would use children and First Amendment genuflection to conflate support for militarism with support for soldiers—and the flag. His letter to the school told the youngsters that wearing the ribbon would give them "a wonderful opportunity to experience one of America's greatest blessings—freedom of expression."

As for the soldiers themselves, many had long ago internalized Vietnam revisionism, as evidenced by a *New York Times* interview with Representative John Murtha (D-PA) in which the paper noted that "troops repeatedly asked [him] whether the *folks back home supported them.*"

"The aura of Vietnam hangs over these kids," said Murtha, the first Vietnam veteran elected to Congress. "Their parents were in it. They've seen all these movies. They worry, they wonder."

Of course they were concerned. Regardless of the fundamental untruths behind the Legend of the Spat upon Veteran and the historically questionable Hands Tied Behind Their Backs Myth, the teenage and twentysomething grunts deployed to the Gulf had grown up in a 1980s pop culture that said those fallacies were verifiable fact. Indeed, Murtha's reference to movies was no throwaway line—filmic fantasy had become our whole frame of reference.

"When we deployed here, people cheered and waved flags," said one soldier, "but if I go back home like the Vietnam vets did and somebody spits on me, I swear to God I'll kill them."

Like aristocrats watching Civil War battles over picnic lunches and iced tea, Americans took in the Gulf War over dinner and beers. From the comfort of our La-Z-Boys™, we got to watch the tracer fire, hear the Scud sirens, and ogle the black-and-white smart-bomb videos (but, of course, see little bloodshed). Yes, the Gulf War was, for those not fighting it, a two-month experiment in Nielsen ratings, and military triumphalism proved to be a huge hit, what with its new troupe of scowling villains (Saddam and the Republican Guard), barrel-chested paragons (Generals Norman Schwarzkopf and Colin Powell), and celebrated G. I. Joes straight out of central casting.

The 1980s equation had been completed. Well aware that entertainment realms and real-world events were taking on a life-imitating-art-imitating-life quality in the *Delta Force* age, Bush had promised a tidy Oscar-caliber conclusion to the Gulf War. He told the country, "I pledge to you there will not be any murky ending," and he appeared to deliver America the contemporary V-E and V-J Day parade we pined for.

"Our country came together with a pride that we hadn't had since the end of World War Two," Bush declared.

In most Americans' minds, the decisive victory seemed to prove that the myths were true, that backstabbing from a hand-tying government and spitting war protesters *was* responsible for the pre-1980s loss in Vietnam. After all, such Vietnam-era dissent was suppressed by politicians and pop culture during the 1980s, and look what happened: America had racked up a series of high-profile victories, capped off by an exciting prime-time cable-television extravaganza called the Gulf War.

Through such seemingly logical deduction, the military *became* America, and to question it anymore or to oppose war was to be a dirty hippie and/or a traitor—the same kind of monster who we're told today insults commanders on the ground, refuses to support the troops, abhors America's just causes, and, oh yeah, just loves providing aid and comfort to our enemies.

When both political parties these days agree on ideas and vie for ownership of those ideas, it's a sign that what they are competing for has become a matter of deep and abiding public consensus. And in our red-versus-blue nation, there are fewer points of national consensus than even the Ten Commandments. By my back-of-the-envelope estimate, I'd say we can, at most, find agreement on hating pedophiles, loving mom, adoring Apple Pie—and, after the 1980s, believing all decisions about war and peace should be made by the military.

What else to conclude when you read the Democratic National

Committee's press release from December 2006? With George W. Bush fast becoming the modern era's most unpopular president and with the war in Iraq already an unmitigated disaster, the opposition party attacked the president not for a lack of leadership or for showing too much deference to the military's inept war planners, but for "refusing to listen to our *military commanders in the field*"—that is, for not deferring to the military's war planners *enough*.

The press release went on to list Bush's most slobbery kisses of the Pentagon ass.

There was Bush's statement in May of 2006: "I have said to the American people: As the Iraqis stand up, we'll stand down, but I've also said that our *commanders on the ground* will make that decision." There was his reiteration of that point a month later, saying that "in terms of our presence" in Iraq, the decisions about whether to stay or leave "will be made by General Casey." And there was his recitation of the key 1980s myths about Vietnam.

"I remember coming up in the Vietnam War and it seemed like that there was a lot of politicization of the military decisions," the Democratic press release recounted Bush saying in April of 2006. "That's not going to be the case under my administration."★

This collection of Pentagon smooches was held up by Bush's political opponents not as an egregious betrayal of constitutional principles that mandate civilian control of the armed forces. On the contrary, they were cited as honorable homilies to the American consensus around junta culture—and reason our country should therefore be angry at news that the president was considering making his own independent military decisions.

When both parties—and, in particular, the ostensible antiwar party—are echoing this kind of fervid militarism, it's a good sign that any argument has ended. Democrats may have been specifically opposing Bush's "surge" proposal to escalate the Iraq War, but by

---

★Two years before these statements, Bush had already admitted that his deferential militarism came straight from eighties backstab mythology about Vietnam. "The thing about the Vietnam War that troubles me, as I look back, was it was a political war," he had said. "We had politicians making military decisions, and it is a lesson that any president must learn, and that is to set the goal and the objective and allow the military to come up with the plans to achieve that objective."

couching their rhetoric in the vocabulary of military deference, they reflected the militarist consensus first solidified in the 1980s.

During the peacetime interlude between the Gulf War that capped off the 1980s and today's Afghanistan and Iraq wars, militarism was certainly lower profile than it had been at the beginning of the Reagan era, but it was just as robust.

Factions on the right, for example, proffered that the military and its culture wasn't merely distinct or distinctly better than the rest of the hand-tying, backstabbing government. Militias and "patriot" groups in the 1990s presented the rituals and panache of the armed forces as explicit expressions of anti-government zeal. To wear camouflage uniforms, play at weekend war games, and run hypothetical deployments in the backwoods of Flyover Country was to display antipathy for the state.

The political left, already weakened, fractured completely. At the top, a newly inaugurated president, Bill Clinton, who once said Vietnam was "a war I opposed and despised," delivered a speech in 1993 calling the conflict "worthy," a riff off Reagan's "noble cause" language.

College kids took the cues. These potential antimilitarist voices of a new peacetime generation were cowed by the same Vietnam myths of the 1980s that Gulf War GIs feared.

"Students at school after school volunteered stories of protesters spitting on soldiers as their central image of the Vietnam-era peace movement," wrote Paul Rogat Loeb in his study of Generation X's post-1980s attitudes about war and opposition to militarism. "At every kind of college, in every corner of the country, the slightest mention of antiwar activism of that time would impel them . . . to describe how the peace marchers [of the sixties] spat on soldiers, called them names, and drove to bases and airports with the sole purpose of heaping contempt on the already scarred young men as they returned."*

9/11 and its aftermath was the coda—rather than evoking self-

---

*As an example: During the Bosnia conflict in 1995, a leaflet distributed at Holy Cross College captured the staying power of the 1980s myths about Vietnam by stating the "hope that no student today will repeat the mistakes of the generation that proceeded us—by spitting on Marines."

reflective questions about the consequences of our bellicosity and the inevitability of blowback, the terrorist attacks elicited ever more '80s-themed militarism.

Elder antiwar icons who had lived through the 1960s and who had tried to fight Reaganism in the 1980s—they suddenly started sounding like unreformed Reaganites when the Twin Towers went down. For example, Todd Gitlin, the former leader of Students for a Democratic Society, lashed out at antimilitarist voices—and on specifically Vietnam terms. In a much circulated newspaper editorial, he said the most vehement opponents of the Afghanistan invasion were unable to feel the "passion of patriotism," and he lamented that "America's anti-war movement [is] a child of the Vietnam era and has viewed every subsequent conflict through that prism."

Likewise, Marc Cooper of *The Nation* magazine said that while "the American left has had reason to be skeptical about the deployment of U.S. military power," the 9/11 attacks "demand a *just response*" of overwhelming military force. He added that in opposing lockstep deference to the military, "The American left—or at least a broad swath of it—is more alienated from its own national institutions than its counterparts in any other developed nation."

He wasn't wrong on that last point. The few who questioned Rambo-style militarism and junta culture in the years after 9/11 did separate themselves from almost everyone else, and certainly from debates over national security—debates that quickly devolved into 1980s talking points.

As the media incessantly beat the drum for war through Super Bowl-esque television graphics and revenge-flavored narratives, reporters "embedded" with American battalions filed propagandistic satellite dispatches that made the messy conflicts in Afghanistan and Iraq seem like the perfectly executed military operations fearured in so many '80s flicks. At home, W. reenacted his father's Gulf War performance by pledging fealty to "commanders on the ground," portraying war opponents as troop-spitters or America haters, and bragging, "I make decisions here in the Oval Office in foreign policy matters with war on my mind."

At the Republican National Convention in 2004, Senator Zell Miller, a former Democrat, keynoted the quasi-religious military-worship session by echoing Reagan's 1980 VFW speech—the one about soldiers "so often blamed for war by those who parade for peace."

Miller said, "It is the soldier, not the reporter, who has given us the freedom of the press . . . it is the soldier, not the poet, who has given us freedom of speech. It is the soldier, not the agitator, who has given us the freedom to protest. It is the soldier who salutes the flag, serves beneath the flag, whose coffin is draped by the flag, who gives that protester the freedom he abuses to burn that flag."

Democrats loyally fell in line with the theme, as one of their leading pollsters, Stan Greenberg, told the party, "The biggest doubt about Democrats coming into this election was on the military: Do they respect the military and will they support spending for the military?"

Despite almost half of Americans having been born after the end of the Vietnam War, Democrats designed their 2004 National Convention to revolve around that conflict, with its most hyped moment coming when the party's Vietnam-vet-turned-presidential-nominee saluted the crowd and said, "I'm John Kerry and I'm reporting for duty." The strategy was political suicide. In reinforcing rather than rejecting the supremacy of modern militarism's Vietnam obsession, Democrats only empowered the old stab-in-the-back revisionism.

The so-called Swift Boat Veterans for Truth, for instance, lambasted Kerry's outspoken opposition to the war after he came home from combat.

"We won the battle," said one Swift Boater. "Kerry went home and lost the war for us."

Former president George H. W. Bush, dispatched to amplify this line on national TV, attacked Kerry's opposition to the Vietnam conflict as "impugning the . . . integrity and the honor of those who were still serving." By speaking out against the war, Kerry "brutalized people that were still serving or who had served," Bush said.

The aggregate effect was to further bolster that 1980s notion that you cannot at once "support the troops" and oppose a war, because opposing militarism allegedly harms soldiers. And when Kerry lost, Democrats interpreted it not as a failure to indict 1980s militarism, but as a failure to show sufficiently loyalty to it.

One Democratic lawmaker started attacking Bush for "grossly miscalculat[ing] what would be needed to win the (Iraq) war" and for deploying "not enough troops" to the battlefield. Another would warn against opposing any and all wars in the future.

"If we become the antiwar party, that's not beneficial," said Representative Lincoln Davis (D-TN), as he urged his fellow party members to only consider "the kind of pro-war Democrat that we ought to be."

Had 2008 commenced a genuinely new era just as Reagan's first election did—had we finally stepped forward from the 1980s—militarism would probably have been the first pillar of 1980s culture to crumble. Iraq has become the quagmire Dick Cheney once predicted it would become,★ Afghanistan is falling apart, Pentagon expenditures continue to burn an ever-bigger hole in the national budget, and at the end of the Bush era, even the troops themselves told pollsters they were souring on America's state of permanent war. Additionally, the 2008 presidential campaign was, at least initially, about a choice between militarism and something, well, different.

On the one side, there was the Republican Party circa 1984.

The party's initial frontrunner, Rudy Giuliani, kicked off the campaign with an ode to stab-in-the-back mythology, stating that "America must remember one of the lessons of the Vietnam War . . . Then, as now, we corrected course and began to show real progress . . . But America then withdrew its support, allowing the communist North to conquer the South . . . The consequences of abandoning Iraq would be worse."

★From the I Shit You Not File: Cheney in 1994 said of President George H. W. Bush's decision not to send troops all the way to Baghdad during the Gulf War: "There would have been a U.S. occupation of Iraq. None of the Arab forces that were willing to fight with us in Kuwait were willing to invade Iraq. Once you got to Iraq and took it over, took down Saddam Hussein's government, then what are you going to put in its place? That's a very volatile part of the world, and if you take down the central government of Iraq, you could very easily end up seeing pieces of Iraq fly off. . . . It's a quagmire if you go that far and try to take over Iraq." This is the same Cheney who later promised an easy invasion and occupation of Iraq when he was vice president.

The GOP's eventual nominee, John McCain, was the guy who said he "thought our civilian commanders were complete idiots" in Vietnam and who had campaigned for president in the 2000 election saying that "the lessons of Vietnam" teach that "never again (should) we send our men and women to fight and die in foreign conflicts unless our goal is victory"—i.e., we have to "let them win."

On the other side was Barack Obama, who seemed to promise more diplomacy, a withdrawal from Iraq, and less '80s-ish militarism in general. But when the campaign entered its final weeks, Obama sharply pivoted to Republicans' unreconstructed 1980s posture, criticizing the Bush White House's Afghanistan escalation plan for being insufficiently war-mongering.

"It is not enough troops, and not enough resources, with not enough urgency," said the Democratic nominee.

Now, during the Obama presidency, that same unflinching militarism once again stares us in the face everywhere we look.

Here it is in a federal budget that puts President Obama on course to devote more money to military operations than any other executive in one term since World War II. There it is with Obama's secretary of defense saying allies "averse to military force" have become "an impediment to achieving real security and lasting peace." Here it is in a Democratic Party press release attacking Republican Michael Steele's (surprising) antiwar comments for *"Undermin[ing] the morale of our troops"* and "rooting for failure." And there it is again on the ubiquitous SUPPORT OUR TROOPS bumper stickers, in the Super Bowl's military-themed festivities, and on your evening news as Dick Cheney attacks war critics for "giving encouragement—*aid and comfort*—to the enemy."

Militarism and junta culture is omnipresent, but especially in the politics of our ongoing wars. A comparison between the Vietnam-era's General William Westmoreland and a onetime "commander on the ground" in Afghanistan shows how much the 1980s interregnum truly changed us.

In terms of both public perception and tactical reality, Westmoreland's war in Asia's southern jungles was an antecedent to General Stanley McChrystal's war in that same continent's central mountains. Messy and unpopular counterinsurgencies, the conflicts were originally predicated on containment strategies and domino theories. Change the isms, and the goals are one and the same: We were once told we couldn't let Vietnam become a haven for the export of communism; now we're told we can't let Afghanistan become a haven for the export of terrorism.

In similar positions during (relatively) similar wars, Westmoreland and McChrystal initially followed the same script on the public stage.

In the late 1960s, Westmoreland became as high profile a figure as his commander in chief. First, he started pushing his constitutional superiors to send more troops to Vietnam. Then, during a trip home, he publicly declared that opposition to the war was "unpatriotic" and "inevitably will cost lives." And finally, he delivered a speech to a joint session of Congress effectively dictating policy by telling lawmakers, "Your continued strong support is vital to the success of our mission."★

McChrystal made much the same moves in 2009, only with even more defiant enthusiasm. He leaked a demand for an escalation to the press, so as to back his commander in chief into a corner. Then he gave a public address to reporters—in a foreign country, no less—pressuring Congress and the president to immediately endorse an escalation without deliberation or delay.

This is where Westmoreland's and McChrystal's experiences diverge, and where the 1980s mentality kicked in.

In 1967, key congressional leaders were disgusted with Westmoreland and President Johnson soon replaced him—a bold move, to be sure, but neither legally inappropriate (the Constitution explicitly vests the president with authority over military officials) nor historically unprecedented (only sixteen years before the Westmoreland removal, President Harry Truman had fired General Douglas MacArthur for insolence).

By contrast, twenty-two years later, congressional leaders and the political establishment all but celebrated McChrystal's initial insubor-

---

★*Time* noted in 1967 that Westmoreland's move was at that time "unprecedented." The magazine reported that "no other military commander had ever addressed a joint meeting of Congress in the midst of a conflict that he was still directing." Today, of course, America all but expects—if not wants—generals to make public moves in juxtaposition to their civilian superiors.

dination and lambasted President Obama for taking time to consider any alternatives to the general's escalation plan.

Senator Kit Bond (R-MO) went for the Hands Tied Behind Their Backs line, criticizing the White House for allowing "political motivations [to] override the needs of our commanders." *The Washington Post* went with Spat upon Veterans language, declaring any deviation from the general's report would "dishonor and endanger this country." The head of the Veterans of Foreign Wars chose the more general "aid and comfort" rhetoric, saying the deliberations meant "the extremists are sensing weakness and indecision within the U.S. government" that will "embolden" the enemy to "intensify their efforts to kill more U.S. soldiers."

Summing up the national chorus for militarism, *The New York Times* predicted that no matter what the civilian political leadership might want, "It will be very hard to say no to General McChrystal."

The *Times*'s prophecy proved accurate. In the same week newspaper reports quoted a Pentagon aide saying that the general felt "stabbed in the back" by Obama administration skeptics, a *New York Times* headline blared "Three Obama Advisers Favor More Troops for Afghanistan." It was a sign that the White House was not resisting McChrystal's petulant bullying, but was instead preparing to fully comply with his demands. The *Washington Post* later reported that while Obama had initially "looked for a way out of the war in Afghanistan, repeatedly pressing (McChrystal and) his top military advisers for an exit plan," those advisers "never gave him" one. Ultimately, rather than insist they comply with his presidential directive, the commander in chief backed down, agreeing to a version of McChrystal's escalation strategy in a speech at the United States Military Academy—a speech preserving the 1980s doctrine that says civilian leaders must acquiesce to military orders.

"It is instructive to pay less attention to what Obama said in his West Point speech and more to where he said it—that is, in front of the designated heirs to an officer class that in recent years has accrued unprecedented influence over policies once thought to be the exclusive domain of elected officials," wrote Kevin Baker of *Harper's*. "Obama's choice of venue provided the perhaps-too-liberal president a reassuringly martial podium, and in doing so it assured the Pentagon of an outcome its officers had in good part already determined."

Indeed, the commander in chief would "let us win" by completely deferring to whatever his military officials desired, which is exactly the way an eighties-thinking America wanted it.

Public opinion data is dramatic on this point. On the general question of escalating the Afghanistan war or withdrawing, nearly every poll taken during the autumn of 2009 found a majority of Americans saying they opposed a troop increase. But when asked whom they wanted to make the final decision, the same majority said the military—not elected officials as mandated by the Constitution. Even more notably, when pollsters presented a buildup plan as coming from the military and not civilian leaders, the numbers on the specific escalation question inverted, with a plurality of Americans suddenly saying they supported it. Remember, in 1981, half of the same country said it did not have even basic confidence in the military as a functioning institution, much less as the sole arbiter of international affairs. Just three decades later, the military's imprimatur can instantaneously shift public opinion on the biggest questions of geopolitical strategy.

But, then, that's the point: We're *not* the same country *because* of the 1980s—and the eighties drumbeat goes on.

McChrystal, for instance, may later have been fired for insulting top administration officials in *Rolling Stone,* but even his removal was imbued with the underlying principle of militarism.

"This is a change in personnel, but this is not a change in policy," the president said when he removed McChrystal, as if to reassure us of the administration's lockstep commitment to war. Obama then promoted General David Petraeus—a man who, according to the *Washington Post,* had responded to previous orders he didn't like by telling colleagues that the White House was "[expletive] with the wrong guy."

Such deference to the Pentagon, even from the commander in chief, undoubtedly "has to do with the Rambo phenomenon," says David Morrell, the author of the book *First Blood,* which inspired the eighties films. "It's 'support our troops' whether (a) war is right or wrong, which is a version of 'our country, right or wrong," he writes. "There's no question we should support our soldiers: [but] what I find troubling is that this support of our armed forces somehow made it necessary to support policies some Americans disagree with—that if you disagree with the war, you're somehow disloyal to the military."★

To put it in the Bush lexicon, you're either with militarism or against the troops, and that eighties psychology leaves the most prescient cautions against the downsides of war inevitably marginalized, precisely as Rambo hoped.

★Morrell's book was published a decade before it became a movie, and the way Hollywood altered his original Rambo character tracks the American public's larger change in mind-set in the 1980s. "After publication of *First Blood* in 1972, while Americans struggled separately with their own experience of the Vietnam War, Rambo became the war's symbol—but not the one Morrell conceived," wrote *History Channel Magazine* in 2003. "Although Rambo gets blown away at the end of *First Blood* the novel, in *First Blood* the movie (1982) he survives to become the buff, bandanna'd warrior of *Rambo II* (1985) and *Rambo III* (1988), turning his noble soldier talents to good purpose against the enemies of America. No longer the tortured, lonely hitchhiker of the book, Rambo has morphed into an oil-slicked action figure toting an assault rifle and stripped to the waist."

OPERATION RED DAWN

Young people have developed incredible hand, eye, and brain coordination in playing these games. The Air Force believes these kids will be outstanding pilots should they fly our jets. The computerized radar screen in the cockpit is not unlike the computerized video screen. Watch a twelve-year-old take evasive action and score multiple hits while playing Space Invaders, and you will appreciate the skills of tomorrow's pilot. . . . What I am saying is that right now you're being prepared for tomorrow. —PRESIDENT RONALD REAGAN, 1983

I'm living the same fight as those guys. Or at least I'm seeing the same fight. . . . I'm happy to tell you that I've never been more engaged in a conflict in my life. —LIEUTENANT COLONEL CHRIS GOUGH ON PILOTING AN UNMANNED AERIAL VEHICLE OVER AFGHANISTAN, 2009

In 1988, I was in sixth grade. My days were an endless cycle of Eggo waffles, yellow Laidlaw buses, cardboard dioramas, homework, and Phillies radio broadcasts. Book bags, Garbage Pail Kids, Huffy dirt bikes, twenty-sided Dungeons & Dragons dice, and East Abington Little League jerseys were my rock-star bling.

This was all defined as conventionally normal. If my parents had any concern about future deviance, it revolved around my penchant for cracking jokes about the eminently hateable Mrs. Green in music class. What was also considered normal, and what my parents were not concerned about at all, was my basement serving as a makeshift armory, war-planning facility, and high-tech military training ground all in one.

In this, my own private, subterranean NORAD, I war-gamed tank assaults on an international terrorist organization; cleaned and brandished my true-to-life urban assault-rifle toy; reviewed live-action videotape footage teaching me how I could help the military fend off an imminent homeland invasion; and ran a first-person computer simulation of a commando mission, one that lasted extralong when I punched in a secret code that made my avatar immortal. If it was a weekday, I could do this all before heading back upstairs, eating dinner, and catching *The A-Team*'s latest prime-time paramilitary op, and if it was a weekend, I was probably first going to see *Iron Eagle II* or *Rambo III* at the local theater before heading down to my bunker to try to reenact those films' climactic massacres.

Now let's be completely clear: I did not consciously *know* I was a devout militarist at the young, impressionable age of twelve. When I ordered my G. I. Joe Snowcat tank to indiscriminately fire one of its six missiles at the Cobra soldiers who so often held my LEGO city hostage, I didn't think that if this were real, it would probably leave a smoldering pile of blood and limbs and innocent victims. All I thought was "Awesome!"

When I rented Hollywood's first PG-13 rated production, 1984's *Red Dawn,* and I saw the teen heartthrobs protect America by racking up execution after execution, I didn't know the movie would also become the Guinness world-record holder for violent acts depicted per minute in a film.★ All I did was cheer.

And when I played *Contra* on my Nintendo NES, I wasn't ques-

---

★Yes, you read that paragraph correctly. *Red Dawn* really was the very first movie to get the PG-13 rating—a rating designed to make sure kids younger than eighteen can watch. Yet, this same film was unlike any R-rated movie in that it showed 134 acts of violence per hour. Indeed, at the time of its release, *Red Dawn* was the most violent motion picture that had ever been run in theaters, according to the National Coalition on Television Violence.

tioning the premise of a game named after violent terrorist death squads in Nicaragua that were being funded by the Reagan administration's illegal CIA cash transfers from Iran. I was just punching in up–up–down–down–left–right–left–right–B–A, then happily mowing down anything and everything that moved.

"Propaganda is most effective when it is least noticeable," writes public relations expert Nancy Snow. "In an open society, such as the United States, the hidden and integrated nature of the propaganda best convinces people they are not being manipulated."

Exactly, and neither I nor my parents were *supposed* to think much about what the 1980s were teaching me and every other kid in our basements-turned-bunkers. We were supposed to just play, and mom and dad were supposed to simply chalk it all up to "kids being kids." It was an easy rationale for parents whose own adult mediasphere was already convincing them that militarism equals patriotism. And anyway, kids' entertainment is just frivolous fun and games, right?

Well, not really.

For a generation that grew up on *Reading Rainbow, Memory,* and Speak and Spell's *E.T.* Fantasy Module (*geranium* has only one *r!*), games and entertainment were teaching tools, and the militarization of childhood that started in the 1980s made the little green men, cap guns, and Boy Scout retreats of old-time Americana look positively pacifist. With the Pentagon shaping movie screenplays, investing in video games, cooperating with toy marketers, and eventually working with baseball-card companies to publish Desert Storm trading cards, 1985's classic sci-fi novel *Ender's Game* seemed more prophecy than fantasy.

Reaganism abetted this dawn of the "the military-entertainment complex," as *Wired* magazine called it. The administration's hawkishness provided the political rationale for parental complicity, and the White House's deregulatory agenda helped television become the most influential—and most invasive—marketer of kids products, more and more of which were violent and military-themed.

Now, the investment is paying off, just in time for the current era's obsession with permanent war.

Today's soldiers, for example, frequently reference their childhood devotion to *G. I. Joe* cartoons and action figures of the 1980s when explaining their decision to enlist.* Similarly, during the Iraq invasion military brass named the search for Saddam Hussein "Operation Red Dawn" because officers said the John Milius film "was a patriotic, pro-American movie [that] all of us in the military have seen." And the Atari- and Nintendo-trained generation of military leaders now employ video-game arcades to recruit and train today's PlayStation and Xbox youth for newly robotized combat.

Considering all this, do you truly think it was mere coincidence that George W. Bush's aides exquisitely re-created the final aircraft-carrier scene from *Top Gun* to commemorate their boss's declaration of Iraq victory? Do you sincerely believe that Bush's "bring it on" taunt had nothing to do with an attempt to access fond memories of Milius one-liners from the 1980s? And can you really argue that it's just happenstance that the Pentagon today airs recruitment ads in movie theaters, ads that portray soldiers as bulletproof *RoboCops* and war as the bloodless arcade game from *The Last Starfighter*?

The answer to those questions should be no. White House strategists and Pentagon propagandists use information and imagery as strategic weapons, and they are well aware that the most valuable of those weapons is cheery childhood nostalgia. They also know that in a country where almost half the population was born after 1979, some of the most compelling of those youthful memories come from the schlock that was originally stockpiled in the 1980s basement.

The B-movie VHS tapes, the shoeboxes of trading cards, the dusty Atari cartridges, the chipped action figures, the faded comic books, even the ripped WRESTLEMANIA T-shirts—all that cheap plastic, pulp, and fabric constituted a curriculum inculcating kids to not only see the military as central to our society, but to psychologically separate the bombast of war from the carnage of casualty, and to fear new

---

*In the October 2008 edition of *The Believer,* journalist Jason Boog found that "a national newspaper search for *G. I. Joe* references turned up 35 obituaries for soldiers killed in Iraq since the war began, in 2003. In each article, family members reminisced how the men had loved to play with the toy soldiers." He quoted Sergeant Tommy Rieman, for instance, saying, "I always wanted to be a soldier at some point, and *G. I. Joe* had a lot to do with that. It's what they did—they were fighting for something good, something right—and they looked cool doing it."

enemies with far more longevity than Nikolai Volkoff and his Soviet comrades.

Assuming you own the 2007 collector's DVD of *Red Dawn* (which I most certainly do); and assuming you have repeatedly watched *Red Dawn Rising,* the documentary about the movie on disc two (which I most certainly have); and still further assuming you once had fairly intense crushes on Lorraine McFly and Amanda Jones (which I most certainly did); then you might remember the documentary's interview with the vivacious Lea Thompson, the actress who played those girl-next-door hotties in *Back to the Future* and *Some Kind of Wonderful,* respectively, and who, even before that, played Erica in *Red Dawn.*

"Kids keep discovering [*Red Dawn*] because it is empowering to kids," Thompson said, wistfully recalling the movie. "And the truth is kids always do fight wars."

The actress was, if inadvertently, admitting just how much the martial cinema of the 1980s was aimed squarely at children, and the question is why?

One answer is the entertainment media's profit-focused "give 'em what they want" impulse. Just as sex sells to adults, shoot-'em-up fantasy started selling to an eighties youth increasingly drawn—and given access—to the spectacle of violent imagery. As one study found, young viewers in the 1980s were "more likely to attend to violent programs than older viewers, with the heaviest violence viewing occurring between the ages of seven and nine."

But another, more ideological factor was the Pentagon.

Lea Thompson was exactly right. Whether as saber-rattling politicians, hawkish voters, or soldiers themselves, kids inevitably grow up and fight wars, and military leaders in the eighties wanted to shape kids' malleable attitudes through the most powerful media instruments available.

"Young men of recruiting age cited movies and television as their primary source of their impressions about the military, so [movies and television] are very important [to the Pentagon]," an army spokeswoman told PBS, citing the Defense Department's extensive surveys of youth attitudes. "It's an opportunity for [kids] to see what the possibilities are and to see what being a soldier would be like."

Out of all "the mid-'80s Armageddon movies" aggrandizing the soldier life for kids, none "has had as much enduring influence as *Red Dawn*," says *Slate*'s David Plotz.

The movie is a classic invasion flick, but with a deliberate twist for recruitment-age teens. It tells the story of youngsters from the fictional town of Calumet, Colorado, who call themselves the Wolverines and who go rogue by mounting a preposterous guerrilla resistance against a massive Soviet assault on the American homeland. To further sex up the adolescent appeal, *Red Dawn* cast '80s teen heartthrobs such as Thompson, Jennifer Grey, Patrick Swayze, Charlie Sheen, and C. Thomas Howell in the lead roles.

Strikingly, *Red Dawn* doesn't hesitate to mix this troupe, fit as they were for a suburban John Hughes comedy, with a hard-edged fanaticism you might find at a militia meeting in the Idaho Panhandle. The film starts out with the bedrock provisos of militarist paranoia, including key pillars of eighties Vietnam-related revision:

- ANTI-GUN-CONTROL EXTREMISM: One of the film's first scenes shows a Soviet thug pulling a gun from an American corpse as the camera pans across a pickup truck bearing an NRA bumper sticker that reads THEY CAN HAVE MY GUN WHEN THEY PRY IT FROM MY COLD, DEAD FINGERS. Later, the Soviets are able to hunt down American resisters through the secret master list of gun owners that the U.S. government allegedly keeps (one of the longtime conspiracy theories among gun enthusiasts).

- RETALIATION/REVENGE ON COUNTRIES THAT DEFEAT THE UNITED STATES: One of the kids' fathers is shown in a concentration-camp cage, yelling to his son to "Avenge me!" by killing as many enemies as possible. His scream could be the name of every back-to-Vietnam flick from the 1980s.

- BACKSTABBING POLITICIANS: The film shows Calumet's mayor as a cowardly and conniving Soviet collaborator who does nothing while his constituents are rounded up and murdered. Additionally, the mayor's son (also student body president at

Calumet High School) presses the Wolverines to surrender and later betrays them. Taken together, *Red Dawn* argues that politicians are all weak-kneed, corrupt, and traitorous.

- UNITED STATES AS EMBATTLED UNDERDOG: In the same way adult politics, media, and entertainment in the eighties tried to recast the U.S. military as a yellow-ribbon-worthy underdog helping supposed "freedom fighters" in Latin America, rescuing POWs from Vietcong, and liberating Kuwait from the supposed Iraq behemoth, *Red Dawn*'s Wolverines are positioned as outgunned insurgents scratching their way to victory against the Russian colossus. "The message of *Red Dawn*," its director, Milius, said, "is to liberate the oppressed"—the "oppressed" somehow being America, the most militarily dominant nation in human history.

Soon after fleeing to the woods for some good old-fashioned Unabomber-like survivalism (including drinking deer blood as a male-bonding exercise), the Wolverines come upon a fallen U.S. pilot who articulates a few more paranoias of eighties militarism:

- STEALTH TERRORISTS ARE ALREADY AMONG US: "The first wave of the (Soviet) attack came in disguise as commercial charter flights," says the pilot in an eerily prescient vision of a 9/11-like onslaught.

- THE NEED FOR A MILITARIZED SOUTHERN BORDER: "Infiltrators came up illegal from Mexico, Cubans mostly," he continues. "They managed to infiltrate SAC bases in the Midwest, several down in Texas. It wreaked a helluva lot of havoc, I'm here to tell ya. They opened up the door down here, and the whole Cuban and Nicaraguan armies come walking right through."*

---

*Slightly Off-Topic Theory of Geographic Noncoincidence: *Red Dawn* devotees no doubt recall that the pilot goes on to tell the kids that the Russian-Nicaraguan-Cuban invasion "rolled right up through the Great Plains." But when the invaders tried to move out to the coasts, the pilot also reports that "we stopped their butt cold" and "held them at the Rockies and the Mississippi" where "the lines have pretty much stabilized." In other words, right-wing Flyover Country protected

- WEAK-KNEED WESTERN ALLIES JUSTIFY THE UNITED STATES SPENDING MORE ON THE MILITARY THAN ALL OTHER NATIONS COMBINED: When the kids ask if Europe is going to help stop the Soviet invasion, the pilot says that Europe is "sittin' this one out—all except England, and they won't last very long."

Recall that four years before this film was released, Ronald Reagan had given voice to many of these theories, saying "the Soviets and their friends are advancing" and chastising the Carter administration for "failing to see any threatening pattern." A teenage flick such as *Red Dawn* so precisely parroting such presidential talking points was clearly more than a coincidence, and more than just an example of Hollywood succumbing to a larger cultural undertow. It was propaganda in its most literal form.

In 1997, after reports that *Red Dawn* was one of Oklahoma City bomber Timothy McVeigh's favorite films, MGM/United Artists vice president Peter Bart revealed to *Variety* that when his company first considered the movie's script, the studio's CEO "declared in no uncertain terms that he wanted to make the ultimate jingoistic movie." The studio subsequently recruited Reagan's recently departed secretary of state, retired general Alexander Haig, to serve on MGM's corporate board, "consult with [*Red Dawn*'s] director and inculcate the appropriate ideological tint." Though the screenplay's first draft strived to lament the tragedies of war, Bart recounted how the studio "demanded to know why [it] should try to remake *Lord of the Flies* when it could instead try for *Rambo*."

Bart wrote, "With this in mind," MGM offered the directing "job to Milius, a voluble, off-the-wall character renowned for his fascination with weaponry and advocacy of right-wing causes. . . . Haig [took] Milius under his wing [and] suddenly Milius found himself

---

the ultraliberal coasts, or, to put it in more contemporary terms, Sarah Palin's God-fearing, taken-for-granted Middle America bit its upper lip and did its patriotic duty by protecting the hedonists, secularists, elitists, cowards, and hippie traitors in Greenwich Village and Haight-Ashbury. If this were another movie, I might say this geographic story line was inadvertent, but this is *Red Dawn,* a film in which no tenet of conservative dogma is left unexploited.

welcomed into right-wing think tanks and inundated with Defense Department analyses of tactical invasion routes."

Foreshadowing the incestuous relationship between government, corporations, military, and media that would expand in later years, Haig was then cited by reporters as an expert on the movie's supposedly laudable lesson about "the essential need to maintain [U.S.] preparedness to fight a war."

True, Haig wasn't active-duty military brass when he worked on *Red Dawn*. But considering his army pedigree and recent tenure as a top official in the then sitting Reagan regime, it's fair to say his work on the film represented the precursor of the more integrated collusion between government and Hollywood that would become overt, and overtly child focused, as the 1980s progressed.

Of course, the military had been working with Hollywood filmmakers since 1927, when it helped produce *Wings,* the winner of the very first Academy Award for Best Picture. Pentagon involvement varied through the first two-thirds of the twentieth century, but it always had kids in its sights. In the 1950s, for example, the military worked with *Lassie* on shows that highlighted new military technology and produced "Mouse Reels" for *The Mickey Mouse Club,* one of which showed kids touring the first nuclear submarine. As investigative journalist David Robb discovered, a Pentagon memo noted at the time that child-focused media "is an excellent opportunity to introduce a whole new generation to the nuclear Navy."

This ultimately peaked in 1968 when the Pentagon underwrote *The Green Berets,* a film combining John Wayne's cowboy appeal to adolescents with a pro–Vietnam War message.

The 1970s saw far fewer Pentagon-backed war films for a public that was fatigued from Vietnam and its aftermath on the evening news. But according to *The Hollywood Reporter,* as Reaganite militarism began ascending, the 1980s saw "a steady growth in the demand for access to military facilities and in the number of films, TV shows and home videos made about the military."

For that access, the military began exacting a price.

A mundane example was 1983's *The Right Stuff.* The film about the early days of the space program mixed eighties reverence for The

Fifties™ with militarist hagiography, some of it meticulously line-edited for teens. Indeed, in correspondence between filmmakers and military brass, the Pentagon agreed to provide access to its facilities in exchange for the removal of cussing between the pilots—all to make sure the film would be seen by potential enlistees. "The obscene language used seems to guarantee an 'R' rating," wrote the Pentagon. "If distributed as an 'R,', it cuts down on the teenage audience, which is a prime one to the military services when our recruiting bills are considered."

The episode underscores the Pentagon's focus on juveniles and the heavy hand it was beginning to use to shape popular culture in the 1980s, and cutting out cuss words was mild compared to its other demands. Increasingly, for filmmakers to gain access to even the most basic military scenery, Pentagon gatekeepers were requiring major plot and dialogue changes so as to guarantee that the military was favorably portrayed, even if those unedited plots and dialogues represented the verifiable truth.*

This was no real secret inside the film industry. In a 1986 *Maclean's* report, military officials acknowledged that when directors came to them asking for permissions, the requests were being denied if those officials felt the armed forces weren't being depicted "heroic enough in their terms."

In *Variety*'s 1994 follow-up story, the Pentagon's official Hollywood liaison, Phil Strub, put it even more bluntly: "The main criteria we use [for approval] is . . . how could the proposed production benefit the military . . . could it help in recruiting [and] is it in sync with present policy?"

According to Strub, Pentagon-Hollywood collusion hit "a mile-

---

*Hard-to-Believe-but-True Example: The Pentagon refused to assist *Thirteen Days*, the 2000 movie about the Cuban missile crisis. Military officials gave the thumbs-down because they abhorred the script's dialogue between the Joint Chiefs of Staff and President John F. Kennedy. Specifically, they didn't like how bellicose the generals seemed—they feared it would make military leaders look like warmongers. Incredibly, Pentagon officials stuck to their rejection even though screenwriters provided them the White House audiotapes proving the screenplay's dialogue accurately represented exchanges that occurred at the time. In other words, the military leadership rejected a screenplay precisely *because* it accurately reflected the military leadership.

stone" with 1986's *Top Gun,* a triumphalist teen recruitment ad about the navy's "best of the best," who, of course, never even think to ask the most basic of the basic questions.* Set to Kenny Loggins's unbearably catchy "Danger Zone" ballad, the narrative's only pressing query seemed to be how many Vietcong planes Maverick's dad blew away in the 1960s, and whether Maverick would get back his Mach-3 bloodlust after losing his buddy Goose to a military contractor's defective cockpit door.[†]

The movie's glaringly incurious characters and story were no accident. The script was shaped by Pentagon brass in exchange for full access to all sorts of hardware—the access itself a priceless taxpayer subsidy. According to *Maclean's,* Paramount Pictures paid just "$1.1 million for the use of warplanes and an aircraft carrier," far less than it would have cost the studio had it been compelled to finance the eye candy itself.

As if that carrot-stick dynamic weren't coercive enough to aspiring filmmakers, the Pentagon in the 1980s expanded the definition of "cooperation" to include collaboration on screenplays as scripts were being initially drafted. "It saves [writers] time from writing stupid stuff," said one official in explaining the new process.

---

*Like, oh, I don't know, why during peacetime these pilots were being ordered into dogfights with Soviet MiGs, what the foreign-policy fallout might be from shooting those MiGs down, or why an American aircraft carrier was menacingly patrolling an undisclosed area "somewhere in the Indian Ocean"?

[†]This always confused me as a kid and now angers me as a more critically thinking adult: During the official inquiry into Goose's death, only Maverick was potentially to blame. But watch the tape—Goose dies not because of Maverick's maneuver, but because his body is ejected into the cockpit door, which should have been fully open and out of the way. Yet, the defense contractor that built the malfunctioning cockpit door is never shown being questioned—only Maverick is under investigation. How is this possible? The facts of this case are really clear: If Maverick ejected and survived, Goose should have survived, too. How does Maverick stand there and not tell the review board about the door malfunction? How does he let them just focus on his plane's flat spin and not on the circumstances surrounding the failed ejection? Maybe this is the real reason it takes Maverick so long to get his game back—the guy was probably haunted by knowing the planes he's being asked to pilot are flying Pintos. He knows that he could have gone Ralph Nader and blown the whistle, and he also knows that by not going Nader, his silence has put him and every other naval aviator at risk. That would freak anyone out (though apparently not enough to get him to turn in his wings and stop flying altogether).

"Stupid stuff" was a euphemism for "stuff the military doesn't like," and soon Pentagon leaders were making explicit threats, such as the one the navy's Robert Anderson issued on PBS.

"If you want full cooperation from the navy, we have a considerable amount of power, because it's *our* ships, it's *our* cooperation," he said. "And until the script is in a form that we can approve, then the production doesn't go forward."

Such a cavalier attitude coupled with the box-office success of the Pentagon-approved *Top Gun* convinced studios in the 1980s that agreeing to military demands and, hence, making ever more militaristic films was a guaranteed formula for success. Consequently, between the release of *Top Gun* and the beginning of the Gulf War, the Pentagon reported that the number of pictures made with its official assistance (and approval) quadrupled, and a large portion of these action-adventure productions (quickly synergized into video games, action figures, etc.) were for teenagers.

Though many parents might have objected to such obscene Pentagon-Hollywood collusion, most had no idea it was taking place. Unlike the proudly Pentagon-financed-and-advertised newsreels made by Hollywood directors during, say, World War II, filmmakers from the 1980s on almost never tell audiences that they are enjoying military-subsidized-and-sculpted productions.* Viewers may think they are watching a purely commercial venture when they are often watching contemporary newsreels.

"Over and over [Pentagon] documents are full of statements where they are targeting children to be future recruits," says journalist David Robb, whose seminal book *Operation Hollywood* examined the ties between movies and the armed forces. "The children and the people who see these films don't know this is an advertisement for the military."

The short-term impact of the military-entertainment complex was enlistment surges correlating to specific eighties box-office hits. As just one (albeit huge) example, recruitment spiked 400 percent

---

*Most often, the only disclosure of Pentagon influence at all is some token fine print in a film's end credits thanking the military leaders for their cooperation.

when *Top Gun* was released, leading the navy to set up recruitment tables at theaters upon realizing the movie's effect.

Medium term, of course, is the *Red Dawn* effect. Contemporary missions are named after the film (and various other militarist fantasies from the eighties), tapping into the hardwired psyches of the "Wolverines who have grown up and gone to Iraq," as Milius recently called the eighties generation.

Then there are the standards that were set for the long haul. Today, the Pentagon offers Hollywood just as much enticement for militarism, and just as much punishment against antimilitarism, as ever. On top of the eighties militarism that is now endlessly recycled in the cable rerun-o-sphere,★ it's a safe bet that whichever Jerry Bruckheimer or Michael Bay† blockbuster is currently being fawned over by teen audiences is at least partially underwritten by the Pentagon, and as a condition of that support, these blockbusters typically agree to deliberately reiterate the morality of the military and war.

By contrast, it's an equally safe bet that for every one of the few antimilitarist screenplays that are made into films, far more are reflexively spiked because their defiant content raises objections from military leaders, which, in turn, means no official Pentagon approval, no taxpayer subsidy, and therefore no movie from budget-conscious studios. As the director of *The Hunt for Red October* recounted, this new reality prompted studios in the eighties to start telling screenwriters and directors to "get the cooperation of the [military], or forget about making the picture." Not surprisingly, that directive has fostered an insidious pressure for pro-militarist self-censorship among a whole generation of screenwriters.

"When you know that you are going to need the military's assistance, and you know that they are going to be looking at your script,

---

★Theory: Regardless of the time or day, *Top Gun* is playing at any given moment on some cable system somewhere in the United States.

†Telling Example: *Wired* in 2008 reported, "After the Pentagon helped rewrite the script, Bay got access to helicopters, warships and—for just $25,000 an hour— F-22 stealth fighters." Overjoyed, Bay's army liaison officer (read: minder) gushed to the magazine, "As far as I know, this is the biggest joint military operation movie ever made."

you write it to make them happy right from the beginning," David Robb writes in *Operation Hollywood*.

Citing the pro-war tilt of the movies the Pentagon has approved in the last thirty years and the antiwar tilt of those the Pentagon nixed in that same time,* Robb poses a haunting question that summarizes the legacy of the military-Hollyood collusion in the 1980s.

"How many of those killed in Iraq joined the military because they saw some movie when they were a kid?" he asks. "How many of the dead Americans joined the military because of some movie that they saw not knowing that the military was the ones that were behind the scenes manipulating the content of the script to make the military look better than it really was? Once they got to Iraq it was too late—it wasn't so glamorous over there."

Top Gun made $353 million at the box office, and made additional cash for the companies whose swag was associated with the movie—from makers of aviator sunglasses and leather bomber jackets to Pepsi, which ran a $2 million promotion campaign offering rebates on *Top Gun* VHS copies with attendant soda purchases. However, no synergized product better actualized the film's technological allure than its video games.

With so many of the movie's high-stress moments featuring Maverick trying to get his cockpit computer locked onto a MiG, *Top Gun* was a natural fit for the PC, Commodore 64, and, most important, the new Nintendo NES. The game let kids feel as if they were right in the F-14, running missions, toggling between missiles and guns, blowing up enemy bogeys.

Selling 2 million copies upon its 1987 release and spurring a Sega arcade rip-off called *Afterburner*, *Top Gun* was the best-performing game of the moment, and what a moment it was for video games. From 1985 through *Top Gun*'s first year on the market, video game sales went from $100 million to $1.1 billion annually.

*Some movies the Pentagon approved: *Air Force One*, *From Here to Eternity*, *Armageddon*, *The Longest Day*, *The Hunt for Red October*, *Pearl Harbor*, *Patton*, and *Top Gun*. Some movies the Pentagon rejected: *Catch-22*, *Dr. Strangelove*, *Full Metal Jacket*, *Memphis Belle*, and *Platoon*.

Top Gun's video-game success was yet another 1980s milestone for selling militarism to children, maybe even a bigger symbolic achievement than the film itself, considering the video-game genre's martial DNA.

As opposed to motion pictures, which began as an independent art form and later stumbled into the Pentagon's sphere of influence, video games were originally sired within the military-industrial complex. The first program, a jerry-rigged analog computer and oscilloscope called *Tennis for Two,* was birthed at the Brookhaven National Laboratory in 1958. Then in 1962 came *Spacewar!*—the primordial *Defender* was a side project of geeks working in an MIT facility built expressly for the development of military technology. A decade later, the first home-video game system, Magnavox's Odyssey, was developed by a former military intelligence engineer then working for a defense contractor.

Video games and "the very creation of the digital computer itself was an enormously subsidized affair, pursued in the interests of maintaining and strengthening American military dominance," wrote *From Sun Tzu to Xbox* author Ed Halter, who notes that in the 1980s "the Department of Defense [would become] the largest underwriter of the development of computer graphics technologies."

Some of those expenditures were focused on subjecting military strategy to technological rigor—think *War Games*'s Buick-size supercomputer automating U.S. responses to various global threats. But much of it was looking to attract new enlistees, sharpen combat skills, and digitize the battlefield—objectives that would result in a military-consumer-market feedback loop in the 1980s and beyond.

Because of the military's elemental role in computer development, it's difficult to know where independent customer demand for military-themed video games begins and Pentagon machination ends. As Atari's rise in the late 1970s and early 1980s shows, the only certainty is that the Reagan era first saw the two impulses intertwine.

Though many Atari programmers working in Silicon Valley at the time were antiwar liberals, many of them also believed that kids, for whatever reason, liked and wanted military games. Thus, when the company released the revolutionary 2600 console in 1977, the wood-paneled unit came with just a single game—a battlefield simulation called *Combat* based on Atari's two earlier hit arcade games, *Tank* and *Anti-Aircraft*.

Of the nine total games that first became available for the 2600, a third (*Combat, Air-Sea Battle,* and *Star Ship*) were war simulations. In the company's ensuing glory years from 1980 to 1983, Atari made bank with military games for both the home system and the arcade— classics like *Space Invaders, Asteroids, Defender, Berzerk, Chopper Command, Vanguard, Zaxxon, Missile Command, Red Baron,* and *Battlezone.*

As the company's revenues hit $2 billion annually, military leaders took notice. Having financed the original creation of the microchips and graphics that firms such as Atari were commercializing, the Pentagon in the 1980s involved itself more directly in the thematic thrust of the games themselves.

Initially, military leaders were interested in games as training tools. In *Army* magazine's 1981 report, generals said *Red Baron*'s first-person cockpit viewpoint could have "something for helicopter gunners," while *Missile Command,* whose players shoot down incoming ballistics, "has controls very similar to the Army's forward-area alerting radar."

By that time, *Battlezone* was already being directly subsidized by the Pentagon. The game, which had players conduct tank warfare through a periscope viewfinder, is known as the mass market's original first-person shooter.★ When it proved a wild consumer success, military officials contracted Atari in 1980 to build a special version for army training facilities, one that retrofit its technical specs to the then new Bradley Infantry Fighting Vehicle. Though the army's customized

---

★Point of Geek Interest and Nerd Controversy: Apparently, some debate continues in gaming circles about which game was the first "first-person shooter" (i.e., the genre that now dominates the video-game world). In his book *From Sun Tzu to Xbox,* journalist Ed Halter puts the dispute to rest: "*Battlezone* was not in fact the first game to use [the first-person] perspective—racing games like Atari's 1976 *Night Driver* and Vectorbeam's 1979 *Speed Freak* had provided first-person views earlier. [But] they definitely did not involve any guns." Halter also cites 1973's *MazeWar* and 1974's *Spasim* (short for "space simulation"), which were probably the very first first-person shooter games. However, because they existed almost exclusively on NASA and military computers, respectively, they were never commercially available. So, yes, it's fair to call *Battlezone* the first first-person shooter game on the market.

version of *Battlezone* never made it to arcades, the game's 3-D graphics and controls contributed to the game-play innovations of the commercial market's later war-fighting hits.

At the same time, the Pentagon was beginning to see what the general running the army's Training and Doctrine Command saw in 1981: "All of the people in those arcades are [potential] volunteers . . . and two-thirds of [arcade] games are military in nature."

Recruiters for the armed forces were suddenly frequenting arcades in malls, citing the similarities between the most popular eighties games, Pentagon combat simulators, and, increasingly, live-action war-making in a technology-focused military.

"The multidirectional locater ball on the *Missile Command* game is pretty close to the system I use for air defense," one naval officer told *The Philadelphia Inquirer* in 1982. "You have enemy aircraft defined on the screen by radar. You have your sight as an electronic cursor directed by the ball. You push a button, the missiles fire, and 'poof,' no more aircraft."

Just as Pentagon gatekeepers were stunningly honest about their efforts to shape teen-thrusted movies, no less a figure than Ronald Reagan was equally frank about the government's militaristic motives in the brave new gaming world that was emerging.

"Without knowing it, you're being prepared for a new age," he said in a speech to students at Epcot Center in 1983. "Many young people have developed incredible hand, eye, and brain coordination in playing these games. The air force believes these kids will be outstanding pilots should they fly our jets. The computerized radar screen in the cockpit is not unlike the computerized video screen. Watch a twelve-year-old take evasive action and score multiple hits while playing *Space Invaders* and you will appreciate the skills of tomorrow's pilot."

His prediction proved accurate in many different ways.

On a literal level, kids were being prepared for games' increasingly audacious attempts to militarize their future job decisions and personal politics. Games did this, first and foremost, by extolling the armed forces as an exciting, high-tech career path. If cockpit adventures such as *Tiger Heli* and first-person shooter missions such as *Op-*

eration Wolf could be enjoyable, then, it logically followed, the same fun could be found in the real-life military adventures those games simulated.★

Along with aggrandizing the soldier life, games were also preparing America for wholly new recruitment methods that set aside hardsell solicitation in favor of devious, almost subconscious appeals to hedonism.

Those early days of recruiters stalking 1980s arcades, while somewhat controversial at the time, would blaze the trail for more manipulative game-centric pitches. As the 1980s video-game craze exploded in the 1990s and beyond, the Pentagon "realized we had to get the flow of information about life in the army into pop culture," said Colonel Casey Wardynski.

He would oversee what the military officially labeled Operation Star Fighter. It was an appropriate moniker, considering the 1984 film it commemorated, *The Last Starfighter,* centered around a video game designed to train and recruit teen soldiers unbeknownst to the players themselves.

That was precisely the kind of tool Wardynski dreamed of, and exactly the game he would make a reality with the 2002 release of *America's Army.* Constructed with a commercial graphics engine and $32 million of Pentagon cash, the free first-person shooter fantasy aimed to recruit "kids to come into the army and feel like they've already been there," as Wardynski put it.

Millions of downloads (and uncountable enlistees) later, the Pen-

---

★It should be noted that this authenticity was manufactured in the 1980s not just by ever-improving graphics and first-person player perspectives, but also in military games' penchant for incorporating real-world military and political themes into their story lines. As a spokesman for the maker of *Contra* said when the game came out in the middle of the Iran-contra hearings, "Coin-op designers take anything remotely in the news and make it a game." Likewise, during the first Gulf War, *The Toronto Star* reported that "a new crop of video games are coming out to cash in" on the casualty-generating combat still in progress. In today's $50-billion-a-year video-game economy, such politicized gameplay now dominates. The very names of today's bestsellers, such as *Call of Duty* and *Just Cause,* continue to sell the post-Vietnam Reaganite vernacular while promoting the idea that militarism is the highest form of patriotism. Others such as *Kuma\War* boast of using "cutting-edge game technology to accurately reconstruct real-war events from the news."

tagon spent $12 million to open a 14,500-square-foot facility in a suburban Philadelphia mall called an Army Experience Center. *Adweek*'s coverage highlighted the pilot project's attempt to stealthily implant itself more deeply into youth culture: "Unlike recruitment centers in office complexes, the (Army Experience Center) is surrounded by retail stores and designed to look hip and modern, with giant plasma screen televisions, brushed stainless steel fixtures, interactive displays, helicopter and Humvee simulators, a gaming area and a cafe."

The success of these efforts are summed up by army veteran Jason Christopher Hartley, the author of the book *Just Another Soldier: A Year on the Ground in Iraq.* "Movies and video games are the lexicon of soldiers," he told *The Believer* magazine in 2008. "It is literally why most of us joined—we just wanted to extend the excitement into real life."

In addition to recruitment, video games in the 1980s began improving military training, which was the reason the Pentagon first got involved in game development.

The Reagan years were preparing soldiers-to-be for future combat with simulators such as *Battlezone* and *Falcon,* which would set the stage later for *Doom* and *Full Spectrum Warrior.* Epitomizing the military-entertainment that came out of the 80s, the latter was named after a Joint Chiefs of Staff report and was developed by a Hollywood-Pentagon venture that sprung from a military report calling for "linking entertainment and defense."

The Pentagon loved this kind of enterprise as their researchers found that the more trainees played, the better they were performing in live combat exercises. And as the 1980s became the 1990s and 2000s, these skills would become less and less simulative and more directly applicable to modern warfare.

In that capstone event of eighties militarism, the Gulf War, much of the American combat was waged electronically through Patriot missiles and smart bombs. Today, one of the military's strongest growth sectors is drone warfare, a form of combat that has soldiers sitting in Las Vegas at glorified arcade machines attacking targets in Afghanistan via video-game-style consoles that control unmanned aerial vehicles (UAVs).

This gets to the deeper figurative truth of Reagan's prophecy about video games: While most of the gaming generation that came of age in the 1980s and beyond will never literally enlist and remote-control bomb Afghan villages, the games we've been playing for the last three decades have prepared us in the same way they've prepared those drone pilots.

Grounded in electronic simulation, video games decontaminate and dehumanize their subject matter. Viscera such as pain, injury, death, and "collateral damage"—i.e., the brutal consequences of war that might make us question militarism—are reduced to pixels if they are even depicted at all, and most times they aren't. Most often a game's player is killed only to instantly reappear unscathed.

The earlier the game, the lower-bit the graphics and therefore the more digitally sanitized the simulacra to the point where children's visual experience of war in the 1980s was often the same as their visual experience of recreational games (think about it: *Combat,* the original program shipped with Atari, a program whose name is a literal synonym of violence, was basically *Pong*).

Hence, from the 1980s on, games led Americans to feel comfortable cheering on militarism, confident that the worst ramifications of any given martial incursion would be a few soldiers and victims having to hit the "reset" button on their Atari-like equipment.

The dynamic was an obvious boon to military leaders who didn't want to contend with an aggression-averse public. Thus, those military leaders encouraged the game-war conflation in the Gulf War, just as they did in all the conflicts that followed.

For instance, delivering good news during Desert Storm, army spokespeople celebrated the war for its "surgical strikes," smart bombs, and limited (American) losses, packaging combat in what *Playboy* at the time aptly called "visions of the Nintendo War." Same thing in the selling of our reinvasion of the Gulf in 2003—preposterous dreams of drone-led victories and "shock and awe" assaults on Iraq's phantom WMDs were interspersed throughout news reports and U.N. presentations that could have been mistaken for Xbox gameplay.*

---

*During rare moments of candor, a few voices of militarism have indirectly admitted the downside of the 1980s success in equating video games with actual war.

Now, as casualties keep mounting in America's new militarist adventures, "It's almost impossible to open a video game magazine or log onto a video game Web site without being besieged by advertisements for the Army," write Heather Chaplin and Aaron Ruby in their book *Smartbomb*. And the armed forces no longer rely on euphemisms (*surgical strike,* etc.) alone to evoke video-game dreams; military recruitment ads now explicitly insist to both future enlistees and the general public that war is a video game.

One television ad from 2007 shows kids playing a military-themed game, only to see the soldier they are controlling on-screen turn to them and ask, "Are you ready to take this to the next level?"

Message: War is just the next exciting level of the video game you are playing.

Another ad shows CGI-enhanced images of soldiers running what looks like *Missile Command* on a Sony PSP and using the game to call in airstrike coordinates. Yet another lauds drones that "fight terrorism and protect America, and in the process, keep the front lines unmanned."

The ads promise that war-as-video-game "is not science fiction—it's what we do every day."

True or not, many in the Atari and Nintendo generation still believe it.

At this point, it should be obvious that the 1980s was the beginning of militarism's multilayered political campaign for the hearts and minds of children.

To the sensitive and diverse national broadcast audience, martial movies and prime-time television programs in the 1980s used com-

---

General Norman Schwarzkopf, for example, interrupted a press conference during the Gulf War to sternly remind America, "The kind of thing that's going on out on that battlefield right now [is] not a Nintendo game. It is a tough battlefield where people are risking their lives at all times." Fourteen years later, it was Senator Chuck Hagel. After buying into the Bush administration's video-game sales pitch and voting for the allegedly easy Iraq War, the Nebraska Republican exasperatedly reminded citizens, "The deadly struggle for Iraq is not a video game, war is not an abstraction."

edy (*Stripes*), drama (*The Right Stuff*), hyperpatriotism (*Top Gun*) and combinations of all three (*The A-Team*) to sand down militarism's sharpest edges and push kids to generally believe that militarism is a good and decent social force.

Video games were one level beneath this. Because they were a computer console or trip to the mall removed from the adult audience, Atari, Nintendo, and arcade messages could be more manifest and unapologetic in their militarism, with less chance of a parental backlash.

The true gutter in this hearts-and-minds endeavor, though, was still one level below that—the shadowy subterranea far away from measured scrutiny where campaigns employ the most deceitful tactics and stalk the most vulnerable populations. In the 1980s, this was the toy culture—a cesspool immersing unsuspecting and unsupervised kids in a toxic discharge that didn't just replicate Hollywood's general celebration of militarism nor merely mimic video games' suggestion that war is harmless fun. Eighties toys and their corresponding cartoons would lead the way in encouraging kids to embrace new ideas about what future militarism is *for* and who specifically America must wage war *against*.

It started when the toy industry in the 1980s experienced a wave of consolidation, wiping out the mom-and-pop toy shops where a discerning store owner may have steered a child away from inappropriate products. In their place came discount megastores such as Toys "R" Us™ that are run by low-wage workers with minimal toy expertise and even less involvement in the product choices that were simultaneously beginning to be hijacked by mass media.

Until the 1980s, TV ads were relatively limited in their reach because public opposition to direct-to-kids marketing had kept the pitches highly regulated. Then came the Reagan years. In 1983, the FCC removed its children-programming guidelines, then in 1984 allowed TV stations to air as many commercials in after-school and weekend hours as they wanted, and then in 1985 formally refused to regulate the Program Length Commercial (PLC).

The FCC's latter vote turned the industry upside down. In the past, toys were typically based off of characters originally created by television programmers and already featured in television programs.

But the new ruling allowed toy companies to reverse engineer the process. They could create and syndicate thirty minute television cartoons about children's products that were first on the toy market. Shows such as *Rubik the Amazing Cube, Dungeons and Dragons, Pac-Man,* and *Strawberry Shortcake*—all based on existing games and toys—could then be promoted as regular, independent programming rather than what they really were: sponsor-engineered product commercials. And fortunately for militarism, these moves to deregulate the television airwaves happened just as manufacturers were accelerating production of war toys to reflect corresponding trends in movies, video games, and politics.

"Think military! That's what several leading toy manufacturers hope the American public will do this year—and hopefully beyond," read an article in a 1982 issue of the industry trade magazine *Toys, Hobbies and Crafts.* "Ushered in along with the [Reagan] presidential administration has been a resurgence of demonstrative patriotism and a renewed interest in the US armed forces. . . . Children [are] exposed on an almost daily basis to military stimuli—in the form of TV news, recruitment ads, classroom studies, movies and comics. . . . Given this new military consciousness, it seems only natural that leading toy companies are putting renewed energy into military-related toy lines."

Not surprisingly, the first FCC-approved PLC* was the quasi-militarist fantasy *He-Man,* based on the *Masters of the Universe* toy line. A huge hit airing on stations covering 82 percent of America in its first season, the show generated 35 million action-figure sales in a year—or almost ninety-six thousand a day. With those kinds of numbers, other toy makers followed.

From *The Transformers* to Chuck Norris's *Karate Kommandos* to *Rambo and the Forces of Freedom,* animated programs soon became the most relied-upon way to sell toys to kids, and these programs' mili-

---

*Historical Asterisk: While *He-Man* was the first *FCC-blessed* PLC, it was not actually the first PLC. That distinction goes to a 1969 ABC cartoon about Mattel's toy cars called *Hot Wheels.* However, it was quickly taken off the air when the FCC deemed the show one giant "commercial promotion" that went "beyond the time [allowed] for commercial advertising." The PLC did not attempt a return until the 1980s.

tarist messages were incessant. According to a 1986 *Advertising Age* report, the average war cartoon was broadcasting forty-one violent acts per hour, with a murder attempted every two minutes. The year before, children were seeing "an average of 800 TV commercials that promoted war toys and about 250 episodes of war cartoons produced to sell these toys," the magazine added, reminding readers that such a sum equals "22 days of classroom instruction in warfare."

The carnage generated big revenues, as *Advertising Age* found in 1986 that "war-toy sales topped $1.2 billion in 1985, up 600 percent in three years." In a separate study, political scientist Patrick Regan reported that 9.5 percent of 1985's toys were war-themed, "the highest ratio of war toys to total toys outside of the World War II period."

Far and away the most successful of the PLCs in the 1980s was *G. I. Joe: A Real American Hero,* whose backstory and plot embodied the country's love-hate, then permanently love relationship with the armed forces.

The G. I. Joe brand traces its birth to the Oscar-nominated 1945 film *The Story of G.I. Joe* and, in 1951, to *Time* magazine, which in honoring "the American Fighting Man" in Korea, named G. I. Joe its Man of the Year. A decade later, an independent toy manufacturer approached Hasbro about creating a Barbie-like toy for boys to complement Gene Roddenberry's pre–*Star Trek* show, *The Lieutenant.*

In 1964, the G. I. Joe doll was born. Hasbro produced four twelve-inch figures to represent the four branches of the armed forces, and in their first few years they were a hit. By the early 1970s, however, the Vietnam War had become a nightmare, and sales of war toys were plummeting. Hasbro tried to adapt by rebranding G. I. Joe as an "adventurer" rather than a soldier. Sales-wise, the shift flopped, and in 1978 with the military's overall image heading for its Gallup poll nadir, G. I. Joe was discontinued.

But not for long.

The same year G. I. Joe died, *Star Wars* pioneered a brilliant new militarist formula. At the time, the movie industry was so afraid combat films would offend the Vietnam-scarred public that studio execs were worried about putting the word *war* in the title of George Lucas's masterpiece. Yet the film found enormous success, just as many video games had, by moving combat out of all-too-real jungle settings and into the bloodless, technologized, and therefore sanitized science fiction of outer space.*

The result: 26 million *Star Wars* action figures were sold in their first year.

Following suit, G. I. Joe characters came back in 1982 at the smaller, four-inch height that *Star Wars* had popularized—and re-duced size wasn't the only change. The brand was synergized first as a comic book, then as a television cartoon, and then as everything from lunch boxes to its own quarterly magazine. Following trends in 1980s movies, G. I. Joe was also patriotized with a new "Real Amer-ican Hero" tagline.

---

*Point for *Star Wars* Fetishists (of which I am one): The public's aversion to ex-plicit war narratives in the late 1970s has to be a big reason the *Star Wars* trilogy goes out of its way to show very little blood—and it really does go out of its way. Save for the early shots showing the charred carcasses of Luke's Tatooine family and the severed arm of a thug at the Mos Isely pub, fleshy carnage—i.e., the most graphic downside of war and violence—basically doesn't exist in George Lucas's war-torn universe. That's not to say that maiming, killing, and death don't hap-pen constantly a long time ago in the galaxy far far away. But it is to say that when such violence does occur, it is mostly shown without the very blood that might turn kids off to it. Now, you can argue that some of the deaths in the original *Star Wars* trilogy were naturally without overt carnage, and sure, X-wing fighters being instantly vaporized or an Imperial commander being choked to death by Darth Vader through a videophone probably wouldn't produce open wounds or graphic hemorrhaging. But when you consider other events, it's clear *Star Wars* filmmak-ers were bending over backward to avoid bloody carnage that might offend par-ents, who were particularly averse to militarism at the time. For example, when Darth Vader whips out a Jose Canseco swing with his light saber and cuts Obi-Wan Kenobi literally in half, Lucas doesn't show, say, Kenobi's intestines hanging out of his writhing and newly legless torso. Instead, Kenobi simply vanishes. Even if you want to claim that was "naturally" bloodless because Kenobi was destined to become an eternal blue-glowing spirit upon his death, how about when Luke gets half his arm cut off? Somehow, there's no blood at all. *Star Wars*'s rooting in the concept of bloodless war might explain why Reagan officials and their sup-porters happily accepted the *Star Wars* reference for their biggest militarist fantasy of all: the so-called Strategic Defense Initiative (SDI), which sought to shoot down intercontinental ballistic missiles from space. Describing the scheme in the mid-1980s, Reagan said, "The Force is with us." At the same time, one political ad by a group backing SDI showed a young girl asking "what this *Star Wars* is all about." As author Edward Tabor Linenthal recounts, "A protective dome magi-cally appeared over the family and their house, enemy missiles bounced harmlessly off the dome, the sun smiled, and the American flag flew overhead." The message was simple: accelerating the arms race in a way that would undermine the deter-rent of mutually assured destruction and escalate tensions with the Soviet Union was as harmless as *Star Wars*'s sanitized combat scenes.

"In the sixties, we went too far," Hasboro consultant Tony Parkinson told *Harper's* in 1982 when explaining the ideological motives behind the newly rebanded G. I. Joe. "We can [now] take pride in America—that's what this toy says: that we're Americans and we're going to protect ourselves. G. I. Joe is what he says he is—a real American hero. This G. I. Joe is a rapid-deployment team, and he's going to need a lot better helicopters than the ones we used in Iran."

To that end, rather than just continuing the brand as the previous four grunts of the 1960s and 1970s, G. I. Joe brand of the 1980s tracked video games by technologizing itself as an entire colorful team of Special Forces using the Pentagon's most futuristic vehicles and arms—"toy items that seem torn from today's headlines," wrote *Advertising Age* in 1986.

Like *Star Wars* and so many other filmic toy fantasies for kids, G. I. Joe's weapons, however lifelike, always avoided the explicit shedding of blood. Yet somewhat paradoxically, G. I. Joe would also mimic video games by subtly incorporating the blood-soaked geopolitics of the 1980s. In various issues of the G. I. Joe comic book, the Joes confront an enemy selling fortresses to South American revolutionaries; invade Afghanistan to help the mujahideen; and rout an Iranian battalion ("So much for the Iranian-American relations!" says one Joe).★

G. I. Joe could pull off this mix of real-world news and entertainment especially well because Hasbro was doing something that even film and video games were only starting to systematically attempt: namely, creating the idea of a new and immortal menace—G. I. Joe's enemy, the Cobra forces—that would go on to justify permanent militarism well after the Soviet Union collapsed.

★Other manufacturers of children's entertainment also followed video games in mixing militarist themes with real-world geopolitics. There was the Transformers' children's book and audiotape called *When Continents Collide,* which showed foreign Decepticon enemies attempting to steal Alaska's oil and ultimately bringing the United States and Russia to the brink of nuclear war. There were toymakers—including *Rambo* cartoon producers—who, according to *AdAge* in 1986, "released action figures with the name 'Mad Dog,' President Reagan's appellation for Libya's leader Mommar Khadaffi." And there was Topps, the maker of baseball cards, which manufactured Desert Storm cards and sold them in retail stores. Noting the success of such child-targeted kitsch in selling militarism, General Colin Powell said in 1991, "A good part of my time is now spent signing the backs of cards."

Cobra Commander was Osama bin Laden and the Cobra organization, of course, was an early version of al-Qaeda—a stateless and (literally) faceless terrorist group conducting attacks from caves, desert encampments and other secret hideouts. Though terrorism was only just becoming a focus of the U.S. military apparatus in the 1980s, Hasbro's brain trust prophetically manufactured an antagonist that was more abstract idea than single nation or bad guy because they believed that would better sell militaristic toys for the long haul.★

"[Executives] decided that the Russians weren't going to work as an enemy," journalist Tom Englehardt told *The Believer* in recounting his visit to Hasbro's offices during the G. I. Joe era. "They were onto terrorism before Paul Wolfowitz and the other neocons. . . . These guys did grasp the future—there wasn't any money in the Russians."

Put the pieces together. Put G. I. Joe's firefights against Iranians with the comic-book story that had them "infiltrate a Persian Gulf nation [to] bring it into the U.S. sphere"; add Hasbro's calculated shirking of a statebound enemy in favor of a stateless terrorist group; further mix in that terrorist group's exotic, Arab-snake-charmer semiotics—and you see that G. I. Joe was preparing the next generation for the Pentagon's post-1980s shift. Rather than aiming at Russians, contemporary militarism would be unleashed against Islam under the guise of a neverending "war on terror." In this way, recalibrating children's war fetish from one that fears Soviets into one that hates Muslims was a farsighted investment by a military-entertainment industry that has always been in the business of fictionalizing current events.

Hasbro in the late 1980s was the lead venture capitalist in this transition. The firm spent tens of millions of dollars a year on G. I. Joe ads, generating $200 million in annual sales, and by 1988 the company declared that a breathtaking two-thirds of all American boys between the ages of five and eleven owned a Joe. With such success, the

---

★As if to stress its desire for a conceptual enemy rather than a tangible one, Hasbro depicted Cobra Commander in both his mirror-mask version and his hooded version as quite literally having no face at all. The goal here was to manufacture an enemy that is an indomitable *idea* that will forever justify militarism (and militarist toys) rather than pitting G. I. Joe against something tangible, defeatable, and therefore finite.

brand and its antiterrorism narrative had created a new cultural market that others aimed to tap.

In the toy world, there would soon be new dolls such as Desert Storm Barbie and Nomad Desert Warrior and board games such as *The Butcher of Baghdad* and *Arabian Nightmare.* In Hollywood, film scholar Jack Shaheen found more than a third of the most anti-Muslim films of the last century were made in the 1980s alone, and many of them "credit the Department of Defense for providing needed equipment, personnel, and technical assistance."

"The movies of the eighties are especially offensive," he said, pointing out that particularly in action/adventure films for kids,★ the Evil Arab became the go-to enemy.

For sheer chutzpah, however, nothing topped the World Wrestling Federation. A hybrid of theater, politics, and sports, the WWF was "a cartoon United Nations, in which the U.S. always has a fighting chance," wrote *Time* magazine in 1985.

On the Good side, there were distinctly American heroes such as Hulk Hogan and Sgt. Slaughter, the latter an ultrapatriotic symbol of militarism dressed in an army uniform and complemented by his own G. I. Joe action figure. On the Bad side, old-school Soviets (Ivan Koloff, Krusher Khrushchev, Alexis Smirnoff, Nikita Koloff, and Nikolai Volkoff) and lumbering Eastern Bloc monsters (Andre the Giant) came to be led by an Iranian madman called the Iron Sheik.

Here was child-oriented, synergized entertainment presenting the Islamic world as a newfangled, even-more-dangerous iteration of the Soviet colossus—a Muslim menace led by an "evil hitman [who] shows no mercy in terrorist attacks on the USA's best," as one wrestling publication described the kaffiyeh-clad Sheik.

★Some good examples of Islamophobia in 1980s kids movies: kaffiyeh-clad nuclear terrorists from Libya stalking *Back to the Future*'s suburbs with a bazooka and a Volkswagen bus; *Raiders of the Lost Ark* and *Indiana Jones and the Last Crusade*'s Nazi-sympathizing Arabs who tried to help Hitler pilfer Jewish and Christian artifacts; the wild-eyed Egyptian cult in *Young Sherlock Holmes; Iron Eagle*'s unnamed Arab nation that effectively abducts an American dad from his kids; the *Star Trek* movies' swarthy, dark-skinned Arab effigies called Klingons, with their guttural language and writing that resembles Arabic; and what Jack Shaheen calls Cannon Films's twenty-six "hate-and-terminate-the-Arab" flicks such as *Delta Force* and its spin-offs.

There it was: The T-word. According to New York University's Rémi Brulin, the eighties was the very moment that it was just starting to enter the lexicon. Not coincidentally, the WWF Terrorist always played Washington General to the U.S. Military's Harlem Globetrotter, as wrestling promoters in the 1980s would sooner let the Junkyard Dog—WWF's chained black slave—reign over the sport than let the Sheik hold the title belt for an extended time. Inevitably, the Sheik and his Muslim iconography would be the punching bag for the camo-wearing Slaughter and his American flag. And lest there be any confusion in kids' minds, the Sarge's victories would be painted in hysterically militarist terms.

"We don't want Iranians around," Slaughter said in 1984. "We're going to clean up America of all this trash."★

If that seems exactly like the political rhetoric you might hear today in a talk-radio rant or on a cable scream show or on the floor of the U.S. Congress or in a newspaper op-ed, that's no coincidence either. Those rants, screams, speeches, and editorials are deliberately using the same diction as Sgt. Slaughter because that's the same lingo we were trained to respond to as eighties kids in our basement.

One of pop culture's lost artifacts that every eighties kid remembers is what the entertainment industry euphemistically called "prosocial messages." During cartoons' commercial interludes, television gave us quick Golden Rule booster shots such as NBC's *One to Grow On*

★Reflecting how American pop culture was painting all Muslims with one broad brush, the same wrestler who played the Iron Sheik was quickly repackaged by the WWF during the Gulf War as the new Iraqi wrestler Colonel Mustafa—all to make sure American wrestling fans had a Saddam acolyte to despise. Few fans seemed to notice the switch, as almost none of them seemed to recall—or even know—that big ethnic, religious, and geopolitical differences distinguish Iran from Iraq. For example, surveys in the 1980s showed roughly three-quarters of Americans believed Iran is an Arab country like Iraq, when in fact it is a largely Persian nation. Worse, many Americans (or at least wrestling fans) didn't know that Iran and Iraq had been mortal enemies at war with each other, even though the Iran-contra affair was, in part, about the United States helping arm Iran in that conflict. All the 1980s pop culture seemed interested in doing was painting the Muslim world as a singular menacing monolith. Thus, in American entertainment, Iranian sheiks (who in reality probably hated Iraqi military officers) could be the same thing as Iraqi colonels (who in reality probably hated Iranian sheiks).

or public service announcements such as G. I. Joe's cheery pontifications that followed every one of the Program Length Commercial's violence-strafed episodes.

This moralizing pablum was, collectively, a smoking gun. Through the bromides, makers of children's entertainment in the 1980s were clearly trying to inoculate themselves against future criticism, and in doing so in such a bald way they were admitting their awareness of their war crimes against youth.

They got one thing right, though. No matter if it was the one telling kids to avoid chatting with weird pedophile-ish strangers or the one imploring prepubescent boys to avoid their natural pyromaniacal proclivities, G. I. Joe's so-called prosocial messages all ended with children saying, "Now we know!" and a Joe reminding them, "Knowing is half the battle!"

No more important axiom was broadcast in the 1980s that was so ignored.

Somehow, militarism remains the assumption in our society. Somehow, permanent war is now the permanent consensus. Somehow, we keep losing far more than half the battle by *not* knowing how we were manipulated into this reality.

Such ignorance is the triumph that public relations expert Nancy Snow was talking about—the victory of propaganda so seamlessly integrated into society that it "convinces people they are not being manipulated" at all.

In terms of sheer ubiquity, 1980s militarism stands alone. Because so many unsuspecting kids became fluent in its vocabulary, America now converses, debates, and even thinks in militarism's varied dialects.

The militarism of eighties cinema speaks to us when a president explains war decisions with Hollywood one-liners such as "Bring them on" and "Mission accomplished," dresses up like Pete "Maverick" Mitchell, and makes a nationally televised flight-deck speech about Iraq look like a casting call for *Top Gun*.

The militarism of the eighties arcade whispers to us both in today's video games and in the proliferation of sanitized drone warfare.

The militarism of eighties toys screams at us in new live-action

G. I. Joe movies, in the recent resurrection of the G. I. Joe comic-book series, and in our ongoing celebration of secret Special Forces missions in exotic locales from Yemen to northwest Pakistan.

And the militarist xenophobia of eighties cartoons and theatro-sports still beckons to us in a WWF-ized conversation about Islam, terrorism, and foreign policy—a conversation epitomized by *New York Times* columnist Tom Friedman, who famously said that post-9/11 America needs to "take out a very big stick" and tell the Muslim world to "suck on this." What else is such now banal rhetoric but a rehashed Sgt. Slaughter diatribe?

If complex foreign policies could be one-liners, if invasions had movie endings, if combat operations were bloodless Atari games, if the War on Terror were a steel-cage match—well, then our eighties attitudes might be appropriate and even constructive. But that just isn't the world we live in.

"There's no reset button," one drone pilot told CBS's *60 Minutes* in 2009, stopping to momentarily consider the dilemmas of his job. "When you let a missile go [and] it's flying toward the enemy to kill somebody or to break something . . . there's no take-back there."

Such self-examination is rare, taboo even, precisely because it highlights the troubling divergence between the eighties-born militarist fantasy and truth. Whether we admit it or not, that divide has life-and-death consequences, even if those consequences are buried under the stoicism and ennui of what today passes for "normal."

"Normal," unfortunately, is the week in 2010 when General Stanley McChrystal told reporters that in Afghanistan, U.S. troops have "shot an amazing number of people and killed a number and, to my knowledge, none has proven to have been a real threat to the force."

Days later, a Pentagon video surfaced showing a Special Forces unit in a helicopter mowing down an unarmed group of Iraqi civilians and journalists. The recorded dialogue was harrowing for its ebullience.

"Light 'em all up. Come on, fire!" one yelled.

"Ha, ha, I hit 'em."

"Look at those dead bastards."

When asked about the inhumane violence, Defense Secretary

Robert Gates brushed it off, saying, "It should not have any lasting consequences."

He was betting that the nation would see the video not as a heinous war crime or proof that American militarism is now totally out of control, but as just some innocuous snippets of eighties movie dialogue, Atari *Combat,* and G. I. *Joe* cartoons.

For too many of us, that's exactly what it is.

PART IV

THE HUXTABLE EFFECT

If David Letterman made a Top 10 List of the Most Taboo Subjects in America, I have to believe militarism would be right near the top. We largely avoid raising objections to it, and the military mostly avoids responding to our occasional queries, other than to let us know those answers are classified: They could tell us, but then they'd have to kill us. Yet, as uncomfortable as we are with questioning the Pentagon, militarism is far less taboo than the issue of race.

Once again, the 1980s frames our thinking. Just as Reaganite hyperpatriotism undermined opposition to militarism after the Vietnam War, so too did the 1980s' celebration of supposed "color blindness" stifle civil-rights-era debates about persistent bigotry.

To know that the decade fundamentally changed our views on race is to simply acknowledge chronology. After all, something major must have intervened between a 1960s that recognized and fought over racial inequality and today's society that pretends "there's not a black America and white America and Latino America and Asian America, there's the United States of America."

That line from Barack Obama's 2004 Democratic National Convention speech is today's motto of racial "transcendence," an at once palliative and poisonous concept that originally came to preeminence in the 1980s—and for a specific reason.

With the passions of 1960s black struggle still simmering, political parties, media outlets, and White America in general were desperate for something to asphyxiate increasingly militant liberation movements in the Brave New World of the 1980s. Hence, they manufactured "transcendence." A double-edged concept rife with promises of "postracial" advancement, "transcendence" was designed to smother the flames of civil-rights crusades and concurrently stoke the embers of white resentment.

It began with little fanfare in the 1970s when then–White House aide Daniel Patrick Moynihan first called for "benign neglect" on race. Having already blamed Jim Crow–era inequality on black "social pathology" rather than the period's institutional discrimination, the future senator told President Nixon that race "has been too much talked about" and called for a period in which "racial rhetoric fades." Moynihan was soon followed by University of Chicago professor William Julius Wilson, who authored the bestselling treatise *The Declining Significance of Race,* downplaying prejudice as a major social ill.

These seemingly high-minded arguments provided the intellectual cover and casuistry that Republican operatives were groping for to foment an election-winning white backlash against Democrats in the 1980s, and the GOP's argot was upgraded accordingly.

"You start out in 1954 by saying, 'Nigger, nigger, nigger!' By 1968 you can't say *nigger*—that hurts you. Backfires. So you say stuff like forced busing, states' rights, and all that stuff," said Republican strategist Lee Atwater in 1981. "You're getting so abstract now [that] you're talking about cutting taxes, and all these things you're talking about are totally economic things, [but] a by-product of them is [that] blacks get hurt worse than whites."

Atwater was opining just a few years before he masterminded that crowning white-hooded achievement of 1980s racism, the Willie Horton ad of the 1988 presidential campaign. Marrying the politics of plausible deniability with the ideology of bigotry, Republican strategists publicly labeled the spot a race-neutral look at furlough policy while privately applauding it for its "wonderful mix of liberalism and a big black rapist,"★ as one GOP official snickered.

★Atwater's two-faced race-baiting was exemplified by his insistence that the Horton ad of the 1988 presidential campaign had nothing to do with race—all while using Horton as a synonym for *black.* Most famously, when discussing the prospect of Democratic presidential nominee Michael Dukakis nominating Jesse Jackson as his vice-presidential running mate, Atwater said, "Maybe he'll put this Willie Horton guy on the ticket after all is said and done." A year later, *The New York Times* reported, "Atwater grows angry at the suggestion that he may have exploited racism in the campaign." The paper quoted him preposterously posturing as the *victim* of racism, saying, "As a white Southerner, I have always known I had

America would experience that kind of duplicitous bigotry and denial throughout the Reagan era and beyond.

Reagan himself perfected the language of what he called "color blindness," an early version of "transcendence" whose imperceptible timbre made it the perfect dog whistle for bigots. In a 1980s that saw black poverty increase faster than it had even under Jim Crow, this dog whistle helped the same Republican politician campaign on neo-confederate promises of "states' rights," trade on minstrelized images of "welfare queens," and yet also appropriate the patois of the civil rights movement. "We want a color-blind society—a society that in the words of Dr. King judges people not by the color of their skin but by the content of their character," Reagan said in a 1986 Martin Luther King Day speech berating affirmative action.

In striving for a "kinder, gentler nation," Reagan's successor, George H. W. Bush, reached for a "kinder, gentler" white denial as epitomized by what was, and was not, in his own 1992 Martin Luther King Day speech. The original draft included a brief mention of Dr. King's struggle in "a nation disfigured by a kind of homegrown apartheid." It also conceded that "racism and bigotry, blind hatred and intolerance, still exist in our land." But these comments were eliminated from the final speech by Republican aides eager to perpetuate the "color-blind" propaganda and pretend prejudice doesn't exist.

The media world joined in. In Hollywood, CBS executives in the 1980s bragged that "television is now color-blind," and when asked about persistent allegations that its media productions were racist, Disney executives feigned an innate inability to even see race, much less confess to the possibility of prejudice.

"We don't have anyone presumptuous enough to talk about complex social problems," the company's spokesperson told the *Los Angeles Times* in 1987.

Likewise in the sports world, even as broadcaster Jimmy the Greek was promoting bigoted theories on black genetics, even as Los

---

to go the extra mile to avoid being tagged a racist." Only on his deathbed in 1991 did Atwater finally apologize for his Willie Horton statement, though even then he clung to the color-blind card, saying he was particularly sorry "because [the statement] makes me sound racist, *which I am not.*"

Angeles Dodgers general manager Al Campanis was praising blacks' "great musculature" but saying they may not "have the background" for management positions; even as a National Basketball Association official said his league was perceived "as being too black"—even despite all this, the same NBA official would go on to say that "it doesn't matter what color [athletes] are" to white audiences, while *Sports Illustrated* praised athletes for "shed[ding] their racial identity."

No cultural commodity, however, did more to advance the notion that America can—and should—get "past" color than Bill Cosby.

The actor and comedian was the first African American to break many barriers: the first to regularly guest-host Johnny Carson's *Tonight* show; the first to costar on a weekly television series in a dramatic role; the first to top the advertising industry's Q ratings, which measure celebrities' overall fame and public approval; the first to be an on-camera pitchman for Fortune 500 companies; and, most significantly, the first to lead a number one television show.

And not just any television show—*The Cosby Show,* aka the most popular and profitable series in the medium's history.

In the 1960s, Cosby had told *Playboy,* "I don't spend my hours worrying how to slip a social message into my act," and he transcoded that apolitical worldview into his Thursday-night performances on NBC. Intimately involved in crafting every aspect of the program, Cosby was adamant in his belief that "if individuals are interested in racial equality and sufferings, then they should simply go to the library and read about it, read about some real people who have suffered, but not watch the show for that reason because that's not what [*The Cosby Show*] is all about."

White America, previously resistant to African American programs, rewarded *The Cosby Show* with unprecedented ratings, and specifically because of Cosby's stance on race.

"It's not like a jive show," said one typical Caucasian respondent in the University of Massachusetts' landmark study of the program's audience. "Other [black] shows are more jive, more soul shows, say as far as the way the characters are with making you aware that they are more separate. . . . Where Cosby is more American down the line."

While such responses garnered Cosby fawning mass media billing as "transcendent," his show incited heated debates among activists, academics, and critics during the 1980s. On one side were those who praised Cosby for showing white audiences a "humanized" black family and giving African American audiences public role models. On the other side were those who attacked Cosby's utopian vision of "color-blind" harmony as purposely avoiding any questions of real-world racial friction.

These same arguments would continue when Cosby was challenged and then surpassed by Michael Jordan in the Q ratings toward the end of the 1980s and into the 1990s.

Upon entering the league in 1984, the Bulls star was being billed in the same "transcendent" terms that Cosby was shrouded in.

Bulls owner Jerry Reinsdorf, for example, said, "Is Michael Jordan black? Michael has no color." Jordan's superagent, David Falk, raved, "If you were to create a media athlete and star . . . spectacular talent, midsized, well-spoken, attractive, accessible, old-time values, wholesome, clean, natural, not too goody-two-shoes, with a little bit of deviltry in him—you'd invent Michael. He's the first modern crossover in team sports. We think he transcends race."

But when Jordan avoided taking political stands on major issues of racial inequality, he was lacerated by critics for his Cosby-esque prevarication.

If these debates sound all too familiar, that's because this 1980s deification of transcendence is precisely the prism through which America sees its newest Q-score star, Barack Obama.

Reporters constantly said Cosby went "beyond" race, just as they now extol Obama's so-called "postracial" appeal. Jordan was billed by his agent as "the first modern crossover in team sports" who is "well-spoken," "clean," and "attractive" just as Joe Biden in 2007 described his future running mate as the "first mainstream African American who is articulate and bright and clean and a nice-looking guy." And whereas the media oxymoronically dogged Cosby and Jordan for their personal views on race while praising them for avoiding race, that same media obsessively monitors Obama "for signs of parochialism or racial resentment," as The New York Times reports—all the while extolling the president for "steer(ing) clear of putting race front and center," as the Times gushed.

The supposition in this "color-blind" vernacular is that non-whiteness is inherently bad, a disease that afflicted minorities should seek to get "past," "steer clear of," be "blind" to, and above all else "transcend."

The Cosby Show, for instance, was praised by whites as "more American" because it avoided "making you aware" that its characters were black, in the same way white historian Douglas Brinkley now praises Obama for aspiring "to be an American leader, not a Black History Month poster." The logical conclusion is that to be "black" is wholly separate from, and maybe even antithetical to, being "American."

Likewise, Jordan and Obama were venerated as uniquely "beyond" race for being simultaneously black and "clean," "attractive," *and* "well-spoken," as if blackness and hygiene, good looks, and smarts are mutually exclusive.

As with Cosby, Jordan, Obama, and almost every other "transcendent" African American on the public stage since the 1980s, the meager national discussion of race still starts and stops with no-win questions about whether individual stars are "too black" (read: frightening to whites) or "not black enough" (read: abandoning their heritage). To ponder the built-in racism of the transcendence brand itself—to consider its origins in the 1980s white backlash, how those origins constructed its persistent prejudice, and what that prejudice does on a societal level—is to flatten out the concave fun-house mirror that caricatures African Americans and then turn that mirror onto White America.

This is the taboo of taboos, the thou-shalt-not commandment of the entire race issue, because it forces whites to at least admit white racism exists, a notion that most denied even as Mississippi burned and Bull Connor billy-clubbed. As race scholar Tim Wise reports, "In 1962, nearly 90 percent of whites said black children were treated equally in terms of educational opportunity," and "in 1963, roughly two-thirds of whites told Gallup pollsters that blacks were treated equally in white communities."

In the 1980s storm of "color-blind" rhetoric and Reaganite claims that whites were actually the ones facing discrimination, this head-in-the-sand denialism dramatically intensified, creating a situation whereby black icons now risk losing their mass audiences if they do not either speak in careful euphemisms about racism or fully triangulate themselves against the African American community.

In his ratings heyday, for example, Cosby could muster only hints about his personal views on racism when he told *Playboy* in 1985, "If I threw a message out hard and heavy, I'd lose viewers." A few years later on CNN, a cautious Jordan allowed that he believed "you're never colorless" in the eyes of White America, but also begged Larry King's television audience to "know that I'm a black American, but I'm still a person, no matter how you look at me." And after Obama was excoriated as a race-baiter for simply stating the painfully obvious fact that "there's a long history in this country" of racial profiling, he felt compelled to publicly brush off the Congressional Black Caucus's demands that he endorse new programs to alleviate disproportionate black joblessness.

In the article that reported Obama's latter rebuke, *The New York Times* piously noted that the president had "learned the pitfalls of talking bluntly about race."

The "pitfall" the *Times* referenced is the same "transcendence" trap originally set in the 1980s to prevent White America from having to face up to reality and responsibility. The trap may pretend to circumvent or obviate hazardous questions, but all it really does is prevent us from finally finding much needed answers.

MOVIN' ON UP?

Magic, Eddie, Prince, are not "niggers." . . . They're black, but they're not really black. They're more than black. It's different. —PINO IN 1989'S *DO THE RIGHT THING*

[Obama] is postracial, by all appearances. I forgot he was black tonight for an hour. —MSNBC's CHRIS MATTHEWS ON PRESIDENT OBAMA'S 2010 STATE OF THE UNION ADDRESS

As a grade-schooler growing up in leafy Montgomery County, Pennsylvania, I never considered the social ramifications of much of anything, and that includes my regular must-see TV staples. I never thought about what I was learning from the tube, probably because I was repeatedly told that the glowing box in our living room was a distraction from learning (read: my homework) that would "turn your brain to bubble gum" (a direct quote from my mom, and our particular household's version of the "you'll shoot your eye out" scold).

To kids, though, the television of the mid-1980s was more than a mind-warping device. It was an educational teleportation machine, instantly taking us to exotic locales and faraway universes. *The Love Boat* brought us to tropical islands (when we were allowed to stay up on Saturdays to watch it). *Miami Vice* and *The Golden Girls* dropped us in balmy South Florida. *Dallas* and *The Dukes of Hazzard* whisked us away to Texas and the Dixie South (okay, maybe not "exotic," but at least twangy and banjo-worthy). And, hell, *Buck Rogers* and *Star Trek* reruns beamed us into outer space.

But arguably no TV destination was more foreign and strange to me and other suburban white kids than the inner city, and more specifically, the black inner city. These were the places we never visited. In supersegregated metropolises such as the one I lived near, if we saw these neighborhoods at all, it was either in a blur from the overpass on the way to the major league baseball stadium, or during Dad's "Roll 'em up, kids!" wrong turn off the highway à la Clark Griswold.

TV, by contrast, seemed to take us right inside this mysterious and off-limits underworld, and my two favorite stops were very different destinations: upscale Brooklyn and postriot Watts.

I was able to visit the former only once a week. At 8:00 p.m. on Thursdays, I and 60 million other Americans visited the Huxtables' New York City brownstone for thirty minutes of *The Cosby Show*'s wholesome Huxtable-ness. My craving for vicarious black family fun was then sated the rest of the week through excursions each day with *What's Happening!!,* the sitcom about a single African-American mother raising two kids named Raj and Dee in working-class Los Angeles. Though the program had gone off the air in 1979, and though it wasn't a top-rated show in its heyday, its reruns★ nonetheless aired every afternoon between *The Jeffersons* and *Sanford and Son* on "The Great Entertainer," otherwise known as Philadelphia's rickety independent station, WPHL-17 (which, for the record, might not have been "great" in the conventional sense, but was definitely an entertainer).

Was my mom correct in predicting that the cathode rays were transmogrifying my cortex into a chewed gob of Hubba Bubba? This I cannot answer with confidence, though based solely on the number of Rerun Stubbs dance moves† I can still recall (and, obviously, perform on command), I suspect she was right.

What I can state with more scientific certainty is that the TV's

---

★Pun intended—we'll get to him in a second.
†I told you we'd get to him.

mystical, Flux Capacitor–like powers of space/time travel were undoubtedly indoctrinating me and the larger white audience in a profound way—and that's not necessarily a good thing.

For instance, we know from the longest-running study of television's social impact that heavy TV viewers typically "become less tolerant of 'outsiders' like blacks," as *The Boston Globe* has reported. We know from surveys that both children and young adults who watched a lot of 80s television disproportionately saw the Huxtables as a realistic representation of the average black family when, in fact, the Huxtables' wealth was the rare exception to a 1980s experiencing an explosion in black poverty.

We know too that "attitudinal data suggests that the more TV we watch, the more we are able to hold contradictory ideas simultaneously," as University of Massachusetts researchers report, and that "one of the most striking features" of the school's landmark *Cosby Show* audience study was viewers' ability to both acknowledge the Huxtables' way-out-of-the-norm economic status and yet believe "that they are a normal, everyday family."

Considering my viewing habits as a nine-year-old, I was a perfect slate for this type of contradictory thinking, a blank wall onto which Hollywood's virtuosos were graffitiing two conflicting cartoons. In my afternoons, *What's Happening!!*'s working-class family was painting me a humorous comic strip of a typical black life. On Thursday nights, *The Cosby Show*'s family seemed to be doing the same, but in economically atypical environs.

Though I didn't know it at the time, the distance between the two settings was representative of a larger televisual transformation that sculpted the parameters of today's discussion—or lack thereof—of race. The shift was dramatic, and it pivoted, like many cultural trends, specifically off *The Cosby Show.*

As the program watched by more viewers than any sitcom in history—a program not only credited with rescuing NBC but saving the entire sitcom form—*The Cosby Show* is the major time stamp of modern television's historical scripture. There is B.C.—Before Cosby—and A.D.—After Dr. (Huxtable)—and the key difference between the two eras is the near-total elimination of the black working class from the small screen. Indeed, between the mid-1970s B.C. and the mid-1980s A.D., while the total percentage of black characters on television significantly jumped, blacks went from being cast in 30 percent of working class roles to being cast in almost none of those roles.

Noting that this happened at the very moment African Americans were losing economic ground in real life, Harvard's Henry Louis Gates wrote in 1989, "When American society could not successfully achieve the social reformation it sought in the 60's through the Great Society, television solved the problem simply by inventing symbols of that transformation in the 80's."

How and why this transformation occurred in the 1980s is the creation story of the now preeminent transcendence brand.

The Washington Post has correctly reported that for most of the first half of the twentieth century in Hollywood, African Americans were limited to hyperracialized "roles as domestics, dancers or savages." That changed when, during the civil rights tumult of the 1960s, NBC executives gave "color blindness" an ephemeral test run in 1965 by offering Bill Cosby his first major role, as Alexander Scott in *I Spy*.

The show was historic, both because Cosby became the first African American to costar in a dramatic television series and because Cosby's character, Alexander Scott, wasn't the stereotypical minstrelized sidekick—he was the straitlaced brains to his white counterpart's breezy insouciance.

Pioneering an early version of what scholars would later call *The Cosby Show*'s "bargain," *I Spy* seemed to make a deal with its white audience: In exchange for accepting an African-American in a dignified role, white viewers were guaranteed that plots never dealt in any way with racial inequality or bigotry.★

★This was a calculated decision from the beginning of the show. In an interview years later, *I Spy*'s white costar, Robert Culp, said he told Cosby, "There are stations in the South that won't carry us," and asked Cosby, "Do you want to do anything about that?" Culp says Cosby told him, "Our statement is a nonstatement." In following this strategy, Cosby was following in the footsteps of another African-American pioneer at the time, Jackie Robinson. As the baseball legend wrote in his autobiography, rather than making overt statements about racism, "I learned that as long as I appeared to ignore insult and injury, I was a martyred hero to a lot of people who had sympathy for this underdog."

That was exactly the pact that undergirded the follow-up to *I Spy,*
1968's *Julia,* a sitcom launched only months after President Lyndon
Johnson's National Advisory Commission on Civil Disorders (i.e.,
the Kerner Commission) criticized television programming as "almost totally white in appearance and attitude." But while *Julia* dealt
with the "appearance" issue in telling the story of an African American widow and her son, it most certainly avoided the "attitude"
question. Discussing the show's story, lead actress Diahann Carroll
told *TV Guide* in 1968 that *Julia* is "presenting the white Negro,"
which she said "has very little Negro-ness."

I Spy and *Julia* were the initial building blocks of the entertainment industry's "don't ask, don't tell" attitude toward race that would
feature African Americans without making value judgments about
the racism African Americans face in their daily lives—racism that
the crucial white audience either supported or ignored and certainly
didn't want indicted in its prime-time TV.

"In the racially tense and stratified United States of the middle
1960s, Diahann Carroll and Bill Cosby lived and worked in mostly
white worlds where whites dare not notice and blacks dare not acknowledge their blackness," wrote sociologist Herman Gray in his
book *Watching Race.*

As the 1960s became the 1970s, Gray writes that this fleeting flir-
tation with color blindness temporarily receded with the ascent of
Norman Lear and his controversial new genre of sitcoms that rejected
transcendence and forcefully responded "to angry calls by different
sectors of the black community for 'relevant' and 'authentic' images
of black people."

Lear's wildly successful *All in the Family* was the genre's forefather.
Its overt ridiculing of Archie "Never Gonna Break Bread with No
Jungle Bunnies" Bunker, its full-throated antiracist social commentary, and its inclusion of the boisterous couple that would later become *The Jeffersons*—all of that flipped Hollywood's previous caution
on its head, replacing the moment's brief "don't ask, don't tell"
mantra with an "always ask, and always tell" reflex.

All in the Family debuted as the number one show in America in
1971, and within a year Lear's follow-up, *Sanford and Son,* was a close
second—an arguably bigger landmark in television history than *All in*

the Family itself, considering the new program used characters and settings that were entirely foreign to much of the white audience. Specifically, rather than raising racial issues through the Bunkers' white family and their Queens neighborhood, *Sanford and Son*'s vaudeville costars, Redd Foxx and Demond Wilson, portrayed poor African Americans struggling to get by with a salvage business in Los Angeles' black ghetto.

From *Good Times* to *That's My Mama* to *What's Happening!!*, *Sanford and Son*'s success prompted a spate of Lear-inspired follow-ups, spin-offs, and replicas that "famously tackled racism, feminism, abortion, divorce, homosexuality, cancer and other topics previously deemed too 'sensitive' for TV," *The Denver Post*'s Joanne Ostrow has written.

These portrayals certainly received their share of scorn. Citing how "J. J. from *Good Times* changed from a thoughtful character with comic insight" into a "Dyno-MITE!"–bellowing buffoon, *The Boston Globe* accused the "ghetto sitcoms" of turning initially "thoughtful" roles "with comic insight" into "colorful, minstrel-like characters." Likewise, Harvard psychologist Alvin Poussaint, an adviser to *The Cosby Show,* said the genre was "a throwback to the old *Amos 'n Andy* approach to blacks . . . full of jivin', jammin', streetwise-style stuff that is the worst kind of stereotyping." According to the Museum of Broadcast Communications, Redd Foxx himself was known to periodically "complain that the white producers and writers [of *Sanford and Son*] had little regard or appreciation of African American life and culture."

But even Foxx conceded that programs such as *Sanford and Son,* which rejected *I Spy*'s and *Julia*'s color blindness, showed white, middle-class America "a lot of what they need to know" about typical black life. And even if critics were correct in saying these shows sometimes reverted to stereotyping, the programming at least humanized African Americans and familiarized whites with quotidian black settings.

Hollywood, however, doesn't exist in a vacuum, and as the civil rights movement's successes went from abstract legislative victories to real-world policies in schoolhouses, factories, and voting booths, the so-called Silent Majority of Richard Nixon, George Wallace, and

Ronald Reagan began mounting its retaliation—and entertainment shifted. Local fights over busing, antiwelfare demagoguery, the Supreme Court's *Bakke* decision highlighting minority-preference programs in higher education—these were the kind of combustible ingredients that ignited a cultural backlash in which more and more whites saw Archie Bunkers as victims, rather than perpetrators, of racism.

The runaway success of the *Rocky* films in the late 1970s and early 1980s exemplified the counterrevolutionary fervor. Rocky "Italian Stallion" Balboa was South Philadelphia's very own Archie Bunker, a white, working-class grunt who gets fired by the black affirmative-action case that runs the local meatpacking plant; gets his gym locker taken by the more physically gifted black boxers; and gets taunted by Apollo Creed, whose snooty diction, intellectual arrogance, and three-piece suits are a blatant caricature of the "uppity" black stereotype. After Rocky heroically vanquishes Creed, he goes on to face another black stereotype named Clubber Lang, an inner-city behemoth played by Mr. T who seethes with animalistic rage, bellicosity, and a predatory lust for white women.* Reviewers called Lang "a white racist's worst nightmare of black brutality," and he was summarily pummeled by Rocky, with the inspirational "Gonna Fly Now" ballad playing in the background.

Not wanting to abandon the sizable black television audience but also aiming to harness the Italian Stallion and the moment's politics of white backlash, television re-embraced the "don't ask, don't tell" posture on race, shifting in those Rocky years to what might be called the "postghetto" programs. Anchored in aspiration and integration, these were the immediate precursors to *The Cosby Show*'s Obama-esque "postracialism," serving as "a bridge between sitcoms depicting the ghetto and those portraying the new black upper class," wrote Henry Gates.

In the late 1970s and early 1980s, *The Jeffersons,* once Archie Bunker's neighbors in Queens, "moved on up" to ritzier Manhattan

---

*At one point, Clubber Lang disrupts a public event by screaming for Rocky's wife to "bring your pretty little self over to my apartment tonight, and I'll show you a real man."

with their economic success. *Benson* was an African American who started as a butler in the California governor's mansion and eventually climbed to the second-highest constitutional office in the state. *The A-Team*'s white characters routinely relied on B.A. Baracus to save the day. *Diff'rent Strokes,* whose apostrophed title awkwardly tried to stress comedic ghetto-ness, was nonetheless about low-income black kids being civilized by benevolent upper-crust WASPs. Same thing for *Webster,* only it wasn't WASPs, it was a white-ethnic NFL player and his trophy wife.

In some ways, this was, according to *Blacks and White TV* author J. Fred MacDonald, "a reversion back to the age of neo-minstrelcy" as each of these shows' characters and story lines as firmly rooted in black stereotypes.

The Jeffersons comedy pivoted off the friction between George's new neighbors and his inability to linguistically or culturally transcend his lagging ghetto (read: black) sensibilities. *Benson* was only able to break into high-level politics after doing time as a glorified custodian. And B.A. Baracus may have been *The A-Team*'s go-to guy, but only for his power of intimidation, a factor enhanced by the fact that his tribalized appearance (Mohawk, bangles, chains, etc.) made him look like a sullen ex-slave.★

Similarly, *Diff'rent Strokes* generated fish-out-of-water laughs that contrasted Arnold and Willis Jackson's outbursts, poor manners, and vernacular ("What you talkin' bout, Dad?") with the haughty social conventions of their white guardians. Their story was topped only by that of Webster Long, an orphan whose situation breezed past mere paternalism and went for a tacit endorsement of the master-slave relationship. In *Webster,* the black child is taken by a wealthy white cou-

---

★This description of B.A. Baracus and his circumstances actually understates his position as *The A-Team*'s resident slave. Not only was he kept around mostly for his muscle, but he is also shown to be so stupid that he allows himself to be dragged by his white superiors from job to job against his will. Recall that B.A. always insists, "I ain't gettin' on no plane," because he fears flying. Rather than respecting that wish, however, B.A.'s slavemasters alternately drug or hypnotize him so he can be transported—like a piece of meat—without complaint. This might explain why Mr. T, the actor who played B.A., complained to *People* magazine in 1983 that Hollywood was still treating him like "a higher-priced slave" and "the house nigger."

ple, who are then shown heroically fighting to prevent the boy's bio-logical uncle from reclaiming him and bringing him back to—gasp!—live on Chicago's African American South Side.

But along with promoting neo-minstrelcy, these shows and others like them were also beginning to sell white audiences on two of the most deceptive arguments of transcendence. The first says African Americans face no racial barriers that cannot be overcome by hard work, subservience, and allegedly universal white benevolence. The second asserts African Americans who do break those barriers are liberating themselves of their race and are therefore different and more laudable than typical black people who continue to toil in the economic and cultural conditions of *Good Times*.

Such hybrid "postghetto" characters straddling minstrelcy and transcendence had their counterparts in the top movies of the era. *Superman III*'s Gus Gorman (Richard Pryor) ends up saving the ultimate epitome of White Power—the Man of Steel—but only after Gorman suppresses his "black criminal" instinct that previously led him to embezzle money from his employer. *The Toy*'s Jack Brown (Pryor) is an out-of-work reporter who teaches a young boy important lessons of the world, but only as the personal slave of the child's KKK-aligned Louisiana father. *Beverly Hills Cop*'s Axel Foley and *Trading Places*' Billy Ray Valentine (Eddie Murphy) right wrongs that privileged whites cannot or will not, but specifically by employing the hustling skills the two characters learned as former street thugs. And *The Empire Strikes Back*'s Lando Calrissian (Billy Dee Williams) is a cross between John F. Kennedy and Willie Horton: a respected and benevolent elite but also a shady creature of the underworld; a successful and altruistic politician and renowned pilot, but also a sexual predator constantly hitting on his best buddy's white girlfriend—yes, Cloud City's very own "mix of liberalism and a big black rapist," which Republican Party operatives would in 1988 see in Horton himself.*

---

*This sounds like an overstatement, I know, but it's not. Go back and watch *Empire Strikes Back*. Within five minutes of Lando's screen debut, he's sexually harassing Princess Leia. His initial greeting to Leia is "Hello, what have we here?"—almost drooling all over his cape as he introduces himself as "the administrator of this facility." A scene later, Lando breathily tells Leia, "You look absolutely beautiful," and asks, "Will you join me for a little refreshment?" He then quickly adds,

For all its success, though, this postghetto genre was suffering by 1983, as B.A. Baracus was the lone African American lead left in the top-ten-rated television programs. So the following year, *The Cosby Show* launched with the ambitious goal of reinvigorating the form.

Cosby aimed to mix the black self-sufficiency of ghetto shows with the self-improvement and integrationist narratives of the post-ghetto programs. He wanted to go from "blaxploitation" to "blaxpiration" by showing a successful African American family and forwarding the idea that, as he said, "If you want to live like they do, and you're willing to work, the opportunity is there."

To paint the picture, Cosby and NBC enthusiastically used transcendence as their brush, employing three shrewd strategies to make the Huxtables look as nonthreatening to whites as possible.

The first tactic homed in on economics. Cosby initially imagined a show about a typical working-class black family—in his proposal, one headed by a limousine driver and a carpenter. But that was scrapped by NBC management in favor of an obstetrician and a high-powered corporate lawyer.

The decision paid off. White audiences explicitly cited the Huxtables' atypical wealth as a comforting, race-mitigating anodyne to majoritarian fears and resentments, and critics followed suit. In its initial review, *The New York Times* in 1984 effusively praised the Huxtables by stating, "This particular family happens to be black but its lifestyle and problems are universal middle-class." A year later, *Newsweek* described "a tightly nuclear, upscale family coping with the same irritations and misunderstandings that afflict their white counterparts."

"They're upper-middle-class, not black," said one white viewer in the University of Massachusetts audience study, a perfect summary of wealth's critical role in the new transcendence brand.

Just as important, Cosby also opted to, as he said, "leave all of that anger and controversy" about ongoing racism and racial disparities aside. It was, again, a calculated decision. He told *USA Today* that he

---

"Everyone's invited, of course," lest the suspicious Han or the audience think he's employing sexual innuendo (which he most certainly is). For the record, Lando is both the only black character and only sexually aggressive character in the original *Star Wars* trilogy.

believed the mass audience couldn't "take it if we began to lay it out and tell the truth" about bigotry.

The result was that in 201 episodes, the show did not include a single plot point about the everyday racism that a black family—even a wealthy one—would almost certainly have faced in real life.* Additionally, save for a few visits to Sandra and Elvin's shabby apartment (which was a source of ridicule), the show barely showed the disproportionately depressed economic status of blacks. And when racism was tangentially referenced, it was either portrayed in the famed March on Washington episode as a thing of the past, or in Theo's END APARTHEID poster as something that only foreign countries such as South Africa still struggled with.

Finally, while *The Cosby Show* proudly played up specific aspects of historic African American culture that had long ago been accepted by whites, the program also played down more contemporary black culture that might scare off those whites.

Thus, episodes teemed with appearances by black music legends, references to black colleges, displays of African American art, and even grandchildren named Nelson and Winnie (after the Mandelas), but that's where it stopped.

As media scholar Linda Fuller reported in her book-length study of *The Cosby Show,* although Theo Huxtable and his friend Cockroach "deliver a riotous rap version of 'Julius Caesar' during one episode, and although there are various Black friends who 'high five' one another, a conscious decision [was] made to refrain from using jive language or nonstandard Black dialect." Indeed, *The Wall Street Journal* reported that in his original audition for the show, Malcolm Jamal-Warner, who played Theo, was scolded by Cosby for "adopting the jive-talking manner that [Warner] assumed TV producers wanted from black actors trying out for sitcoms."

---

*As evidence that the program truly did go out of its way to avoid a discussion about racism, *Cosby Show* writers avoided the issue even when it would have fit perfectly into the show's plot. Case in point is the episode when Vanessa complains about being mistreated at school. For a moment, it sounds as if she is going to recount some act of discrimination, which would have seemed perfectly normal. Instead, she ends up complaining that her problem "wouldn't have happened if we weren't so rich."

The three-pronged formula hit paydirt, as the University of Massachusetts study found that white viewers were drawn to the show specifically because of the Huxtables' "transcendence."

"I like the fact that they're black and they present a whole other side of what you tend to think black families are like," said one white viewer.

"When we see Bill Cosby," said another, "I don't look at a black person."

"You're able to relate to them as people regardless of their color," said yet another.

Such enthusiasm meant unprecedented commercial success. *The Cosby Show* attracted roughly half of the entire national television audience, raked in $1.5 million in ad revenues per show, and was a top-five rated program for seven of its eight years on the air. In one of those years, 1986, nineteen of the twenty-five most watched programs on television were *Cosby* episodes. Coming less than two decades after the end of Jim Crow and in the same decade as Reagan's white backlash, this was no small achievement for an African American program, and many iconic black voices hailed its ascent.

Alvin Poussaint, the Harvard psychologist who consulted on the program's scripts, said, "This show is changing the white community's perspective of black Americans" and "doing far more to instill positive racial attitudes than if Bill came at the viewer with a sledgehammer or a sermon."

Ralph Ellison, renowned author of *Invisible Man,* said *Cosby* "cuts across race and class" by rejecting "the distorted view" that all African Americans "are poor."

Coretta Scott King called the show "the most positive portrayal of black family life that has ever been broadcast," adding, "With one out of three black families living below the poverty line, it is inspiring to see a black family that has managed to escape."

That notion of "escape" carried a deeper meaning that just living conditions. *The Cosby Show* was making the larger case that if African Americans simply worked hard and pretended racism didn't exist, they could "escape" their race in the eyes of whites and therefore accumulate the wealth and acceptance that the Huxtables had somehow managed to amass.

In making that argument, the show was drawing a clear distinction between the "racial" working-class African Americans (Fred Sanford, Rerun, and J. J., etc.) and the "postracial" Huxtables. And the fact that those "racial" character types were almost completely omitted from the Huxtables' lives suggested to the white audience that no less a respected black figure than Bill Cosby was endorsing that audience's views about what is—and is not—an acceptable, venerable African American.

Hollywood eagerly replicated *The Cosby Show*'s postracial vision as the After Dr. Huxtable age commenced at the end of the 1980s with spectacles such as *The Fresh Prince of Bel Air*. The Will Smith production was *Diff'rent Strokes* but with an important twist: It was as if the black Huxtables, rather than the white Drummonds, had rescued Willis Jackson from the supposed horrors of working-class black culture. Instead of jokes about the friction between poor, nontranscendent black kids and white adults, it was gags about the clashes between the nontranscendent black nephew and his transcendent black relatives.

The burlesque was a final chapter in a historic journey: The early 1970s of *Good Times* celebrated the black working class; the early 1980s of *The Jeffersons* celebrated that working class starting to pull its way out of the ghetto and toward transcendence; the mid-1980s celebrated the Huxtables having used transcendence to complete that climb; and the 1980s ended with a program celebrating a transcendent black family in Bel Air valiantly saving their West Philadelphia kin from his decidedly nontranscendent *Good Times* roots.

The completion of this full-circle voyage affirmed the crucial and disturbing value judgment that still defines White America's views on race today.

"It's the Cosby decade! America loves black people!"

That was the exclamation of Mark Watson, the white college grad from *Soul Man,* one of 1986's top-grossing movies, and, for its preposterous decision to put C. Thomas Howell in blackface, one of that year's most controversial films.

When Mark blurted out his glib declaration, he was trying to justify using tanning pills to make himself look black so as to land Harvard Law School's African American scholarship. On the merits he was half-right. It most definitely was the Cosby decade. But, in part, because of that, America learned to love only *certain* black people—those that "transcended" their race.

Bill Cosby had started a trend. In its 1987 article headlined "TV's Disappearing Color Line," *U.S. News and World Report* said he had "created opportunities for other blacks" who were emulating his show's posture on race—icons such as Oprah Winfrey, Bryant Gumbel, and Michael Jordan, the latter of whom was quoted in *The New York Times Magazine* reassuring its mostly white readership that he "aspires to be seen as 'neither black nor white.'"

According to University of Massachusetts researchers, by rewarding these transcendent eighties personalities with huge ratings, big ticket sales, and widespread fame, white audiences were enunciating their appreciation for "a 'nice' blackness" (i.e., rich, nonconfrontational, etc.) as contrasted with the "not-so-nice blackness" (i.e., working-class, intolerant of racism, etc.) of the ghetto shows—and that insipid distinction soon spread.

Looking back at eighties politics, for example, Pulitzer Prize–winning columnist Leonard Pitts noted that America began seeing civil-rights-era black leaders as embodying the negative "politics of grievance and lament." Pitts said whites had started embracing "a new generation" of black politicians such as Los Angeles mayor Tom Bradley and Virginia governor Doug Wilder, who sought to make race "incidental."

Media-wise, it was the same contrived dichotomy. On the very television networks that featured the "nice blackness" of Cosby, Winfrey, Bryant, and Jordan, journalists were trotting out the "not-so-nice" analogue, framing current events in the same racialized inflection that was dominating 1980s' sports clichés. Come the evening news, every issue was inevitably held up as the earnest, gritty, gutty lunch-pail sensibilities of Rocky Balboa and Larry Bird versus the angry, showy-but-undisicplined, overtalented-but-underachieving Clubber Lang and Magic Johnson.★

★This Lunch Pail vs. Showtime paradigm—and its attendant racism—came, in particular, out of 1980s basketball, and not just from the white-black rivalry of Larry

"Nightly television news reports of 'rampaging' hordes of urban black youth robbing and raping helpless and law-abiding white victims came to us in the Bernhard Goetz and Central Park jogger cases in New York City, television documentaries such as CBS's *The Vanishing Black Family* presented case studies of mostly black and female welfare parents who were usually uneducated, unemployed, and single; [and] reality-based crime shows such as *Cops* showcased the apprehension and arrest of black inner-city crack cocaine users," wrote sociologist Herman Gray.

This televisual contrast between images of transcendent black celebrities and nontranscendent black masses was leading whites to a seemingly logical conclusion: namely, that "blacks are solely responsible for their social conditions, with no acknowledgement of the severely constricted life opportunities that most black people face," wrote Gates in 1989.

That narrative was amplified by a *Cosby*-mimicking prime-time lineup that was, according to the National Commission on Working Women's 1989 report, "portraying an artificial world of racial harmony where whites and blacks almost always get along and no one is poor."

Political leaders in the 1980s, ever the opportunists, cited this whitewashed tableau to insist that the Huxtables proved antiracist initiatives were no longer necessary.

In 1986, President Reagan's undersecretary of education delivered a high-profile speech declaring, "*The Cosby Show* and the values it promotes may ultimately be more important to black children's

---

Bird and Magic Johnson. In *Michael Jordan, Inc.*, University of Maryland professor David Andrews notes that during the 1982 NCAA Championship game, "The media alluded to the fact that the [University of North Carolina's] white coach, Dean Smith, infused his players with a sense of his superior knowledge of the game, whereas his black counterpart [Georgetown's John Thompson] merely assembled a group of players and allowed them to do what came naturally, that is, to rely on their natural physical attributes." The framing survives today. As the *Rocky Mountain News'* Paul Campos exhibited in a 2008 column about sports-page terms such as *gritty, gutty, hard-nosed, lunch-bucket ethic,* and *intelligent,* the "idea is that white players must overcome their lack of God-given athletic talent through good moral character, and in particular the classic Puritan virtue of hard work," while black players can get by on their genetic—and therefore, unearned—abilities.

success than a bevy of new federal programs." A few years later, Brent Bozell, chairman of the conservative Media Research Center, criticized civil rights leaders for telling African Americans "that they have little hope of making it on their own, that they can only make it with government assistance [and that] America, as a whole, owes them something.

"This Neanderthal, left-wing message has done almost irreversible harm to black Americans," he said, adding that "influential television programs" such as *The Cosby Show*—not civic institutions or better schools or capital investment—"make the difference in poor black communities."

At the same time, what seemingly critical analysis of bigotry survived in this "postracial" phantasmagoria helped construct the now ubiquitous "white savior" paradigm.★

In 1986's *Soul Man,* for example, only a white C. Thomas Howell—not a black student—finds the courage to punch out the racists at his school. In 1987's *Cry Freedom,* a film ostensibly about blacks' antiapartheid struggle in South Africa ended up concentrating attention on the white journalist who chronicled the events, ultimately becoming "a movie about black suffering in which the hero is white," as the *Miami Herald* pointed out.

Nineteen eighty-eight's *Mississippi Burning* downplayed the big-

---

★Yes, the "white savior" story really is ubiquitous, even in sci-fi. Writing for the website io9.com, Annalee Newitz shows how 2010 Oscar nominees *Avatar* and *District 9* both feature humans as "the cause of alien oppression and distress," then show "a white man who was one of the oppressors switches sides at the last minute, assimilating into the alien culture and becoming its savior." This "is also the basic story of *Dune,* where a member of the white royalty flees his posh palace on the planet Dune to become leader of the worm-riding native Fremen." Same thing for "*Enemy Mine,* where a white man and the alien he's been battling (played, of course, by a black actor, Louis Gossett) are stranded on a hostile planet together for years. . . . Eventually they become best friends, and when the alien dies, the human raises the alien's child as his own." She goes on to note, "This is a classic scenario you've seen in non-scifi epics from *Dances With Wolves* to *The Last Samurai,* where a white guy manages to get himself accepted into a closed society of people of color and eventually becomes its most awesome member." Notably, the "white savior" genre is different from the "white collaborator" idea. In "white savior" fables, whites don't just join the cause of equality in solidarity with minorities, they actually lead minorities when those minorities are supposedly incapable of leading themselves.

otry of average white Mississippians during the Jim Crow era and advanced the image of helpless African Americans waiting to be rescued by white FBI agents. This, even though the historical record of the infamous murder of black civil rights activists showed the FBI was either dreadfully inept or complicit in the crimes.

And, of course, there were 1980s miniseries. NBC's 1989 recap of the Howard Beach white-on-black race crimes revolved around the heroism of the white prosecutor, while CBS's *Unconquered* was supposedly about Martin Luther King, but, as *Newsweek* reported, was really a drama "that deal[t] mostly with the pressures of a white family caught up in the civil-rights struggle."

Between the nice/not-so-nice contrast and the savior hagiography, the 1980s was building a powerful and deceptive fable. Rather than being nudged toward self-reflection and remorse, white America was being told that Huxtable-level wealth was common among blacks; that such wealth was universally available to blacks who were willing to follow the Huxtables' transcendent values; that whites deserve approbation for saving blacks from racism; and that because racism was supposedly eliminated, governmental initiatives to combat bigotry were obsolete.

According to polls, these fictions took firm hold in the public psyche. *The Cosby Show* audience study, for instance, found that the program's grounding in Huxtable transcendence meant "the overwhelming majority of white [*Cosby*] viewers felt racism was a sin of the past." They believed that "if Cliff and Clair" can make it, "then so can all blacks," and those that don't succeed "only have themselves to blame." The University of Wisconsin found in 1985 that white college kids who were heavy television watchers grossly overestimated black economic success in America. A March 1988 *Newsweek* poll found four out of five whites said they saw no need for affirmative action programs to combat discrimination, and a 1991 poll by the magazine found only about a third supporting any congressional action to help African Americans. Summing up the trends, the *Los Angeles Times* reported that polling during the 1980s showed whites simply "no longer feel blacks are discriminated against in the schools, the job market and the courts."

If ever there was proof that culture could shape perception in spite of facts, these surveys were it. As a few brave newspapers re-counted in 1989's requisite end-of-the-decade recaps, the Reagan era did not construct the utopia of racial equality that whites were led to believe it had. On the contrary, the 1980s was a comparatively terri-ble time to be a regular, nonfamous, nonrich black person in Amer-ica, no matter what kind of Huxtable-ian "values" or work ethic one exhibited.

Calling the decade "black folks' worst nightmare," the *St. Peters-burg Times* recounted a massive jump in African American poverty and unemployment from past eras, "a shrinking black middle class," and a spate of high-profile white-on-black hate crimes. Concurrently, the *St. Louis Post-Dispatch*'s eighties retrospective was headlined "Blacks Feel the Breaks." It reviewed how "the strong right arm of the fed-eral government" was once again "raised against minorities."

The paper recounted, "The Supreme Court—peppered with several of President Ronald Reagan's appointees—issued numerous rulings that made it more difficult for blacks to get a foot in the work-place door. In high-profile legal battles, Reagan's administration was on the side of segregationist schools, of white parents trying to block school desegregation and of whites and men trying to stop affirmative action."

With cross-burning expressions of overt racism no longer socially acceptable, Reaganites draped this legal backlash in coded phrases such as *states' rights, local control,* and *color blindness,* presenting a world supposedly ravaged by *reverse discrimination* against whites. Whether deliberately or not, the rhetoric was buttressed by pop culture stars whose success seemed to underscore the demagoguery's truth. Tran-scendent black heroes, increasingly ubiquitous on television, seemed to verify that regular African Americans' economic troubles had nothing to do with racism, and that to even contemplate the opposite was to pantomime a *Bonfire of the Vanities* cartoon embodying other code words such as *rabble-rouser, reverse racist, troublemaker,* and *race hus-tler* that were in vogue in the 1980s.

Of course, this thinking is inherently based on a vile if unstated assumption of strident, torch-horse-and-hood racism: namely, that the trait needing to be "transcended"—blackness—corresponds to an intrinsic, even genetic, "pathology."

The theory is seductive in its illusory logic. It correctly accepts that persistent mass trends (like, say, disproportionate black poverty) cannot be explained as the mere product of individual actions. After all, accidents, mistakes, and poor decisions afflict every human population regardless of color. But beneath this patina of empiricism is the willfully ignorant insistence that institutional racism cannot account for mass trends, either. That leaves congenital "pathology" as the only possible culprit, a Jimmy the Greek line of reasoning that assumes blacks are "bred" for failure.

Though first popularized in contemporary America by Pat Moynihan in the 1960s, this kind of bigotry has been around in some form since at least Nazi eugenics. But it made a big post-civil-rights-era resurgence in the 1980s with the rise of transcendence and what race scholar Tim Wise calls "enlightened exceptionalism"—a form of prejudice that "manages to accommodate individual people of color, even as it continues to look down upon the larger mass of black and brown America with suspicion, fear, and contempt."

Such is the spirit of *Soul Man*'s declaration that "America loves black people!" because "It's the Cosby decade!" or, as a Princeton sociologist told *Sports Illustrated* in 1991, "We must be good people— we love Michael Jordan." Extrapolating from the old "my best friend is black so I can't be a racist" motto, the 1980s used zealous affinity for transcendence as a rationale for denial and an alibi for white prejudice.

This is the "racism masquerading as liberalism" that the University of Massachusetts found in white *Cosby Show* viewers who embrace the show's "bargain"—the one that "accept[s] the Huxtables as people who are 'just like us'" while "reject[ing] the majority of black people who are not like the Huxtables and, by implication, not 'like us.'"

This is what Michael Jordan's agent was talking about when he said, "People don't look at Michael as being black—they accept that he's different because he is a celebrity."

And this is the daringly honest revelation of the most famous interchange in Spike Lee's 1989 masterpiece, *Do the Right Thing*. After Pino, the white racist pizza chef, lists transcendent African Americans such as Magic Johnson, Eddie Murphy, and Prince as his favorite pop culture stars, his black coworker asks him how that can be when "all you ever talk about is 'nigger this' and 'nigger that.'"

"It's different," Pino replies. "Magic, Eddie, Prince, are not 'niggers.' . . . They're not really black. I mean, they're black, but they're not really black. They're more than black."

That crass attitude is what transcendence is all about, and why since the 1980s, African Americans on the public stage must agree to the same bargain that *The Cosby Show* first negotiated.

Which brings us to the debates over Barack Obama's "postracial" image.

As *The New York Times* noted in 2009, the first African American president has repeatedly been "criticized as either too black or not black enough," and he is constantly questioned with an eye on his skin color. Is he sufficiently concerned about the disproportionate pain the black community is bearing in the Great Recession, or is he "not listening" to African Americans, as black congressional leaders assert? Does he "run from race like a black man runs from a cop" as one of his leading black critics, Michael Eric Dyson, argues? Or, as one of his chief defenders, Melissa Harris-Lacewell, writes, is Obama "stunningly similar to Martin Luther King"?

These volleys elucidate the parameters of twenty-first century transcendence, yet as new as these queries seem, *The Cosby Show* was the source of an eerily similar exchange.

In 1985, *Ebony* reported that some prominent voices were asserting that the show was "not being 'black enough'" in its refusal to "deal with more controversial issues, such as poverty and racism and interracial dating," and its "focus on a Black middle-class family when the vast majority of Black people survive on incomes far below that of the Huxtables." Condensing the different threads of criticism into two brutal blows, *The Village Voice* first said the Huxtables were not "black in anything but their skin color," and then criticized Cosby's character for being a father who "no longer qualifies as black enough to be an Uncle Tom."

The pushback was equally caustic. The Associated Press in 1986 reported that in response to allegations that the show was "not delving deeply enough into racial problems and prejudice," Cosby "says he doesn't have any greater responsibility in that area than Bob Newhart does." The actor later told the *Los Angeles Times,* "There's no need to rap my show if you're not going to make [white] shows behave accordingly—you can't have two sets of standards." He also bridled at the conflation of "white" with achievement, telling *USA Today,* "To say that [the Huxtables are] acting white means that only white people can [succeed]."

This back-and-forth certainly raised important questions about whether public figures bear any responsibility to their communities or to a particular social agenda, and Cosby is undeniably correct that African Americans are treated differently on this score than their white counterparts. As one network programming director told the *Los Angeles Times* in 1985, the expectation is that "whenever there's a black person in the cast, we have to deal with heavy social issues."★

But in putting all of the culpability for television's distorted racial imagery on African Americans and none of it on white America, the "too black"/"not black enough" argument obscures the troubling fact that Cosby and every other icon of transcendence are *forced* to play by the postracial rules that incite such destructive arguments, rules that network chieftans and the white audience demand.

In the 1980s, cautious entertainment executives more often than not fell "back on their dreadful, unspoken belief that white viewers don't want to watch a series about black reality," wrote *Los Angeles Times* entertainment reporter Rick Du Brow. That meant categorically rejecting the old Norman Lear model in favor of a less provocative, more "color-blind" template. Exemplifying the attitude, one

---

★A good example of this double standard's longevity came in recent years in the very different way the media treated the Falcons' black quarterback, Michael Vick, and the Pittsburgh Steelers' Ben Roethlisberger when they were confronted with allegations of illegal dog fighting and sexual misconduct, respectively. "Black athletes who had never seen a dog fight in their lives were asked about Michael Vick as if they all had pit bull tournaments happening in their backyards," wrote *The Nation*'s Dave Zirin. "No one will be asking [white QB] Drew Brees if he ever tries to have bodyguard protected sex with 20-year olds. No one will press [white QB] Peyton Manning on whether a culture of pickup trucks, Kenny Chesney music, and white baseball caps may have led Big Ben [Roethlisberger] down this regrettable road. Such pop-sociological stupidity is a burden white athletes never have to face."

NBC executive told the newspaper, "We can't do *Do the Right Thing* every week."

If this dynamic was discussed at all, it was inevitably shrouded in opaque circumlocution. Cosby, wrote *The New York Times* in a typical 1988 article, was being compelled to "play the prime-time program game of trying to appeal to the widest possible audience, which means offending as few people and groups as possible."

"Widest possible audience," "offending as few people as possible"—when it comes to race, that's Establishment-speak for "whites" and their unrelenting desire for the wholesale absolution that the transcendence brand affords.

This explains the growing infatuation in the 1980s with a racialized permutation of organized labor's atavistic "Which side are you on?" question. While fetishizing the difference between the postracial black heroes it loved and the racial black commoners it still despised, white America began constantly evaluating whether its public figures were secretly connected to the latter.

In 1988, this frenzied compulsion manifested itself via a Republican presidential campaign that became a singular exercise in making the Democratic Party look as if it were secretly led by Jesse Jackson and determined to free imprisoned black rapists through revolving doors. That same year, Eddie Murphy touched off a controversy—and was met with harsh criticism by media and the Hollywood glitterati—for using an Academy Award appearance to break the rules of transcendence and mention the conspicuous absence of black Oscar winners.

A few years later, the infatuation focused on Michael Jordan, who was alternately hounded about his off-court gambling and his voting preferences in his home state's U.S. Senate race between the race-baiting incumbent, Senator Jesse Helms (R–NC), and black Charlotte mayor Harvey Gantt. Months after that, the virus spread to Bill Clinton. Trying to separate himself from the Democratic Party's racialized branding, the 1992 presidential candidate publicly chastised a black hip-hop artist, creating a whole new political tactic known as the Sister Souljah Moment.

Among these episodes, Jordan's infamous rationale in staying away from the Senate contest—"Republicans buy shoes, too"—was particularly telling. Though the comment was disturbing for its indifference, Jordan's basketball forefather, Julius Erving, perceptively noted that had the Bulls star intervened, there would have been "a pretty heavy downside" in terms of "alienating" a huge portion of the "general public" (read: white audience).

In spirit, the defense was similar to the one offered by *Mississippi Burning* director Alan Parker, who countered criticism of his film's white-savior narrative by saying the story "had to be fictionalized"—specifically, "the two heroes in the story had to be white. That is a reflection of our society as much as of the film industry," he told *Time* magazine. "It could not have been made any other way."

How can we know this sentiment was accurate? How can we tell that white appeasement—whether from athletes, politicians, movies, or any other cultural commodity—is crucial to popular success? How can we validate the University of Massachusetts study's disturbing conclusion that "to confront the uncomfortable realities of racism" is to commit "commercial suicide"?

The answer goes back to perhaps the most telling response from the school's study of *The Cosby Show* audience. When asked if anything about the program's lead was at all irksome, a white respondent homed in on a deep fear that the actor was not really the transcendent figure he presented himself as.

"Does he support Jesse Jackson? That really upsets me," the viewer said. "I have to question Cosby's philosophy and principles and everything if he can stand behind someone like Jesse Jackson. I don't see Bill Cosby in the pure sense that I saw him years ago. Then you read about him giving money to the Negro College Fund and you wonder, you don't want to watch a show that's against you, you know—against the white race."

Since the 1980s, this has been the Great White Anxiety—a fear that African Americans will use the basic legal protections they gained during the 1960s to seize their deserved rights of genuine equality and, in doing so, pit themselves "against the white race." Hence, whites' unslakable desire to make sure postracial blacks and powerful white political leaders aren't secretly cavorting with "angry" non-transcendent "not-so-nice" African Americans.

This explains why the 1980s narratives of "transcendence," the "white savior," and white victimization remain so pronounced in whites' entertainment, consumer and voting choices. Many whites intrinsically believe those illusions and caricatures are the Great White Hope that will alleviate the Great White Anxiety—illusions and caricatures that will deny inconvenient truths about racism, defang black antagonism and, most significantly, preserve self-serving contradictions.

The double standards are everywhere. White directors can have white film heroes angrily beat African American stereotypes to a pulp, but as *Taxi Driver*'s white screenwriter, Paul Schrader, admitted in 1989, a black director "doesn't have the privilege to be that angry—society won't let him . . . it's just not allowed." White activists can scream about "reverse discrimination" and "states' rights" and be honored as courageous populists, but black leaders can't say peep about ongoing discrimination for fear of being branded as craven "race hustlers." Leading white politicians can criticize the supposed scourge of black privilege, deviously reference history's past "race hustlers," and lambast their black opponents for not attracting "hardworking Americans, white Americans." But if black politicians are shown to have nontranscendent friends or even so much as admit racism still exists, they run the risk of political immolation.

Those hypocrisies may seem like recollections of ancient history. But they describe the Reagan era as well as they describe the Obama epoch's postracial present.

The resurrection of the 1980s' nice/not-so-nice racial memes began in earnest in 2006, when *Time* magazine columnist Joe Klein warned readers that electing a Democratic Congress would install a government of, by, and for the supposed Clubber Langs, who he said were poised to assume power chairmanships.

"The ugly truth," wrote Klein, "is that [prospective Judiciary Committee chairman John] Conyers is a twofer: in addition to being foolishly incendiary, he is an African American of a certain age and ideology, easily stereotyped. . . . He is one of the ancient band of left-liberals who grew up in the angry hothouse of inner-city, racial-preference politics in the 1960s."

At the same time, Barack Obama was being presented as the opposite stereotype, a rising star carrying the decidedly Cosby-esque banner of "post-racial transcendence" from the 1980s. CNN had called him "very Huxtable" after his speech at the 2004 Democratic

National Convention; *Politico* raised the prospect that his presidential candidacy could "reach Huxtable cult status"; and one pundit trumpeted the rise of the "Huxtable voter." And like clockwork, out came eighties attacks to challenge that eighties brand.

It started after the release of a key CNN poll showing Obama gaining on Hillary Clinton in the upcoming New Hampshire Democratic primary. Hours after the numbers hit newswires, Clinton's New Hampshire cochair Bill Shaheen floated the not-so-nice black narrative about Obama, telling reporters that the Illinois senator was an unacceptable Democratic nominee because he would be portrayed as the ominous black crack dealer who stalks the nightmares of Soccer Moms and Office Park Dads everywhere.

"One of the things Republicans are certainly going to jump on is his drug use," Shaheen said. "It'll be, 'When was the last time? Did you ever give drugs to anyone? Did you sell them to anyone?'"

The next month, Clinton herself floated the white-savior idea, telling reporters that Obama's historic candidacy was providing "false hope" because Dr. King's dream only "began to be realized when President Johnson passed the Civil Rights Act." She added that "It took a president to get it done," reinforcing the assertion that blacks only got ahead because of brave whites.

That same week, another Clinton surrogate, African American billionaire Robert Johnson, melded the two themes in an introductory speech for his candidate.

"Hillary and Bill Clinton have been deeply and emotionally involved in black issues when Barack Obama was doing something in the neighborhood that I won't say what he was doing, but he said it in his book," Johnson said, portraying the Clintons as white saviors, again highlighting Obama's past drug use, and, for dramatic effect, adding an inner-city ("neighborhood") tinge.

From there, it was on to the South Carolina primary and the attempt to use Obama's victory in that contest to sow white anxiety that he wasn't the postracial candidate he was billed as.

"Bubba: Obama Is Just Like Jesse Jackson" was ABCNews.com's headline, quoting Bill Clinton saying, "Jesse Jackson won South Carolina in '84 and '88. Jackson ran a good campaign. And Obama ran a good campaign here."

The Associated Press followed up with a report about Clinton strategists who "said they believe the fallout [from the South Carolina campaign] has had the effect of branding Obama as 'the black candidate.'"

Next up, eighties-style white victimization from a political icon who knew a thing or two about Reagan-era politics.

"If Obama was a white man, he would not be in this position," said 1984 Democratic vice-presidential candidate Geraldine Ferraro, then serving as Clinton's New York campaign chairwoman. "He happens to be very lucky to be who he is. And the country is caught up in the concept."

The comment was an update of Ferraro's statement in 1988 that "if Jesse Jackson were not black, he wouldn't be in the [presidential] race." The argument, of course, runs counter to the overwhelming white dominance of American politics. As Obama said in response, "Anybody who knows the history of this country . . . would not take too seriously the notion that [being black] has been a huge advantage."

That's undeniably true. But Ferraro, a 1980s icon well schooled in racialized politics, wasn't going for truth. She was deliberately aiming to dredge up the "reverse racism" meme that had worked so well in the past. Thus, when confronted with criticism of her rhetoric, Ferraro dug in by telling reporters, "I really think they're attacking me because I'm white." Responding to calls for an apology, she went even further by declaring: "If anybody is going to apologize they should apologize to me for calling me a racist."

All of this peaked when reporters uncovered video of Obama's pastor, Jeremiah Wright, railing on racism and criticizing white crimes against blacks.

ABC News reported that Clinton aides began "pushing the Wright story" aggressively, the campaign's obvious hope being that Wright would finally destroy Obama's transcendence. Reliably, double standards stood firm. Reporters didn't ask Republican John McCain why he solicited the endorsement of John Hagee, the pastor who called the Catholic Church "the great whore." They didn't ask why Clinton was so friendly with the Reverend Billy Graham, who had been caught on tape spewing rancid anti-Semitism. All they wanted to know was whether Obama's relationship with Wright meant he was a covert Black Panther, and conservatives such as Pat Buchanan fanned the flames. He used the controversy to deride "black hustlers" and insist that descendants of those "brought from Africa in slave ships" owe whites a thank-you.

"Where is the gratitude?" he asked in a syndicated column titled "A Brief for Whitey."

It was yet another excuse to again dredge up all the 1980s narratives on race, and, at least for Clinton, the rehash had a precise electoral objective—and impact.

According to exit-poll data, racial resentment against blacks was a key factor keeping her presidential candidacy alive. In such states as Pennsylvania, Kentucky, and West Virginia, between 10 percent and 20 percent of white Democratic voters said race was an important factor in their vote, and Clinton won those voters by overwhelming margins. In the critical state of Ohio, Clinton's 8-point victory was made possible by the 12 percent of the electorate who said race was a key factor in their vote and who voted for her.

In case anyone thought Clinton's eighties-reminiscent race strategy wasn't a calculated ploy, Clinton and her campaign put that notion to rest when they proudly cited the racism they were successfully stoking as yet another race-based argument against Obama's overall electoral viability.

Warning Democratic primary voters that Obama might not be able to win Pennsylvania in a general election, Pennsylvania governor Ed Rendell, a key Clinton campaign surrogate, told the *Pittsburgh Post-Gazette,* "There are some whites who are probably not ready to vote for an African American candidate."

Clinton herself echoed that comment after the North Carolina and Indiana primaries, and also, for good measure, threw in a line equating whiteness to work ethic. She told *USA Today* that she believed "Obama's support among working, hardworking Americans, white Americans, is weakening," and said she was excited that "whites in both states who had not completed college were supporting me."

When Obama overcame this assault and won the nomination anyway, the general election was more of the same eighties rehash, as conservatives waged an all-out assault on his transcendence. Their goal was straightforward: to turn Obama from postracial into plain old racial, knowing that the now dominant transcendence brand casts the latter as fundamentally at odds with what Sarah Palin called "the real America" or "the pro-America areas of this great nation."

Republicans unleashed a rat-a-tat-tat barrage of birth-certificate conspiracy theories, references to middle names, mentions of Kenyan ancestry, allegations of madrassa indoctrination, and whispers about tapes of Michelle Obama supposedly criticizing "whitey." In pop culture terms, all of it aimed to revive our enduring memories of *What's Happening!!* and *The Cosby Show* and then tell us Obama was really Rerun Stubbs, not Cliff Huxtable.

Along with this kitchen-sink strategy came the ongoing effort to racialize every shred of news, even good news for Democrats. For example, when Republican Colin Powell made headlines by crossing party lines to endorse Obama, Rush Limbaugh attacked Powell's announcement as an act of racial solidarity and reverse racism against whites. On the rare occasion Obama responded to these kind of attacks by saying the obvious—that some of his opponents were bothered that he "doesn't look like all those other presidents on those dollar bills"—the McCain campaign tried to steal transcendence for itself by doubling down on "reverse racism" and criticizing Democrats for "play[ing] the race card . . . from the bottom of the deck—it's divisive, negative, shameful, and wrong."

White race-baiters feigning outrage at racism—it was Republicans' standard Kabuki theater since Ronald Reagan pilfered the rhetoric of the civil rights movement to attack affirmative action. Most often in 2008, it was used by bobbing-and-weaving Obama opponents trying at once to race-bait, avoid a real discussion of racism, and also look color-blind.

"The last thing we need now is a heated national conversation about race," wrote conservative *New York Times* writer Bill Kristol in a typical column after the Wright kerfuffle, a column that counseled America to take Moynihan's advice and endorse "benign neglect" on the race issue.

Just as often, though, it has been Obama supporters—and even Obama himself—who have unwittingly imparted credibility to the eighties lens.

When former Tennessee Democratic Party chairman Bob Tuke

promoted Obama as the candidate who "is emancipating white voters," he was overtly reinforcing the Reaganite fantasy that whites
have for too long been the victims of black oppression.

When "in his own Bill Cosby moment, Obama used Father's
Day as an opportunity to renew old comments critical of absent black
dads," as *The American Prospect* reported, he was adding credence to
one of the most destructive messages of *The Cosby Show*, the one that
seems to blame black people exclusively for their failings.

When Obama responded to the Wright controversy by in part
sympathizing with the "anger [that] exists within segments of the
white community," he was implying that black and white gripes are
equivalent, even though in historical terms, blacks have a hell of a lot
more to be upset about than whites.

And when *The New York Times* reported that "Obama's black advisers caution that no one should expect him to behave like a civil
rights leader" and that Al Sharpton "says [Obama] is smart not to ballyhoo 'a black agenda,'" those black leaders were only further (if inadvertently) demonizing a civil rights program and black agenda that
deserves legitimacy.

But while Obama is not without fault, to blame him or his supporters for the transcendence brand is to mimic the old "too
black"/"not black enough" debates over *The Cosby Show*, and again
let white America off the hook. Just as Bill Cosby would have committed "commercial suicide" by using his show to challenge the
white audience's racism, Obama would be committing political suicide by using his campaign and presidency to do the same—and that
undeniable truth has unduly handcuffed him.

Not only does he have to "try to confine his racial references," as
The New York Times reported, he also must mimic Cosby by avoiding
an unvarnished discussion of seemingly nonracial issues in a way other
candidates didn't.

"If Obama started talking like John Edwards and tapped into
working-class, blue-collar proletarian rage, suddenly all of those
white voters who are viewing him within the lens of transcendence
would start seeing him differently," said Charles Ellison of the University of Denver's Center for African American Policy. That's because once Obama parroted attacks on greed and inequality, he

would "be stigmatized as a candidate mobilizing race," said Manning Marable, a Columbia University history professor.

Transcendence and white appeasement have, then, been Obama's only hope in a country still deeply mired in the 1980s.

In its political postmortem titled "Before Obama, There Was Bill Cosby," *The New York Times* stated the obvious about the 2008 election's grounding in the racial psychology of the 1980s. Noting that a "debate has heated up over who, or what, in arts and entertainment presaged" Obama's historic run, the paper said many experts believe there was a "Huxtable Effect" that "had succeeded in changing racial attitudes enough to make an Obama candidacy possible."

"There were a lot of young people who were watching (*The Cosby Show*) who are now of voting age," said Alvin Poussaint, the *Cosby Show* consultant and Harvard psychologist. "Kids were raised on that show, and people are still watching it [and] we have had a carryover effect."

Undoubtedly, the "post-racial" concept popularized by the Huxtables defined the euphoric response to Obama's candidacy in the final weeks of the campaign—a response that echoed the reaction to *The Cosby Show*'s success a generation earlier.

In an August 2008 report, *The New York Times Magazine* trumpeted "the end of black politics"—as if feting the conclusion of some long national nightmare. When the polls closed in November and America learned it had elected its first black president, *The Wall Street Journal*'s editorial board said the vote showed that "we can put to rest the myth of racism as a barrier to achievement in this splendid country." Republican Rudy Giuliani said "we've achieved history tonight and we've moved beyond. . . . the whole idea of race and racial separation and unfairness."

In sum, just as America thought Cliff and Clair Huxtable's success meant that racism had disappeared, so too did the nation tell itself the same fable about Obama—even though Obama himself once railed against this kind of thinking.

That's right, after being elected Harvard's first black *Law Review* president in 1990, Obama explicitly warned against this type of enlightened exceptionalism that holds up the individual success of one atypical African American as proof that racism and inequality no longer exist.

"It's crucial that people don't see my election as somehow a symbol of progress in the broader sense, that we don't sort of point to a Barack Obama any more than you point to a Bill Cosby or a Michael Jordan and say, 'Well, things are hunky-dory,'" he told the Associated Press at the time.

Why, then, had his election to a much higher office elicited exactly that misguided response?

Because unlike his ascent to the editorship of a legal journal, the presidential campaign took place in the larger crucible of a national pop and political culture whose postracial ingredients are designed to evoke *Soul Man*'s Mark Watson, that ultimate white *Cosby Show* devotee of the 1980s. Once again steeped in the transcendence brand's warm exoneration, we told ourselves after the campaign that "It's the Obama decade!" and therefore it must mean "America loves black people!"

The effect of such a delusion was evinced by major polls released in the immediate aftermath of Obama's election. A CNN/*Essence*-magazine poll in June 2009 found just 17 percent of whites agreeing that "racial discrimination against blacks is a serious problem." This figure jibed with an ABC/Washington Post poll from January finding that just 22 percent of whites believed racism is "a big problem," and further finding that "83 percent of whites think blacks in their area have an equal chance to get a job for which they're qualified."

But just as in the 1980s, these views do not reflect basic reality.

One way to see that is to consider gross inequities in joblessness and wages. During the recent Great Recession, the black unemployment rate has been roughly twice as large as the white unemployment rate, and that disparity is the same when comparing blacks and whites of the same educational background. Additionally, the Brookings Institution found that whereas wages for white males have remained flat since the 1970s, wages for black males declined by 12 percent in the same time. The study also found "only 31 percent of black children born to [middle-class] parents . . . have family income greater than their parents, compared to 68 percent of white children from the same income bracket." And according to Brandeis researchers, from 1984 to the present, America witnessed a quadrupling of the wealth gap between whites and blacks who started at the same income levels.

For the "social pathology" bigots and postracial denialists who say those numbers prove only economic inequality but not racism, behold the recent studies documenting the ongoing and specific discrimination against African Americans.

In 1999, for example, Rutgers scholars evaluated federal data from 160,000 employers and found that minorities face a one in three chance of being discriminated against in a job hunt. In 2001, researchers in Milwaukee and New York tracked black and white job applicants with equivalent résumés and "concluded that a white man with a criminal record had about the same chance of getting a job as a black man without one," according to *The Atlantic Monthly*. An MIT/University of Chicago study in 2004 found that "compared to whites, African Americans are twice as likely to be unemployed [and] earn nearly 25 percent less when they are employed." The same survey found that job seekers with "white names receive 50 percent more callbacks for interviews" than job seekers with the same résumé and a "black sounding" name.

This is the reality that transcendence concealed in the 1980s and hides today. It would certainly be easy to treat Obama the way critics treated Cosby and singularly blame the president's dogged pursuit of postracial iconography for failing to consistently challenge the ugliness of persistent racism. After all, *The New York Times* is absolutely right that Obama "has sought to transcend, if not avoid, the issue of race" altogether—and that's putting it mildly. In his first year alone, he publicly chided his own attorney general for saying America is a "nation of cowards" when it comes to discussing race, then made headlines telling a radio interviewer that despite criticism from black congressional leaders, "I can't pass laws that say I'm just helping black folks"—as if that's what they were even requesting.

But as the *Times* so delicately put it in a review of Obama's first year in office, race "can be an incendiary issue in American politics."

The paper was referencing the president's response to the now famous 2009 arrest of Henry Louis Gates—the same Henry Louis Gates who had written so eloquently about the problems with "color blindness" in the 1980s. When asked about the arrest at a White House press conference, Obama dared to say the white police officer "acted stupidly in arresting somebody when there was already proof that they were in their own home"; then further stated "that there's a long history in this country of African-Americans and Latinos being stopped by law enforcement disproportionately"; then added that "race remains a factor in the society."

Despite the fact that these declarations are self-evident, indisputable truths, Obama was instantly excoriated in 1980s terms. Fox News chairman Rupert Murdoch called the president's comments "racist," radio host Glenn Beck said Obama had exposed himself as "a guy who has a deep-seated hatred for white people or the white culture"; and Rush Limbaugh said, "Here you have a black president trying to destroy a white policeman."

It was the beginning of the Summer of Race. Soon, conservatives were claiming that Obama's Latina Supreme Court nominee, Sonia Sotomayor, was a "racist" and "an affirmative action appointment"; that his environmental adviser, Van Jones, was one of those not-so-nice black nationalists; that his legislative agenda was "Reparations by Way of Health Care Reform" and "affirmative action on steroids," as an *Investor's Business Daily* house editorial put it.

In light of the blitz, to blame Obama for seeking "to transcend, if not avoid, the issue of race" is to yet again avoid blaming the real culprit: the white America that since the 1980s demands reticence on race from all black public figures as the price of public support.

Sure, as a purely tactical matter, you can credibly argue that Obama's Cosby-esque deal with white America is a self-defeating Faustian bargain. Survey data show roughly six in ten whites openly admit to believing in at least one bigoted stereotype, and a recent study showed that when asked about health care legislation, a significant number of whites expressed less support for the exact same bill if it was coming from President Obama rather than from a white Democratic president. A black leader who tries to circumnavigate that intense bigotry by avoiding race may be emboldening the bigotry inevitably coming his way.

Similarly, American politics is increasingly steered by a largely white Tea Party movement whose supporters are, according to polls, disproportionately motivated by racial resentment. An African American leader who goes out of his way to downplay that right-wing racism to the point of rebuking former president Jimmy Carter for criticizing it—well, that only helps the Tea Party opposition play its duplicitous dog-whistle games.

But no matter what Obama does, he is in a no-win situation because he still exists in a 1980s nation. This is a country that sees Bill O'Reilly's call for war against those trying "to break down the white, Christian, male power structure" and then delivers him prime time's best cable ratings.

Here in twenty-first-century America, a newspaper can lament "that bright, dying star, the American WASP" and cite "Barack Obama's inauguration" as supposed evidence of whites' "long downward spiral," and we reward that paper, *The Wall Street Journal,* with the highest circulation in the land.

Here, white Democratic politicians can win primary victories in the biggest states on the shoulders of white resentment. Meanwhile, Republican politicians like Rudy Giuliani can in one moment cite transcendence as evidence that "we've moved beyond [the] whole idea of race and racial separation" and in another moment tell voters at the site of New York's 1986 white-on-black race murder that electing another black mayor would bring back "the fear of going out at night and walking the streets." They can do all of this without facing ostracism or even mild scorn from transcendence-obsessed media leaders such as Chris Matthews, MSNBC's *Family Guy* clone who reacted to Obama's 2010 State of the Union address by telling the national television audience, "I forgot he was black tonight for an hour."

Matthews was trying to praise the president, but in doing so, the beefy visage of average-white-guy-ness inadvertently exposed how the "Reagan Democrat" demographic he represents still looks at black people during the other 8,759 hours of the year. For a country that remains anchored in the 1980s, it was a valuable glimpse into a [dare I say] transcendent truth—one exposing the dishonesty of the transcendence brand itself.

THE END OF HISTORY?

Marty: Where the hell are they?

Doc: The appropriate question is, "When the hell are they?" —*BACK TO THE FUTURE,* 1985

At the end of the 1980s, political theorist Francis Fukuyama issued what would become a renowned prophecy:

"What we may in fact be witnessing is not just the passing of a particular period . . . but the end point of mankind's ideological evolution."

Having now read this book, you know there is ample proof to suggest Fukuyama was right, and the evidence just keeps coming.

Pulling up *The Dallas Morning News'* website in the weeks between initially writing and now editing those last few chapters, I came upon a story about the Texas state school board approving curriculum standards that the 1980s would be proud of. The board will "require a more positive portrayal" of the 1950s conservative hero Senator Joseph McCarthy, as well as positive references to the 1980s chief Fifties™ nostalgists, activists such as Phyllis Schlafly and organizations such as the Heritage Foundation and the Moral Majority. The new rules will also compel students to learn of the supposedly negative "unintended consequences" of sixties achievements like the Great Society and affirmative action.

In neighboring Louisiana, where British Petroleum has been putting on a remake of 1989's *Exxon Valdez* disaster, all eyes remain on President Obama and President Obama alone. Despite the 24–7 media storm surrounding BP's catastrophic oil spill, few bother to discuss the kind of collective changes we will all need to make to end our hydrocarbon addiction and eliminate the need for such dangerous deepwater drilling in the future. Driving SUVs, eating steak dinners, and blasting air-conditioning, the Americans paying attention to the disaster only want to know when the Jump Man president will Just Do It, go rogue against his own inept government, and singularly save the planet from an oily apocalypse.

According to a recent study, though, many of us probably haven't been paying attention at all, too consumed by 1980s-inspired self-absorption to even care what's going on in the Gulf of Mexico. *The New York Times*'s website says it all: "The Culture of Narcissism" screams the headline of a story about the growing sense of selfishness and self-centeredness among college graduates. They'll surely flock to campus speeches by Sarah Palin's daughter, Bristol. The latest star in the "famous for being famous" tradition that emerged from the 1980s, Bristol "is joining the speakers circuit," reports the Associated Press, and she'll be paid up to $30,000 a speech in a nation still mindlessly addicted to celebrity for celebrity's sake.

Speaking of addictions, some more mouse clicks remind me that our other vice—eighties militarism—is as debilitating as ever.

In Connecticut, the Democratic U.S. Senate candidate, Attorney General Richard Blumenthal, has been making news lying not only about being deployed to Southeast Asia as a reservist during the Vietnam War (he wasn't), but regurgitating the Legend of the Spat upon Veteran from the 1980s.

"When we came back, we were spat on; we couldn't wear our uniforms," he reportedly told one audience, before telling another, "I remember the taunts, the insults, sometimes even physical abuse."

In D.C., eighties militarism shapes budget and foreign policies, with few raising any objections. "The Senate approved a $58.8 billion wartime spending bill even as House Democrats ordered still more cuts from their jobs and economic relief package," writes *Politico,* in a story that is as summarily ignored as a *Washington Post* piece about the

Obama administration "significantly expanding largely secret U.S. wars" in Somalia, Yemen, and northwest Pakistan.

Meanwhile, outside the Beltway, Pabst Blue Ribbon is reprising martial branding strategies from the eighties, leaking its plan to militarize the domestic alcohol market with "a whole beer brand around troops."

"When you see Red White & Blue (beer) at your barbecue, you (will) know that money's supporting people who have died for our country," one Pabst executive tells *Businessweek*.

And just as I entertain the possibility that all the '80s-style racism of 2008's presidential campaign and 2009's Tea Party summer is dying down, here comes good ol' Arizona singeing my Web browser with its burning cross.

The Arizona Republic reports that officials are calling for a public school's outdoor mural to be repainted so that the children pictured are white, not Latino. The push comes after passersby kept screaming racial epithets at the Latino and Black students painted in the mural. That white backlash was originally fomented by a city councilman and radio host who accused the schoolkids of being insufficiently postracial and "excit[ing] some kind of diversity power struggle" simply by having the gall to paint a picture of nonwhites.

The episode follows the passage of two state laws that are stirring the simmering pot of racial hatred. The first statute basically criminalizes the act of looking Latino, with its requirement that police arrest anyone they suspect is in the country illegally.★ Another cuts state funding to public schools that offer ethnic studies classes. The Associated Press reports that according to the bill's backers, such classes promote "racial resentment toward whites." The sound and fury surrounding the new statute has set off yet another national debate

---

★This sounds like an exaggeration but, sadly, it's not. The original law only prohibited law enforcement officials from "solely" considering a person's race, color, or national origin in detaining them—meaning that a person's race, color, or national origin can be a major consideration in an arrest. Furthermore, when one of the nation's leading anti-immigration activists, California congressman Brian Bilbray, was asked how police would determine suspicion under this law, he told MSNBC, "They will look at the kind of dress you wear, there is different type of attire, there is different type of—right down to the shoes, right down to the clothes."

about the need for transcendence in the face of alleged reverse racism against Caucasians, and in typical eighties fashion those Caucasians are casting their crusade as the highest form of civil rights activism.

"Martin Luther King gave his famous speech in which he said we should be judged by the quality of our character, rather than the color of our skin," said the bill's chief sponsor. "African American studies for the African American kids, Indian studies for the Native American kids, and Asian studies for the Asian kids [are] dividing them up just like the old South . . . They're teaching them to emphasize ethnic solidarity, what I call ethnic chauvinism. And I think that's exactly the wrong thing to do in the public schools."

In this, a quick, unscientific sampling of news over a few balmy weeks, we see that the 1980s remains central to our society, our politics, our everything. Yet, even knowing that, can we really be sure Fukuyama was correct when he suggested that the 1980s represents "the end of history"?

No—at least not yet.

In the last few years, we've witnessed a few fleeting signs that the 1980s may be weakening and that we may eventually move on to a new historical chapter.

For instance, every Tea Party rally that takes its cues from the 1980s by memorializing The Fifties™ and bewailing The Sixties™ is, in a small way, helping to resuscitate a valuable principle from the actual 1960s, one that the 1980s tried to crush: the principle that collective grassroots protest matters in a democracy.

To be sure, those Tea Party protests, however democratic, often represent white racial resentment lingering from the 1980s. But Pew polls show that on race, the younger generation may shift America's overall attitude away from the 1980s over the long run. These "millennials" are far more ethnically diverse, tolerant, and supportive of genuine multiculturalism (as opposed to eighties "color blindness") than older demographics.

When it comes to militarism, yes—ancient Reagan-style hubris infuses the ongoing Iraq and Afghanistan wars and the indiscriminate violence U.S. forces have used around the globe. But military officials and the general public—including conservatives—are beginning to gently question some of the basic militarist assumptions of the 1980s.

In March of 2010, for example, *The Washington Post* reported that Admiral Mike Mullen, the chairman of the Joint Chiefs of Staff, "outlined a new U.S. approach to war [that] replaces overwhelming firepower with more restrained use of force to safeguard civilian lives." Weeks later, Army Chief of Staff George Casey gave a speech admitting that the "era of persistent conflict" was taking a heavy toll on soldiers. At the same time, Gallup polls have recently shown a plurality of Americans believe the Reagan-bloated defense budget is now too big—a plurality eventually that includes the far right. *Politico* reports that in response to Defense Secretary Robert Gates's modest push for military frugality, "Key tea party players, on and off Capitol Hill, are expressing a willingness to put the Pentagon budget on the chopping block if it will help rein in federal spending and eliminate a projected trillion-dollar-plus budget deficit."

Even the Gordon Gekko mind-set, though still powerful, is at least being rhetorically challenged. As just one example, consider President Obama's 2009 Arizona State University speech telling students to reject the "old, tired me-first approach":

> You're taught to chase after all the usual brass rings; you try to be on this "who's who" list or that Top 100 list; you chase after the big money and you figure out how big your corner office is; you worry about whether you have a fancy enough title or a fancy enough car. That's the message that's sent each and every day, or has been in our culture for far too long— that through material possessions, through a ruthless competition pursued only on your own behalf—that's how you will measure success. . . . But at this critical juncture in our nation's history, at this difficult time, let me suggest that such an approach won't get you where you want to go; it displays a poverty of ambition—that in fact, the elevation of appearance over substance, of celebrity over character, of short-term gain over lasting achievement, is precisely what your generation needs to help end.

To many readers, that passage probably seems altogether radical, a recitation of subversive truisms rarely ever uttered in mixed company anymore, much less by a president in a public address. But it only appears that way in comparison to the eighties outlook that we've internalized as the norm. By historical standards, it's not radical at all.

Before the 1980s, this was a country that valued more than the individual. Franklin Roosevelt asked us "to forgo higher wages" and to accept that "profits are going to be cut down" to defend the common good. John F. Kennedy later told us to "ask not what your country can do for you, but what you can do for your country." We responded each time to that call for solidarity.

This was also a nation that at least struggled openly with the downsides of institutional militarism and racism. Dwight Eisenhower warned us against the dangers of the "military-industrial complex"; the movement against the Vietnam occupation asked us to question our assumptions about war; and the civil rights movement forced us to look honestly at the hideousness of Jim Crow.

Today, the quandaries we face are so massive and so global that we need to excavate the values the 1980s tried to bury, and that requires us to face up to the destructive shortcomings of the 1980s mind-set which created and perpetuated those crises in the first place. That doesn't mean we can't still laugh at eighties TV reruns and flock to remakes of eighties movies and rock out (as I do) to eighties music during the workday (the *Rocky IV* soundtrack is my favorite). It does, however, mean questioning what that decade was telling us, and understanding why the 1980s outlook is now so outdated and inappropriate for the challenges at hand.

This was the canary-in-the-coal-mine lesson that we should have taken to heart from that memorable 1980s send-off, the series finale of *The Cosby Show,* which aired during the 1992 Rodney King riots.

As if deliberately reinforcing the fusion of entertainment and real life that had started in the 1980s, Los Angeles mayor Tom Bradley attempted to use the program and its soothing message as an instrument of public policy, imploring his constituents to "observe the curfew and watch *The Cosby Show.*" But the televisual juxtaposition highlighted the short-term tactic's failure—and the larger inconvenient truth. As images of the "transcendent" Huxtables aired alongside images of burning ghettos, television was telling us that for all the hype and promise, the brands, outlooks, and mindsets of the 1980s are not the solution—they are the problem.

By ignoring that lesson at the end of the 1980s, we've let Marty McFly's harrowing question linger for far too long.

"What happens to us in the future?" he asked. "Do we become assholes or something?"

ACKNOWLEDGMENTS

Though books have the author's name on the cover, every book I've written is the product of an entire team of editors, family members, friends, colleagues, and co-workers. This one is no exception, so here are my thank-yous, with the description of the role you served put in distinctly 1980s terms.

To my literary agent and friend, Will Lippincott: If the writer confronting a blank page is the overmatched Rocky taking on a bigger, better opponent, then you are my Mickey Goldmill.

To my editor, Luke Dempsey, and his deputy Ryan Doherty: This manuscript came in looking like the team from *Hoosiers*— undisciplined, disorganized, and all over the place. You were my Norman Dale and Shooter Flatch. You've taken a writer of Hickory's decent-but-unspectacular ability and squeezed more out of me than I ever thought I could muster.

To Joel Marlin, Erin Yourtz, Aaron Kleiner, Jay Marvin, Mike Nelson, Alex Miller, John Turk, Fred Savage, and John Kupetz: Sam Malone had the crazy crew at *Cheers* to bounce his insane ideas off of. I had all of you for this book—and I wouldn't trade any of you for any of them, not even for Cliff Clavin or Norm Peterson.

To both moms and both dads: I see every great '80s parent in you, from the Keatons to the Huxtables to the Griswolds. What ties them all together is that they love and accept their kids, no matter what— and that moral support throughout this project was crucial.

To Steven and Jeff, aka Jim Kirk and Sardo Numspa: As two of the Sirota family's Three Amigos, you were, in many ways, the inspiration for this book.

To Monty: That's all that really needs to be said, as Chandler Jarrell proved in *The Golden Child*.

To Emily: I know I sometimes seem like I'm only happy going Mach 2 with my hair on fire, but that's not true. I'm only really happy when I'm with you, and this book would have crashed and burned without you. You take my breath away.

NOTES

INTRODUCTION

Atari Reboot Is Underway: "Atari Reboot Is Underway," *Los Angeles Times,* August 3, 2010.

fighting for the number one spot: MTV Movies Blog, June 13, 2010.

leading comedy in America: Box Office Mojo, March 26, 2010–March 28, 2010.

becoming feature-length films: "Classic 1980 Atari Game 'Missile Command' Is Preparing to Launch as a Movie?" MTV Movies Blog, February 19, 2010.

had their own A&E reality shows: Gene Simmons's *Family Jewels* and Dee Snider's *Growing Up Twisted.*

Cosby moments: "Obama Assails Absent Black Fathers," *American Prospect* (Tapped blog), June 16, 2008.

majority of American households possessed a television: U.S. Census Bureau, Table 1090, Utilization of Selected Media.

nearly half had video-game systems: Barry Gunter, *The Effects of Video Games on Children,* 1998, p. 16.

just fifty conglomerates controlled: Paul Wellstone, *Federal Communications Law Journal,* May 1, 2000.

the next hundred years: Heather Chaplin and Aaron Ruby, *Smartbomb,* 2006, p. 2.

perceptions of the world even more than reality: "Re-run: Why So Many Americans under 30 Are Greeting a Black President as Old News," *Boston Globe,* January 11, 2009.

PART I: LIKING IKE, HATING WOODSTOCK

rejecting the counterculture: "What He Left Behind," *Baltimore Sun,* July 7, 2004.

top-five-rated program: ClassicTVHits.com.

switched at birth: "In a Sitcom for Its Time, Teen-Agers Knew Best," *New York Times,* July 5, 1998.

me working for a nonprofit: *Family Ties* episode "Keaton and Son," October 18, 1984.

revamp the program's entire structure: "What He Left Behind," *Baltimore Sun,* July 7, 2004.

young people immediately saw as strengths: Interview with Gary David Goldberg, August 15, 2009.

grossing more than a quarter billion dollars: Box Office Mojo.

DIE, HIPPIE, DIE!

Rocky Horror Picture Show: "Top Grossing Movies of 1975," Internet Movie Database.

three of the top-rated seven television shows: *All in the Family* (no. 1), *Maude* (no. 4), *Sanford and Son* (no. 7), ClassicTVHits.com.

Two of the top three grossing films were *Back to the Future:* "Top Grossing Movies of 1985," Internet Movie Database.

replaced atop the television charts: ClassicTVHits.com.

primarily a phenomena of the last quarter of the 20th century: "Generational Identity and Memory in American Newsmagazines," *Journalism,* May 2003.

glut of new Eisenhower biographies: Daniel Marcus, *Happy Days and Wonder Years,* 2004, p. 63.

hit number one on the charts: Billboard Top 100 Singles Chart, February 23, 1980.

Hard Rock Cafe: Hard Rock Cafe corporate history.

dates from an antediluvian choir: "Reagan's Combative Rhetoric Is Working Against Him," *Washington Post,* August 24, 1980.

the center seemed to hold: Ronald Reagan, November 3, 1980.

spiritual revival to feel once again: Kiron K. Skinner, Annelise Anderson, Martin Anderson, and George P. Shultz, *Reagan: A Life in Letters,* p. 259.

a storehouse of images of an idyllic America: Garry Trudeau, *Doonesbury,* October 28, 1980.

intellectually, emotionally, Reagan lives in the past: "Man of the Year: Ronald Reagan," *Time,* January 2, 1981.

shots from Woodstock of young people cavorting in the mud: Daniel Marcus, *Happy Days and Wonder Years,* 2004, p. 114.

Getting a popular fix on the more elusive: Interview with Todd Gitlin, August 25, 2009.

filthy speech advocates: Rick Perlstein, *Nixonland,* 2008, p. 83, quoting from Reagan's May 12, 1966, speech.

military and moral inferiority: Ronald Reagan, March 8, 1983.

patriotism is back in vogue: "Decade Shock," *Newsweek,* September 5, 1988.

liked cars and girls and rock and roll: Daniel Marcus, *Happy Days and Wonder Years,* 2004, p. 31.

the Year of the Yuppie: "The Year of the Yuppie," *Newsweek,* December 31, 1984.

chase yuppies with a vengeance: "The Big Chilling of the Networks," *Adweek,* April 15, 1985.

Yuppievision: Jane Feuer, *Seeing Through the 80s,* p. 44, quoting from a November 18, 1987, *Rolling Stone* article.

Yupper Classmen: *Esquire,* February 1988.

twice the number that could identify the nation's secretary of state: Ibid., p. 102, quoting a 1985 Roper poll.

in the back seat of a limousine: "The Year of the Yuppie," *Newsweek,* December 31, 1984.

former flower children laughing: Jane Feuer, *Seeing Through the 80s,* pp. 43–51.

facing up to the responsibilities of adulthood: "Growing Pains at 40," *Time,* May 19, 1986.

the more things change, the more they remain the same: "Decade Shock," *Newsweek,* September 5, 1988.

My Back Pages: *Family Ties,* October 16, 1988.

too young to be in those settings in the actual 1960s: Jane Feuer, *Seeing Through the 80s,* p. 67.

The Great Sellout: Gil Troy, *Morning in America,* 2005, p. 334.

smoke pot, wear crap, and smell bad: *South Park,* March 16, 2005.

states rights: Ronald Reagan, August 3, 1980.

three civil rights workers had been murdered: "Reagan Breaks from the Gate with a Rush," *U.S. News and World Report,* August 25, 1980.

afraid to let [U.S soldiers] win: Ronald Reagan, August 18, 1980.

expelled God from the classroom: "A Disciplined, Charging Army," *New Yorker,* May 18, 1981, quoting Ronald Reagan's speech to the National Religious Broadcasters on October 3, 1980.

invalidation of traditional political and social practices: Daniel Marcus, *Happy Days and Wonder Years,* 2004, p. 38.

to bring down the government: "Watt's Media Campaign Hits Snags," *Washington Post,* April 11, 1983.

blame America first: Jeanne Kirkpatrick, August 20, 1984.

turn the clock back to 1954 in this country: Susan Faludi, *Backlash,* p. 242.

return the republic to the status quo of an earlier day: Daniel Marcus, *Happy Days and Wonder Years,* 2004, p. 62, quoting Rowland Evans and Robert Novak in their 1981 book, *The Reagan Revolution.*

Teach Your Children: "Packaging the Presidency," *Time,* November 12, 1984.

fundamental re-examination of the '60s: "Decade Shock," *Newsweek,* September 5, 1988.

People don't see their experience as symbolic of an era: George Bush, August 18, 1988.

having babies and raising a family: "Kitty Dukakis Stings G.O.P. with Her Attack," *New York Times,* September 25, 1988.

Norman Rockwell vision of America: "Bush Attacks Democrats on Crime Policies," *Washington Post,* October 7, 1988.

he had called the military draft "illegitimate": "Clinton's 1969 Angst," *Newsday,* February 13, 1992.

made it into the national conversation overnight: ABC News, April 3, 1992.

satirizing him as a tie-dyed hippie: *Saturday Night Live,* October 10, 1992.

Not everyone joined the counterculture: "Marilyn Quayle Says the 1960's Had a Flip Side," *New York Times,* August 20, 1992.

go in there and redeem the sixties generation: Daniel Marcus, *Happy Days and Wonder Years,* 2004, p. 165, quoting *Rolling Stone* in 1992.

The era of Big Government is over: Bill Clinton, January 27, 1996.

ending welfare as we know it: Bill Clinton, August 22, 1996.

total bizarreness, total weirdness: "How 'Normal' Is Newt?" *Newsweek,* November 7, 1994.

countercultural McGovernicks: "The Time to Come: Apocalypse Newt," *Oregonian,* November 13, 1994.

be the bridge to an America: Bob Dole, August 15, 1996.

restore honor and dignity: CNN interview with George W. Bush, March 9, 2000.

necessary for a healthy society when Eisenhower was president: Daniel Marcus, *Happy Days and Wonder Years,* 2004, p. 181, quoting Gary Bauer's *Wall Street Journal* letter on June 27, 1994.

as it was in 1960: Ibid., p. 184, quoting Charles Murray in the November 18, 1996, *New Yorker.*

doctored photo of Kerry at a sixties antiwar rally: "Kerry Takes New Fire over Vietnam," CNN, February 12, 2004.

threw his military medals at the U.S. Capitol: "Kerry Hits Back on Medals, Calls It 'Phony Controversy,'" *Washington Times,* April 27, 2004.

testifying against the Vietnam War at a congressional hearing: Factcheck.org, August 23, 2004.

It's never stopped being 1968: National Journal's *Hotline,* April 7, 2004.

black-and-white reruns from The Fifties: "Religion on Television," Museum of Broadcast Communications.

full-blown World War II nostalgia industry: *Journalism,* May 2003.

a strong sense of loyalty and service, modesty and achievement: "War, Remembrance and Reward," *Time,* May 29, 2000.

are loath to revisit what they see as a disastrous time: "Anti-war Movement Wrestles with 1968," *Politico,* February 27, 2008.

Echoes of 1968 Return to Haunt the Divided Democrats: "Echoes of 1968 Return to Haunt the Divided Democrats," *Guardian,* March 23, 2008.

a cover showing Michelle Obama as Angela Davis and Barack Obama as a terrorist: *New Yorker,* July 21, 2008.

did something that I deplore forty years ago: Barack Obama, April 27, 2008.

a stand-in for that desire: "Crowds Adore Obama," *Los Angeles Times,* December 11, 2006.

Obama won office by capitalizing on our profound nostalgia: "Naomi Klein on How Corporate Branding Has Taken over America," *Guardian,* January 16, 2010.

the sense that the country that they grew up in is *slipping away:* "Debate Over Tea Party Protest Numbers Masks the Real History Made," Rick Moran, freedomworks.com, September 13, 2009.

grow up in a different country than I grew up in: "Boehner Says GOP Support Unlikely for Baucus Health Plan," PBS, September 17, 2009.

keep America *the way it was* when we grew up: "Oakhurst Joins Nation Tea Party Protest," *Sierra Star,* July 9, 2009.

real outrage from real people who just want their country back: Glenn Beck, Fox News, September 25, 2009.

shin[ing] the spotlight on the Communist Party: "Glenn Beck Misses Joe McCarthy," Salon.com, March 11, 2010.

Something happened in the 1950s where everything went down: Fox News, September 28, 2009.

deviating from this nation's legacy: CNN, September 14, 2009.

Things we had in the fifties were better: "Tea Party Supporters Doing Fine, but Angry Nonetheless," *New York Times,* April 17, 2010.

get back to where our country was one hundred years ago: CNN, September 12, 2009.

It's kind of a time for another Eisenhower: "Petraeus, Scarborough Eyed for '12," *Politico,* September 4, 2009.

not by exercising judgment but by indulging in ideology: "Getting Iraq Wrong," *New York Times Magazine,* August 5, 2007.

too angry in tone: "Centrist Democrats Take on Left over Iraq," *Politico,* July 31, 2007.

they had it in them to rise and grow again: "America the Ugly," *Wall Street Journal,* September 11, 2007.

PART II: THE JUMP MAN CHRONICLES

I never really thought about it: "Sarah Palin Book Signing," New Left Media, November 20, 2009.

I'll do whatever he says: "Crowe Reveals a Beautiful Mind for Telling Jokes," *New York Daily News,* May 19, 2006.

you want to follow him somewhere: *Charlie Rose Show,* December 21, 2006.

I see him as a leader: "The Brand Called Obama," *Fast Company,* March 19, 2008.

THE JOHN GALT OF OCEANIA

all that is right with or heroized by America: "Making of a Landslide," *Newsweek,* November 1984.

every time he touched the basketball: Jim Naughton, *Taking to the Air,* 1992, p. 226, quoting Bulls assistant coach Tex Winter.

put the ball on the floor: Ibid., p. 28, quoting Milwaukee Bucks head coach Del Harris.

Michael, save us: Ibid., p. 195, quoting Bulls assistant coach John Bach.

seventeen of its twenty-three teams lose money: Donald Katz, *Just Do It,* 1994, p. 31.

tape-delayed television: Jim Naughton, *Taking to the Air,* 1992, p. 94.

$19 million in his rookie season: Walter Lafeber, *Michael Jordan and the New Global Capitalism,* 2002, p. 119.

the Bulls have tripled their audience: Ibid., p. 52.

one-third of the league's entire attendance increase: Jim Naughton, *Taking to the Air,* 1992, p. 8.

Bulls will be worth close to $200 million: Walter Lafeber, *Michael Jordan and the New Global Capitalism,* 2002, p. 119.

In 1983, Nike: Jim Naughton, *Taking to the Air,* 1992, p. 83.

annual earnings growth rate of nearly 100 percent: Ibid., p. 85.

one of the most profitable businesses in America: Donald Katz, *Just Do It,* 1994, p. 68.

Philip Knight has run out of breath: *Washington Post,* February 9, 1992, quoting *Fortune* in 1984.

$2.5 million contract: "Basketball's 'Whopper' Has Whale of Record in Sight," *Christian Science Monitor,* April 5, 1985.

a hero business: Donald Katz, *Just Do It,* 1994, p. 101.

the results could be magical: Ibid., p. 6.

fifth-largest sneaker firm in the world: Jim Naughton, *Taking to the Air,* 1992, p. 90.

Superman in Shorts: Walter Lafeber, *Michael Jordan and the New Global Capitalism,* 2002, p. 75.

conquer the world: Ibid., p. 75, quoting *Sports Illustrated* on December 23, 1991.

alleviated Chicago's spiritual malaise: "Chicago's Tallest Institution," *Chicago Tribune,* November 5, 1989, quoting Jim O'Donnell in *The Arlington Heights Herald.*

God disguised as Michael Jordan: "Jordan Miracle Not Enough," *Chicago Tribune,* April 21, 1986.

athlete as a global brand: "McCormack and Palmer Changed the World of Sports and Business Forever," *Golf,* December 16, 2008.

players practice their dunks: "Individualism Hurting NBA," *Contra Costa Times,* March 6, 2005.

billion-dollar fantasy sports industry: "Fantasy World," *Sports Illustrated,* June 21, 2004.

I saw *Rambo* last night: "39 American Hostages Free After 17 Days," *New York Times,* July 1, 1985.

Where we are going, we don't need roads: Ronald Reagan, February 4, 1986.

forty-eight-inch vertical leap: "How Does Michael Fly?" *Chicago Tribune,* February 27, 1990.

inked multiple endorsement deals: "The Selling of Michael Jordan," *New York Times,* November 9, 1986.

Entertainment Promotions: Donald Katz, *Just Do It,* 1994, p. 81.

Murphy Brown's new baby would sport Air Jordan stuff: Ibid.

most widely recognized athlete: Walter Lafeber, *Michael Jordan and the New Global Capitalism,* 2002, p. 65.

most-wanted product spokesman: Robert Goldman and Stephen Papson, *The Nike Culture,* 1998, p. 75.

Michael Jordan tied with God: "Role Models, Part I: Looking to Athletes for Moral Leadership," Associated Press, June 20, 1994.

the most famous man on Earth: "The Jordan Murder," *Washington Post,* August 18, 1993.

as one of the two greatest men in history: Ibid.

loom with no identification necessary: "Jordan's Star Rises Higher and Higher," *Chicago Tribune,* June 6, 1993.

appeared in a Hanes television ad: "Sheen, Jordan Pitch Hanes," *Adweek,* May 28, 2008.

three times as much on marketing: Robert Goldman and Stephen Papson, *The Nike Culture,* 1998, p. 13.

People already know a lot about him: "High-Performance Marketing," *Harvard Business Review,* July 22, 1992.

supporting cast: "Bulls Toe the Line," *Washington Post,* May 20, 1991.

doesn't matter: "Cheney: 'Full Speed Ahead' on Iraq," ABC, November 3, 2006.

God wants me to be president: "Understanding the President and His God," *New York Times,* April 29, 2004.

I don't feel like I owe anybody an explanation: "Bush at War: Bob Woodward's New Book Takes a Behind-the-Scenes Look at the Bush Presidency," CBS, November 17, 2002.

God-touched speech: "God Is Back," *Wall Street Journal,* September 28, 2001.

God's agent of wrath: "Man with a Mission," *Weekly Standard,* October 8, 2001.

More Power to Self: "Bush Grants Self Permission to Grant More Power to Self," *The Onion,* August 1, 2006.

Just give me the ball: "Battle Plans," *New Yorker,* November 17, 2008.

hungry for something new: "Big Crowds for Obama," *McClatchy Newspapers,* December 10, 2006.

society was looking for something positive: "Michael: Try as You Might, There Will Never Be Another One Like Him," *Denver Post,* June 14, 1998.

united by their affection for the president: "The Party of Obama," *Washington Monthly,* January 2010.

primary focus is to advance the president's agenda: "OFA's Mitch Stewart and Jeremy Bird Speak to TPMDC," TalkingPointsMemo.com, November 11, 2009.

complete evaporation of liberal opposition: "In Polls, Much Opposition to Health Care Plan Is from Left," Fivethirtyeight.com, December 7, 2009.

JUST DO IT

6 percent of Americans: "Researchers Shine Spotlight on Narcissistic Personality Disorder," *Psychiatric News,* August 1, 2008.

rise in cosmetic surgeries: "Cosmetic Surgery Is on the Rise," *WebMD,* February 20, 2004.

7 million (!) pieces of reflective Mylar: "Now It's Your Turn," *Time,* December 16, 2006.

tenth-largest industry in America: Dave Zirin, *What's My Name, Fool?* p. 17.

the best man or woman plays and wins a contest: Ibid., p. 14.

just fuck it: Donald Katz, *Just Do It,* 1994, p. 138.

octogenarian who runs seventeen miles a day: Ibid., p. 145.

ancient call to a way of life: "A Sense of Cool: Nike's Theory of Advertising," *Harvard Business Review,* August 1992.

a blood-splattering jab: Nike ad, "Search and Destroy."

courses that I am not allowed to play: Robert Goldman and Stephen Papson, *The Nike Culture,* 1998, p. 113.

spread like a disease: "Swoosh! Inside Nike," CNBC, February 15, 2010.

launching its own "U.B.U." campaign: "Spots Put Free Spirits into Reeboks," *New York Times,* June 17, 1988.

updating the countercultural anthem: "Burger King Campaign: 'Break Rules,'" *New York Times,* September 28, 1989.

Fire Your Broker: "The New Commandments," *Advertising Age,* June 1, 2001.

capture the sentiment of empowerment: "Bank on It," *Brandweek,* January 8, 2001.

acquiring wealth, power, prestige: "GOP Battler Lee Atwater Dies at 40," *Washington Post,* March 30, 1991.

regards business success as utterly glamorous: "Business on the Big Screen," *New York Times,* April 12, 1987.

American Dream began to take on hyperbolic connotations: "Rethinking the American Dream," *Vanity Fair,* 4, 2009.

Be All That YOU Can Be campaign: "Top 100 Advertising Campaigns," AdAge.com.

first hit the bestseller list: Micki McGee, *Self Help, Inc.,* 2005, p. 56.

created a separate bestseller list: Steve Salerno, *Sham,* 2005.

relax television advertising rules: Micki McGee, *Self Help, Inc.*, 2005, p. 62.

$120 million worth of audiotapes: Ibid.

$80 Million Man: Steve Salerno, *Sham*, 2005.

$10 billion in revenue a year: "Do Self-Help Books Actually Help?" *Waco Tribune-Herald*, March 13, 2007.

between 12 and 15 million Americans: "Selling Self-Help," *American Demographics*, March 1992.

We are the new televangelists: Micki McGee, *Self Help, Inc.*, 2005, p. 59.

"Rev. Eric Butterworth, 86," *New York Times*, April 22, 2003.

a "me" nation: "The 'Me' Decade and the Third Great Awakening," *New York Magazine*, August 23, 1976.

culture of narcissism: Christopher Lasch, *The Culture of Narcissism*, 1979.

debt skyrocketed both because of declining wages: "Household Income and Debt Trends Since 1980," CreditSlips.com, February 16, 2009.

declined by 33 percent: Robert Putnam, *Bowling Alone*, 1995, p. 43 (Figure 5).

participation in community organizations dropped by 45 percent: Ibid., p. 60 (Figure 10).

decline in *demand* for union representation: Henry S. Farber and Alan B. Krueger, "Union Membership in the United States: The Decline Continues," Princeton University, August 1992.

labor is taking a beating: Robert Putnam, *Bowling Alone*, 1995, p. 82, quoting Peter J. Pestillo in the *Monthly Labor Review* from February 1979.

electronic trading detached the buyer from the seller: "Do CDOs Have Social Value?" *New York Times*'s Room for Debate blog, April 27, 2010.

30 percent more than in 1982: "Study Finds Students Narcissistic," Associated Press, February 27, 2007.

more self-promoting, narcissistic, overconfident and attention-seeking: "Are Social Networks Making Students More Narcissistic?" *USA Today*, August 25, 2009.

three-quarters of college freshmen: "Financial Concerns of First-Year College Students Have Wide Impact, Annual Survey Finds," *UCLA News*, January 21, 2010.

22 percent jump since 1980: U.S. Census Bureau, Table 276, citing the Higher Education Research Institute, UCLA, *The American Freshman: National Norms*.

27 percent increase from 1976: "Today's College Freshmen Have Family Income 60% Above National Average, UCLA Survey Reveals," UCLA Newsroom, April 9, 2007.

two in five Harvard seniors: "Harvard Graduates Head to Investment Banking, Consulting," *Harvard Crimson,* June 22, 2008.

about everybody having their own spotlight: "LeBron James' Decision: The Transcript," ESPN.com, July 8, 2010.

no reason why they shouldn't earn $1 million to $200 million: "Financial Giants Donating Little to Obama," *New York Times,* October 2, 2009.

shame and nervous self loathing: "On ESPN and 'Replaceable' People," RollingStone.com, September 11, 2010.

but to instead go shopping: "He Told Us to Go Shopping. Now the Bill Is Due," *Washington Post,* October 5, 2008.

continuing to visit the communities and beaches of the Gulf Coast: Barack Obama, May 27, 2010.

rodeo clown: "Fox News's Mad, Apocalyptic, Tearful Rising Star," *New York Times,* March 29, 2009.

alcoholic-turned-teetotaler: "Glenn Beck to Republican Party: Repent," *Los Angeles Times,* February 21, 2010.

individual, individual, individual: "It's Time to Stand Up for Individual Rights," FoxNews.com, May 5, 2009.

We're not all in this together: Ibid.

serve a cause greater than themselves: John McCain, September 27, 1999.

make common sacrifice for the greater good: Howard Dean, February 17, 2003.

unplanned late-eighties screenwriters' strike: "With Writers on Strike, Expect More Reruns and Dose of Reality," *San Diego Union-Tribune,* February 6, 2007.

Cops as the first reality TV show: "The Original Reality Show: 'Cops' Still Runs," CNNfn, November 14, 2003.

take his wife on a romantic weekend: "Romantic Weekend," Season 1, Episode 105, *Hogan Knows Best* (VH1), August 16, 2005.

permanent commentator spot: "Let's Make It Real," *New York Times,* July 31, 2010.

something that nobody can live up to: "Triumph of the Swoosh," *Sports Illustrated,* August 16, 1993.

a welfare class that lives for having children: "Tea Party Supporters Doing Fine, but Angry Nonetheless," *New York Times,* April 17, 2010.

conservation may be a sign of personal virtue: Dick Cheney, April 30, 2001.

$500,000 is not a lot of money: "U.S. Plans $500,000 Cap on Executive Pay in Bailouts," *New York Times,* February 3, 2009.

investment community feels very put-upon: "Financial Giants Donating Little to Obama," *New York Times,* October 2, 2009.

Squeaking By on $300,000: "Squeaking By on $300,000," *Washington Post,* August 16, 2009.

Richard Heene set up a hoax so as to get his own show: "Balloon Boy Story and Reality TV Culture: What Are Parents Thinking?" *Christian Science Monitor,* October 21, 2009.

specifically to hype their upcoming appearance: "The Salahis Will Be on *Real Housewives;* White House Crashing Will Be Part of Series," Mediaite.com, June 15, 2010.

mostly for the purpose of landing on TV: "Cable Guise," *New York Times,* December 6, 2009.

leading candidate for the Republican nomination: "GOP 2012: Huckabee 29% Romney 24% Palin 18%," Rasmussen Reports, October 16, 2009.

is really really wonderful: Interview with Mike Huckabee, *Fox News Sunday,* November 29, 2009.

allows her to be both at the same time: "Cable Guise," *New York Times,* December 6, 2009.

TV personality over a community organizer: "David Vitter: 'I'll Take a TV Personality over a Community Organizer,'" Salon.com, April 10, 2010.

seem great because they are famous: Daniel Boorstin, *The Image,* 1961.

OUTLAWS WITH MORALS

doesn't mean I should raise your kids: "Wreaking Havoc As a Role Model," *Washington Post,* May 4, 1993.

most subversive sneaker commercial of all time: "Wreaking Havoc—and Selling Sneaks," *New York Times,* June 2, 1993.

spit on a fan: "NBA Fines Barkley $10,000 for Spitting on a Fan," *Oregonian,* March 29, 1991.

jokes about beating his wife: "Not a Good Guy? Wait a Minute," *Washington Post,* February 27, 1991.

tangled with sports governing bodies: Associated Press, February 4, 1994.

full of cockiness and pride and guts: "The Selling Pre," *Oregonian,* April 16, 1995.

shak[ing] 'em up at the country club: 1990 Nike commercial.

that player has to represent something more: Donald Katz, *Just Do It,* 1994, p. 221.

lob a nuke into the men's room of the Kremlin: "Tentacles of Rage," *Harper's Magazine,* September 2004.

outlaws with morals: Robert Goldman and Stephen Papson, *The Nike Culture,* 1998, p. 58.

I know what to do the next time: "Reagan, After *Rambo:* 'I Know What to Do,'" Associated Press, June 30, 1985.

detests rapacious health insurance corporations: "On Health Care, 51% Fear Government More Than Insurance Companies," Rasmussen Reports, October 10, 2009.

keep your government hands off my Medicare: "S.C. Senator Is a Voice of Reform Opposition," *Washington Post,* July 28, 2009.

receive payment from the government: "Tea Party Supporters Doing Fine, but Angry Nonetheless," *New York Times,* April 17, 2010.

indictments of government officials spike by 150 percent: Gil Troy, *Morning in America,* 2005, p. 252.

The nine most terrifying words in the English language: Ronald Reagan, August 13, 1986.

heroes for the eighties: Ronald Reagan, January 25, 1984.

equals Ronald Reagan's respect for the *Communist Manifesto:* "*The A-Team* Draws Fire," *People,* January 30, 1984.

14 million households: "TV Ratings: 1983–1984," ClassicTVHits.com.

second-highest-rated program in 1980: "TV Ratings: 1980–1981," ClassicTVHits.com.

third-most-popular program on television: "How TV Hit 'The A-Team' Was Born," *New York Times,* April 28, 1983.

large following of teen-agers and children aged 6 to 11: Ibid.

7 million "preteens": "*The A-Team* Draws Fire," *People,* January 30, 1984.

audience of 14 million: Ibid.

most violent show ever to air in prime time: "How TV Hit 'The A-Team' Was Born," *New York Times,* April 28, 1983.

ordered to rob the Bank of Hanoi to help end the war: "The A List," *Newsday,* June 6, 2010.

remove the shotguns and replace them with walkie-talkies: "Extra Special," *Entertainment Weekly,* March 18, 2002.

the first, second, and eighth top-grossing films of their years: Box Office Mojo figures from 1982, 1984, and 1989.

made more than $1 billion: *E.T.:* $792 million; *Ghostbusters:* $292 million; *Ghostbusters II:* $215 million; *Nightmare on Elm Street:* $25 million; *Nightmare on Elm Street 2:* $29 million; *Nightmare on Elm Street 3:* $44 million; *Nightmare on Elm*

Street 4: $49 million; *Nightmare on Elm Street 5:* $22 million; *Nightmare on Elm Street 6 (Freddy's Dead):* $34 million; *Nightmare on Elm Street 7 (Wes Craven's New Nightmare):* $18 million; *Nightmare on Elm Street 8 (Freddy vs. Jason):* $82 million; *Nightmare on Elm Street 9 (2010 remake):* $112 million. Source: Box Office Mojo.

Where's the outrage: "Dole Is Imploring Voters to 'Rise Up' Against the Press," *New York Times,* October 26, 1996.

one contractor for every thirty soldiers: Austin Knuppe, "Empire 'On the Cheap': Privatization, Outsourcing and Post–Cold War U.S. Foreign Policy," Hauenstein Center for Presidential Studies.

half of all Americans stationed in Iraq and Afghanistan are contractors: "Obama Has 250,000 'Contractors' in Iraq and Afghan Wars, Increases Number of Mercenaries," Jeremy Scahill's RebelReports.com, June 1, 2010.

profoundly skeptical of the law-enforcement establishment: "Video: Crime Pays in Prime Time," *Time,* September 17, 1984.

when he becomes a Top Gun instructor himself: "*Top Gun,*" *Onion AV Club,* August 31, 2009.

that means that it is not illegal: Richard Nixon, May 19, 1977.

anything [administration officials] do is in our national interest: "6 U.S. Copters, Crews in Bolivia Jungle for Drug Lab Crackdown," *San Diego Union-Tribune,* July 17, 1986.

Boland Amendments: "Deutch Taps Hill Operative for CIA," *Washington Times,* May 15, 1995.

I am in awe of the presidency: Oliver North, Iran-Contra Hearings, July 10, 1987.

put on a bravura performance: "The Colonel Stands His Ground," *New York Times,* July 12, 1987.

sent the money down to help the Freedom Fighters: "Scandal Is a Rubik's Cube," *Miami Herald,* December 14, 1986.

largest spontaneous popular response: David Thelen, *Becoming Citizens in the Age of Television,* 1996, p. 19.

true patriot: "Assessing the Performance," *Time,* January 20, 1987; "Reagan Not Off the Hook on Iran-Contra Affair," *National Journal,* July 25, 1987.

overturned on legal technicalities: "Charges on North Dismissed," *Boston Globe,* September 17, 1991.

$20 million: "Incumbents Not Only Ones in the Money," *USA Today,* November 8, 1994.

cameo appearances on prime-time television: "Prime Time Goes North," *Dallas Morning News,* October 7, 1995.

power to set aside any statute: "Bush Challenges Hundreds of Laws," *Boston Globe,* April 30, 2006.

than two-thirds supported the administration's decision to go to war: "War with Iraq Justified, Even If No WMD," FoxNews.com, June 6, 2003.

55 percent of Americans: "Civil Liberties," Gallup.com, September 2006.

19-percentage-point gap: "Public, Political Left At Odds Over Interrogation," Resurgent Republic, May 16, 2009.

questioning the value of the intelligence: "Why Bush's 'Enhanced Interrogation' Program Failed," ThinkProgress.org, citing Pentagon and intelligence officials.

no need for Congress to even investigate: "Our Poll, Your Questions," CBSNews.com, April 28, 2009.

born of the corrupt Chicago political machine: "McCain Ad Takes on Obama and 'Chicago Machine,'" *Chicago Tribune,* September 22, 2008.

fundamentally different path: "Obama's Reagan Comparison Sparks Debate," WashingtonPost.com, January 17, 2008.

too much government involvement in the market: George W. Bush, November 13, 2008.

Pew and CNN polls: Pew Research Center survey conducted by Opinion Research Corporation, September 19 to September 22, 2009; CNN/Opinion Research Corporation Poll, September 19 to September 21, 2008.

antigovernment protest: "Joseph Stack and Right-Wing Terror: Isolated Incidents or Worrying Trend?" Newsweek.com, February 18, 2010.

Tea Party movement was more popular among voters: "Tea Party More Popular than Dems, GOP," MSNBC's FirstRead.com, December 16, 2009.

PART III: WHY WE (CONTINUE TO) FIGHT

America's limited-government ideals into practice: Sean Paige, *Huffington Post,* February 7, 2010.

one-third of the Springs' entire economy: "Colorado Springs Economy Remains at Mercy of the Military," *Colorado Springs Business Journal,* August 24, 2007.

all-time low in Gallup's polling: "Military, Police Top Gallup's Annual Confidence in Institutions Poll," Gallup.com, June 19, 2003, citing Gallup poll from November 1981.

85 percent of Americans: "Military, Police Top Gallup's Annual Confidence in Institutions Poll," Gallup.com, citing Gallup poll from 1991.

I'm always skeptical of government: "'Intruder' Sought Navy Intrusion," *Los Angeles Times,* January 19, 1991.

greeted as liberators: Dick Cheney, September 14, 2003.

KICKING THE VIETNAM SYNDROME

as if we were doing something shameful: "Reagan Endorses U.S. Role in Vietnam, Calling It 'A Noble Cause,'" Associated Press, August 18, 1980.

evidence of Reagan's reckless pugilism: "Reagan's Combative Rhetoric Is Working Against Him," *Washington Post,* August 24, 1980.

that most bitter and divisive conflict: *Forbes,* September 15, 1980.

can't see the bad impact: "Reagan's Packagers Worry About Loose Ends," *New York Times,* September 7, 1980.

cause for which our men fought was *just:* Ronald Reagan, November 11, 1988.

column in *The Washington Post*'s style section: "The Wall and Scars Unhealed," *Washington Post,* November 20, 1988.

Deny culpability when that policy is exposed: "Stabbed in the Back! The Past and Future of a Right-Wing Myth," *Harper's Magazine,* June 2006.

you were trying to rehabilitate the American attitudes: Bernard Von Bothmar, *Framing the Sixties,* 2010, p. 88.

blamed for war by those who parade for peace: Ronald Reagan, August 18, 1980.

spat on their field gray uniforms: Jerry Lembcke, *The Spitting Image,* 1998, p. 86.

conservative parties in Paris: Ibid., pp. 88–89.

demonstrations are prolonging the war: "Ronald Reagan vs. Robert Kennedy," *U.S. News and World Report,* June 17, 2004, quoting the CBS television debate between Senator Robert Kennedy and Governor Ronald Reagan on May 15, 1967.

effete corps of impudent snobs: Richard Reeves, *President Nixon: Alone in the White House,* 2001, p. 139.

lending comfort and aid: CBS television debate between Senator Robert Kennedy and Governor Ronald Reagan on May 15, 1967.

Americans will die tonight: Rick Perlstein, *Nixonland,* 2008, p. 431.

94 percent of Vietnam vets: Jerry Lembcke, *The Spitting Image,* 1998, p. 68, quoting a 1971 Harris Poll.

impossible to find a "hawk": Ibid., p. 53, quoting the Veterans' World Project at Southern Illinois University.

G. I. Joe comic strips showed vets: Ibid., p. 141.

peacenik character deferentially apologizing: "The Military-Toy-Industrial Complex," *The Believer,* October 2008.

afraid to let them win: Associated Press, February 25, 1980.

because they'd been denied permission to win: Ronald Reagan, February 24, 1981.

literally with one arm tied behind you: Bernard Von Bothmar, *Framing the Sixties,* 2010, p. 79.

too much authority was put in civilian hands: "Vietnam Revisited," *Christian Science Monitor,* March 3, 1983.

the war is unwinnable: "Frederick C. Weyand Dies at 93," *Los Angeles Times,* February 15, 2010.

calling me baby killer: "*Newsweek* Throws the Spitter," *Slate,* January 30, 2007.

second-highest-grossing film of 1985: Box Office Mojo.

"Movie Bloodlines Lead to Rambo's Children," *New York Times,* March 1, 1987.

television had no time to bring the carnage: "1968 Like a Knife Blade, the Year Severed Past from Future," *Time,* January 11, 1988.

blamed the loss of the Vietnam War on the media's critical reporting: Gregory Sieminski, "The Art of Naming Operations," *Parameters,* Autumn 1995.

we tried to fight for our national interests: "Vietnam Echo in Nicaragua," *Miami Herald,* April 8, 1986.

Jane Fonda's apology: "Jane Fonda Regrets 'Hurt' Caused by Vietnam Deeds," *Christian Science Monitor,* June 17, 1988.

learned some lessons from the Vietnam War: "Forgive Fonda? Yes. Forget? Never!" *Miami Herald,* June 19, 1988.

unless we are prepared to win: Ronald Reagan, November 11, 1988.

preparations for the next one: "The Wall and Scars Unhealed," *Washington Post,* November 20, 1988.

militarization of the image of the presidency began: "A Senseless Salute," *New York Times,* April 14, 2003.

"At Ease, Mr. President," *New York Times,* January 27, 2007.

back on their feet and standing tall: "Military of U.S. 'Standing Tall,' Reagan Asserts," *New York Times,* December 13, 1983.

Newsweek fronted covers: Michael Ryan and Douglas Kellner, *Camera Politica,* 1988, pp. 178 and 211.

We Keep America on Top of the World: "CBS Makes Big Splash of Its News," *Los Angeles Times,* May 24, 1985.

good soldiers and gutless politicians: "Millennialism in the Mass Media: The Case of *Soldier of Fortune* Magazine," *Journal for Scientific Study of Religion,* 1992.

Springsteen heartland of America approach: "Making a Loud Noise," *Newsweek,* April 13, 1987.

archconservative columnist George Will: "Bruce Springsteen's U.S.A.," *Washington Post,* September 13, 1984.

message of hope: Associated Press, September 19, 1984.

manipulated and exploited: "How the Boss Recaptured the Flag," *Toronto Star,* June 26, 2004.

Chrysler reportedly bid $12 million: "Are Fans Fed Up with Rock Tie-Ins?" *Adweek,* September 19, 1988.

the pride is back: "Chrysler Revs Up Ad Budget, Seeks Media Mileage Too," *Adweek,* September 23, 1985.

the torrent of applications: "Armed Forces: Proud and Prepared," *U.S. News and World Report,* April 22, 1985.

designed to shape domestic and international perceptions: Gregory Sieminski, "The Art of Naming Operations," *Parameters,* Autumn 1995.

can now make major cuts in defense spending: "58% Say Cold War Is Ending, 45% Back Arms Cuts, Poll Finds," *Washington Post,* November 23, 1989.

kick the Vietnam Syndrome: "Bush Promises to Heal War's Wounds," United Press International, March 4, 1991.

troops will have the best possible support: George H. W. Bush, January 16, 1991.

ought to turn it over to the *military commanders:* "Views on the Gulf: Lawmakers Versed in Vietnam," *New York Times,* September 16, 1990.

support the service personnel currently engaged in the conflict: "Yellow Ribbons, Mixed Messages," *Chicago Tribune,* February 5, 1991.

Operation Yellow Ribbon: Jerry Lembcke, *The Spitting Image,* 1998, p. 22.

experience one of America's greatest blessings: "Bush Replies to School's Ribbon Policy," *Chicago Tribune,* February 26, 1991.

They've seen all these movies: "Views on the Gulf: Lawmakers Versed in Vietnam," *New York Times,* September 16, 1990.

I swear to God I'll kill them: "Troops in Gulf Talk of War, and of Vietnam and Respect," *New York Times,* September 30, 1990.

there will not be any murky ending: George H. W. Bush, November 29, 1990.

came together with a pride: George H. W. Bush, January 15, 1990.

press release from December 2006: "DNC: Bush No Longer Listening to Commanders on Troop Levels in Iraq," Democratic National Committee press release, December 20, 2006.

allow the military to come up with the plans: "President George W. Bush Discusses Various Political, Social and Economic Issues," NBC News, February 8, 2004.

a war I opposed and despised: "A Letter by Clinton on His Draft Deferment," *New York Times,* February 13, 1992.

delivered a speech in 1993: Bill Clinton, April 1, 1993.

Paul Rogat Loeb, *Generation at the Crossroads,* 1995, p. 77.

repeat the mistakes of the generation: Jerry Lembcke, *The Spitting Image,* 1998, p. 22.

every subsequent conflict through that prism: "America's Left Caught Between a Flag and a Hard Place," *San Jose Mercury News,* November 2, 2001.

more alienated from its own national institutions: "Liberals Stuck in Scold Mode," *Los Angeles Times,* October 14, 2001.

war on my mind: "President George W. Bush Discusses Various Political, Social and Economic Issues," NBC News, February 8, 2004.

the soldier, not the reporter: Zell Miller, September 1, 2004.

Do they respect the military: "Kerry Presents Himself as a Patriot with a Different View," *New York Times,* June 4, 2004.

I'm John Kerry and I'm reporting for duty: John Kerry, July 29, 2004.

Kerry went home and lost the war: "Friendly Fire: The Birth of an Attack on Kerry," *New York Times,* August 20, 2004.

brutalized people that were still serving: *PBS Newshour* interview with George H. W. Bush, September 2, 2004.

not enough troops: "Senator Lautenberg's Remarks During Debate Over the Levin Iraq Resolution," Office of U.S. Senator Frank Lautenberg, June 21, 2006.

the kind of pro-war Democrat that we ought to be: "Centrist Democrats Take on Left over Iraq," *Politico,* July 31, 2007.

Cheney once predicted it would become: "Dick Cheney Iraq 'Quagmire' Video Hits the Web," *Telegraph* (UK), August 21, 2007.

troops themselves told pollsters: "Poll of Military Finds Dimmer View of Iraq War," *Military Times* (reprinted in *The Seattle Times*), December 30, 2006.

consequences of abandoning Iraq would be worse: "Toward a Realistic Peace," *Foreign Affairs,* September–October 2007.

civilian commanders were complete idiots: "'Faith' Focuses on McCain's Harrowing POW Ordeal," *Oregonian,* May 29, 2005.

unless our goal is victory: "McCain's Vietnam," *Nation,* December 15, 1999.

not enough urgency: Barack Obama, September 9, 2008.

any other executive in one term since World War II: "Defense Budget Portends Difficult Trade-offs," *National Journal,* August 12, 2009.

impediment to achieving real security: "Gates Calls European Mood a Danger to Peace," *New York Times,* February 23, 2010.

"Dems Say Steele Is 'Rooting for Failure.' Really, Dems?" *Washington Post*'s PlumLine.com, July 2, 2010.

Super Bowl's military-themed festivities: "NFL, Military Continue Super Bowl
    Traditions," American Forces Press Service, January 29, 2009.

giving encouragement—*aid and comfort*—to the enemy: "Dick Cheney Slams
    President Obama for Projecting 'Weakness,'" *Politico,* December 1, 2009.

send more troops to Vietnam: "Westmoreland Asks for More Troops,"
    History.com's *This Day in History,* June 18, 1966.

publicly declared that opposition to the war: "Gen. William C. Westmoreland: A
    Commander Caught in the Mire of Vietnam," *Los Angeles Times,* July 19,
    2005; Randall Bennett Woods, *Fulbright: A Biography,* p. 447.

support is vital to the success of our mission: "The War: Cards on the Table,"
    Time, May 5, 1967.

leaked a demand for an escalation: "McChrystal: More Forces or 'Mission Fail-
    ure,'" *Washington Post,* September 21, 2009.

public address to reporters: "McChrystal Rejects Scaling Down Afghan Military
    Aims," *New York Times,* September 12, 2010.

disgusted with Westmoreland: Randall Bennett Woods, *Fulbright: A Biography,*
    p. 447; "General Commanded Troops in Vietnam," *Washington Post,* July 19,
    2005.

override the needs of our commanders: "Frustration over Obama's Afghanistan
    War Policy," Associated Press, September 23, 2009.

dishonor and endanger this country: "Wavering on Afghanistan?" *Washington
    Post,* September 22, 2009.

intensify their efforts to kill more: "VFW National Commander Urges Decisive
    Action in Afghanistan," press release from the Veterans of Foreign Wars, *Octo-
    ber* 15, 2009.

hard to say no to General McChrystal: "In Afghanistan Assessment, a Catalyst for
    Obama," *New York Times,* September 21, 2009.

"stabbed in the back" by Obama administration skeptics: "Another Afghan War:
    Media Leaks Spark Administration Fight," *McClatchy Newspapers,* November
    12, 2009.

Three Obama Advisers Favor More Troops for Afghanistan: "Three Obama Ad-
    visers Favor More Troops for Afghanistan," *New York Times,* November 10,
    2009.

agreeing to the escalation: Barack Obama, December 1, 2009.

looked for a way out of the war: "Bob Woodward Book Details Obama Battles
    with Advisers over Exit Plan for Afghan War," *Washington Post,* September
    22, 2010.

no other military commander had ever addressed a joint meeting: "The War:
    Cards on the Table," *Time,* May 5, 1967.

had in good part already determined: "The Vanishing Liberal," *Harper's Magazine,* April 2010.

opposed a troop increase: CNN/Opinion Research Corporation Poll taken October 30 to November 1, 2009, found 56 percent "oppose sending more troops to Afghanistan"; Pew Research Center survey taken October 28 to November 8, 2009, found 59 percent either supporting a decrease in U.S. troops in Afghanistan or troop levels remaining the same—but not greater; CBS News poll taken November 13 to November 16, 2009, found 59 percent support reducing troops in Afghanistan or troop levels remaining the same—but not greater.

not elected officials: CNN/Opinion Research Corporation Poll taken October 30 to November 1, 2009, found 52 percent wanting Obama to "follow the recommendations of the generals in charge of U.S. forces in Afghanistan," and not "take other matters into account as well"; NBC News/Wall Street Journal Poll taken October 22 to October 25, 2009, found 62 percent "have more confidence" in the "generals running operations in the country" to make escalation decisions than in "the president and secretary of defense."

suddenly saying they supported it: "More Favor Afghan Escalation—When It's Presented As McChrystal's Plan," *Washington Post*'s PlumLine.com, November 18, 2009, quoting Quinnipiac poll released on November 18, 2009.

a change in personnel, but this is not a change in policy: Barack Obama, June 23, 2010.

[expletive] with the wrong guy: "Bob Woodward Book Details Obama Battles with Advisers over Exit Plan for Afghan War," *Washington Post,* September 22, 2010.

you're somehow disloyal to the military: "From Rambo to Iraq: Why We Now 'Support Our Troops,'" TheHistoryChannelClub.com.

OPERATION RED DAWN

first PG-13 rated production: "The PG-13 Hit Machine," *Detroit News,* April 29, 2004.

"Tom Cruise's son joins cast of Red Dawn remake," *Guardian* (UK), August 11, 2009.

Nancy Snow, *Information War,* 2004, p. 22.

Desert Storm trading cards: "U.S. War Against Terrorism Is in the Cards," *Ft. Lauderdale Sun-Sentinel,* February 8, 2001.

the military-entertainment complex: "War Is Virtual Hell," *Wired,* March–April 1993.

all of us in the military have seen: "Red Dawn Imitated Art," *USA Today,* December 17, 2003.

half the population was born after 1979: "Bush, Clinton, Bush . . . Clinton?" Associated Press, September 28, 2007.

more likely to attend to violent programs than older viewers: "Predictors of Children's Interest in Violent Television Programs," *Journal of Broadcasting and Electronic Media,* Spring 1997, quoting "The Extent to Which Viewers Watch Violence-Containing Programs," *Current Psychology: Research and Reviews,* 1996.

primary source of their impressions about the military: "U.S. Military Helps Create Hollywood Films on War and Warriors," *PBS Newshour,* October 6, 2006.

as much enduring influence as *Red Dawn:* "Red Dawn," *Slate,* October 8, 2008.

to liberate the oppressed: "Red Dawn Imitated Art," *USA Today,* December 17, 2003.

Soviets and their friends are advancing: Ronald Reagan, August 18, 1980.

Timothy McVeigh's favorite films: "Unraveling of a Frayed Life," *New York Times,* December 31, 1995.

tactical invasion routes: "Doing It McVeigh's Way," *Variety,* June 16, 1997.

preparedness to fight a war: "The Night of 'Red Dawn,'" *Washington Post,* August 9, 1984.

winner of the very first Academy Award: "Wings: The Impact of the Silent Era Film 'Wings' on Future Air Force War Movies," *History Today,* July 1, 1995.

kids touring the first nuclear submarine: "Operation Hollywood: Interview with David Robb," *Mother Jones,* September 20, 2004.

introduce a whole new generation to the nuclear Navy: Ibid.

underwrote *The Green Berets:* "The Celluloid Cold Wars," *Washington Post,* June 25, 1978.

steady growth in the demand for access to military facilities: "Hollywood Storms Pentagon with Post-War Project Deployment," *Hollywood Reporter,* June 19, 1991.

when our recruiting bills are considered: "Operation Hollywood: Interview with David Robb," *Mother Jones,* September 20, 2004.

Heroic enough in their terms: "America Takes the Reds to the Movies," *Macleans,* June 23, 1986.

is it in sync with present policy: "Fast-Dancing with the Top Guns," *Daily Variety,* June 24, 1994.

"a milestone" with 1986's *Top Gun:* "Operation Hollywood," *The Passionate Eye,* documentary aired on the Canadian Broadcasting Corporation on October 24, 2004.

$1.1 million for the use of warplanes: "America Takes the Reds to the Movies," *Macleans,* June 23, 1986.

time from writing stupid stuff: "Fast-Dancing with the Top Guns," *Daily Variety,* June 24, 1994.

the production doesn't go forward: "U.S. Military Helps Create Hollywood Films on War and Warriors," *PBS Newshour,* October 6, 2006.

number of pictures made with its official assistance: "Hollywood Storms Pentagon with Post-War Project Deployment," *Hollywood Reporter,* June 19, 1991.

don't know this is an advertisement: "Operation Hollywood," *The Passionate Eye,* documentary aired on the Canadian Broadcasting Corporation on October 24, 2004.

recruitment spiked 400 percent: Ed Halter, *From Sun Tzu to Xbox,* 2006, p. xix.

Wolverines who have grown up and gone to Iraq: "Director Flattered as Iraq Stars in 'Red Dawn' Sequel," *Los Angeles Times,* December 16, 2003.

make them happy right from the beginning: "Operation Hollywood," *The Passionate Eye,* documentary aired on the Canadian Broadcasting Corporation on October 24, 2004.

$353 million at the box office: Box Office Mojo.

$2 million promotion campaign: "High Flyer," *Promo,* May 1, 2005.

2 million copies upon its release: "Moving Toward a Video Foreign Policy," *Oregonian,* March 18, 1988.

was birthed at the Brookhaven National Laboratory in 1958: "Brookhaven Honors Video Game Made First," *New York Times,* November 9, 2008.

for the development of military technology: Heather Chaplin and Aaron Ruby, *Smartbomb,* 2006, p. 39.

developed by a former military intelligence officer: "His Home Video Games Clicked Invent," *Investors Business Daily,* September 8, 2010.

working for a defense contractor: "Video Games: Out of the Lab and into the Living Room," CBC News, October 16, 2008.

largest underwriter of the development of computer graphics: Ed Halter, *From Sun Tzu to Xbox,* 2006, p. 151.

nine total games that were first available for the 2600: Steven L. Kent, *The Ultimate History of Video Games,* 2001, p. 183.

revenues hit $2 billion annually: Heather Chaplin and Aaron Ruby, *Smartbomb,* 2006, p. 64.

something for helicopter gunners: Ed Halter, *From Sun Tzu to Xbox,* 2006, p. 139.

contributed to the game-play innovations of later war-fighting hits: John Sellers, *Arcade Fever,* 2001, p. 43.

games are military in nature: Ed Halter, *From Sun Tzu to Xbox,* 2006, p. 138.

pretty close to the system I use for air defense: Ibid., quoting the *Philadelphia Inquirer* on May 9, 1982.

you're being prepared for a new age: Ronald Reagan, March 8, 1983.

anything remotely in the news and make it a game: "Moving Toward a Video Foreign Policy," *Oregonian,* March 18, 1988.

new crop of video games are coming out: "Game Companies Are Cashing in on Television's Gulf 'Nintendo War,'" *Toronto Star,* February 9, 1991.

flow of information about life in the Army: Heather Chaplin and Aaron Ruby, *Smartbomb,* 2006, pp. 214–215.

officially labeled Operation Star Fighter: Ibid., p. 217.

$32 million of Pentagon cash: "America's Army Bill: $32.8 Million," *Gamespot,* December 8, 2009.

feel like they've already been there: "It's a Video Game, and an Army Recruiter," *Washington Post,* May 27, 2005.

a gaming area and a cafe: "Army Deploys 'Experience Center,'" *Adweek,* August 29, 2008.

extend the excitement into real life: "The Military-Toy-Industrial Complex," *The Believer,* October 2008.

named after a Joint Chiefs of Staff report: Ed Halter, *From Sun Tzu to Xbox,* p. 230.

linking entertainment and defense: James H. Korris, "Full Spectrum Warrior: How the Institute for Creative Technologies Built a Cognitive Training Tool for the Xbox," Institute for Creative Technologies; "Toy Soldiers," *Guardian* (UK), December 1, 2005.

better they were performing in live combat exercises: Heather Chaplin and Aaron Ruby, *Smartbomb,* 2006, p. 202; "Gaming Technologies Improve Soldier Readiness," Defence Talk, April 9, 2010; "Navy Says Video Games Can Boost 'Fluid Intelligence' of Warfighters," *Popular Science,* January 27, 2010.

visions of the Nintendo War: "The Men from DARPA," *Playboy,* August 1, 1991.

"Schwarzkopf Details Strategy," *Los Angeles Times,* February 28, 1991.

"The Political Veteran," *Washington Post,* November 15, 2004.

besieged by advertisements for the Army: Heather Chaplin and Aaron Ruby, *Smartbomb,* 2006, p. 215.

experienced a wave of consolidation: Gary Cross, *Kids' Stuff,* 1997, p. 170.

In 1983, the FCC removed its children-programming guidelines: "FCC Votes Down Children's Programming Quota," Associated Press, December 23, 1983.

in 1984 allowed TV stations to air as many commercials: "FCC Eases Rules for Broadcast TV," *New York Times,* June 28, 1984.

in 1985 formally refused to regulate the Program Length Commercial: "FCC Rejects Protests on Kids' Shows," *Los Angeles Times,* April 12, 1985.

already on the toy market: Gary Cross, *Kids' Stuff,* 1997, p. 199; "Licensed Characters: TV's Cartoon Controversy," *Chain Store Age,* February 1, 1984.

promoted as regular, independent programming: "Is It a Program or a Commercial?" *Washington Post,* October 15, 1983.

renewed energy into military-related toy lines: "The Littlest Arms Race," *Harper's Magazine,* April 1983, quoting the July 1982 edition of *Toys, Hobbies and Crafts.*

He-Man was the first *FCC-blessed* PLC: Tom Engelhardt, "The Shortcake Strategy," *Watching Television,* 1986, pp. 75–77.

35 million action-figure sales in a year: Ibid.

days of classroom instruction in warfare: "Toy Companies' Link with TV Grows," *Advertising Age,* January 16, 1986.

"Toy counterterrorists vs. toy-counter terrorists," *Advertising Age,* May 5, 1986.

highest ratio of war toys to total toys: "The Military-Toy-Industrial Complex," *The Believer,* October 2008, quoting Patrick M. Regan's article "War Toys, War Movies, and the Militarization of the United States, 1900–85" from the February 1994 *Journal of Peace Research.*

complement Gene Roddenberry's pre–*Star Trek* show: "Operating G.I. Joe," *St. Paul Pioneer Press,* August 29, 1995.

rebranding G. I. Joe as an "adventurer": Karen J. Hall, "A Soldier's Body: GI Joe, Hasbro's Great American Hero, and the Symptoms of Empire," *Journal of Popular Culture,* 2004, p. 34.

worried about putting the word *war:* Tom Engelhardt, *The End of Victory Culture,* 1995, p. 264.

26 million *Star Wars* action figures: Ibid., p. 269.

we're Americans and we're going to protect ourselves: "The Littlest Arms Race," *Harper's Magazine,* April 1983.

torn from today's headlines: "Toy Counterterrorists vs. Toy-Counter Terrorists," *Advertising Age,* May 5, 1986.

rout an Iranian battalion: "The Military-Toy-Industrial Complex," *The Believer,* October 2008; "The Littlest Arms Race," *Harper's Magazine,* April 1983.

there wasn't any money in the Russians: "The Military-Toy-Industrial Complex," *The Believer,* October 2008.

infiltrate a Persian Gulf nation: "The Littlest Arms Race," *Harper's Magazine,* April 1983.

$200 million in annual sales: "Toy Counterterrorists vs. Toy-Counter Terrorists," *Advertising Age,* May 5, 1986.

two-thirds of all American boys: Gary Cross, *Kids' Stuff,* 1997, p. 204.

board games: "Going to War with a Stick," *Eugene Weekly,* December 16, 2004.

a third of the most anti-Muslim: Jack Shaheen, *Reel Bad Arabs,* 2001; twenty-four of the sixty-four listed on the "Worst List" are from the 1980s.

needed equipment, personnel, and technical assistance: Ibid., p. 15.

movies of the eighties are especially offensive: Ibid., p. 22.

a cartoon United Nations: "Hype! Hell Raising! Hulk Hogan!" *Time,* April 15, 1985.

shows no mercy in terrorist attacks: Jeffrey J. Mondak, "The Politics of Professional Wrestling," *Journal of Popular Culture,* Fall 1989, quoting *Wrestling World* from June 1986.

just starting to enter the lexicon: "Salon Radio: Remi Brulin Transcript," Salon.com, March 14, 2010.

We're going to clean up America of all this trash: Brendan Maguire and John F. Wozniak, "Racial and Ethnic Stereotypes in Professional Wrestling," *Social Science Journal,* 1987.

three-quarters of Americans believed Iran is an Arab country: Jack Shaheen, *Reel Bad Arabs,* 2001, p. 29.

recent resurrection of the G. I. Joe comic book: "Larry Hama Relaunches his '80s 'G. I. Joe' Series,'" *USA Today,* April 14, 2010.

suck on this: *The Charlie Rose Show,* May 30, 2003.

there's no take-back there: "Drones: America's New Air Force," *CBS 60 Minutes,* August 16, 2009.

shot an amazing number of people: "Tighter Rules Fail to Stem Deaths of Innocent Afghans at Checkpoints," *New York Times,* March 26, 2010.

Look at those dead bastards: "Wikileaks Reveals Video Showing US Air Crew Shooting Down Iraqi Civilians," *Guardian* (UK), April 5, 2010.

should not have any lasting consequences: "Gates: WikiLeaks Video 'Painful to See' but Won't Have 'Lasting' Impact," *Huffington Post,* April 11, 2010.

PART IV: THE HUXTABLE EFFECT

there's not a black America and white America: Barack Obama, August 5, 2004.

social pathology: "The Negro Family: The Case For National Action," Office of Policy Planning and Research, United States Department of Labor, Chapter IV. The Tangle of Pathology, March 1965.

racial rhetoric fades: "Moynihan the Maverick," *U.S. News and World Report,* February 16, 1976; Moynihan memo to President Richard Nixon, January 16, 1970.

blacks get hurt worse than whites: "Impossible, Ridiculous, Repugnant," *New York Times,* October 6, 2005.

put this Willie Horton guy on the ticket: "Willie Horton and the Making of an Election Issue," *Washington Post,* October 28, 1988.

Atwater grows angry at the suggestion: "GOP Chairman Lee Atwater: Playing Hardball," *New York Times,* April 30, 1989.

naked cruelty: "Lee Atwater, Tough Ex-Head of GOP, Dies," *Los Angeles Times,* March 30, 1991.

mix of liberalism and a big black rapist: "Did Gore Hatch Horton?" *Slate,* November 1, 1999, quoting Sidney Blumenthal's book *Pledging Allegiance.*

We want a color-blind society: "President Says No Room for Quotas in Color-Blind Society," Associated Press, January 18, 1986.

disfigured by a kind of homegrown apartheid: Bernard Von Bothmar, *Framing the Sixties,* 2010, p. 112.

television is now color-blind: "TV's disappearing Color Line," *U.S. News and World Report,* July 13, 1987.

presumptuous enough to talk about complex social problems: "Black Image: We're Not There Yet," *Los Angeles Times,* September 9, 1987.

great musculature: "Campanis Questions Ability of Blacks," *Los Angeles Times,* April 7, 1987.

as being too black: "Reach Out and Touch Someone," *Sports Illustrated,* August 5, 1991.

shed[ding] their racial identity: Ibid.

first African American to break many barriers: Linda K. Fuller, *The Cosby Show: Audiences, Impact and Implications,* 1992, p. 14.

the most popular and profitable series: "Cos and Effect," *Los Angeles Times,* April 26, 1992.

slip a social message into my act: "This Is How We Lost to the White Man," *The Atlantic,* May 2008, quoting *Playboy* from 1969.

go to the library and read about it: "The Cosby Phenomenon," *Sun Herald* (Australia), April 2, 1989.

not like a jive show: Sut Jhally and Justin Lewis, *Enlightened Racism: The Cosby Show, Audiences, and the Myth of the American Dream,* 1992, p. 47.

surpassed by Michael Jordan in the Q ratings: Jim Naughton, *Taking to the Air,* 1992, p. 150.

Michael has no color: David L. Andrews, *Michael Jordan, Inc.*, 2001, p. 107,
   quoting "Here Comes Mr. Jordan," *TV Guide*, April 22, 1995.

first modern crossover in team sports: "In an Orbit All His Own," *Sports Illustrated*, November 9, 1987.

first mainstream African American who is articulate: "Biden's Description of
   Obama Draws Scrutiny," CNN.com, January 31, 2007.

signs of parochialism or racial resentment: "Post-Race," *New York Times*, August
   10, 2008.

putting race front and center: "For Obama, Nuance on Race Invites Questions,"
   New York Times, February 9, 2010.

more American: Sut Jhally and Justin Lewis, *Enlightened Racism: The Cosby Show,
   Audiences, and the Myth of the American Dream*, 1992, p. 47.

not a Black History Month poster: "Book Review: 'The Bridge,'" *Los Angeles
   Times*, March 28, 2010.

two-thirds of whites told Gallup pollsters: Tim Wise, *Between Barack and a Hard
   Place*, 2009, p. 33.

I'd lose viewers: *Playboy* interview with Bill Cosby, December 1, 1985.

you're never colorless: CNN, November 1, 1993.

long history in this country: Barack Obama, July 22, 2009.

brushing off the Congressional Black Caucus's demands: "A Frustrated Caucus
   Keeps Complaints Quiet," *Washington Post*, March 12, 2010.

pitfalls of talking bluntly about race: "For Obama, Nuance on Race Invites
   Questions," *New York Times*, February 9, 2010.

MOVIN' ON UP?

60 million other Americans: *Washington Post*, April 1, 1985.

become less tolerant of 'outsiders' like blacks: "Why So Many Americans Under
   30 Are Greeting a Black President as Old News," *Boston Globe*, January 11,
   2009.

children and young adults: Ibid.; Linda K. Fuller, *The Cosby Show: Audiences, Impact and Implications*, 1992, pp. 99–100, quoting Barbara M. Brown, Erica W.
   Austin, and Donald F. Roberts, "'Real Families' Versus 'Television Families,'"
   paper presented at the International Communication Association, 1987.

able to hold contradictory ideas simultaneously: Sut Jhally and Justin Lewis, *Enlightened Racism: The Cosby Show, Audiences, and the Myth of the American
   Dream*, 1992, p. 16.

almost none of those roles: Ibid., p. 59.

inventing symbols of that transformation: "TV's Black World Turns—But Stays
   Unreal," *New York Times*, November 12, 1989.

roles as domestics, dancers or savages: "Passions Over 'Purple,'" *Washington Post,* February 5, 1986.

our statement is a nonstatement: Robert Culp interview with the Archive of American Television, November 6, 2007.

martyred hero to a lot of people: "Playing the Game They Loved," *New York Times,* August 7, 1983.

almost totally white in appearance and attitude: "More Diversity on TV These Days, but Blacks are Usually Rich, Untroubled," Associated Press, August 23, 1989.

has very little Negro-ness: Joanne Morreale, "Critiquing the Sitcom: A Reader," 2002, p. 138; Christine Acham, "Revolution Televised: Prime Time and the Struggle for Black Power," 2004, p. 114.

blacks dare not acknowledge their blackness: Herman Gray, *Watching Race,* 1995, p. 76.

"relevant" and "authentic" images: Ibid., p. 77.

number one show in America in 1971: "TV Ratings: 1971–1972," ClassicTVHits.com.

a close second: "TV Ratings: 1972–1973," ClassicTVHits.com.

previously deemed too "sensitive" for TV: "DVDs Salute Comedy Pioneer Lear," *Denver Post,* June 5, 2009.

minstrel-like characters: "Searing Look at TV's Portrayal of Blacks," *Boston Globe,* May 14, 1992.

full of jivin', jammin', streetwise style stuff: *Psychology Today,* July 21, 1986.

little regard or appreciation: Museum of Broadcast Communications website.

a lot of what they need to know: "Redd Fox, TV's 'Sanford,' Dies of Heart Attack at 68," *Los Angeles Times,* October 12, 1991.

three-piece suits are a blatant caricature: Michael Ryan and Douglas Kellner, *Camera Politica,* 1988, p. 111.

worst nightmare of black brutality: "The A-Team's Mr. T," *People,* May 30, 1983.

a bridge between sitcoms: "TV's Black World Turns—But Stays Unreal," *New York Times,* November 12, 1989.

reversion back to the age of neo-minstrelcy: "TV's Blacks: Little More Than Minstrel Shows?" *Syracuse Post-Standard,* June 7, 1992.

looked like a sullen ex-slave: Mark Crispin Miller, "Deride and Conquer," from the book *Watching Television,* 1986, p. 213.

prevent his biological uncle from reclaiming him: *Washington Post,* March 26, 1984.

KKK-aligned Louisiana father: "'The Toy' Isn't Any Fun," *Washington Post,* December 11, 1982.

if you want to live like they do: "He Has a Hot TV Series, a New Book—and a Booming Comedy Empire," *Time,* September 28, 1987.

limousine driver and a carpenter: "Before Obama, There Was Bill Cosby," *New York Times,* November 8, 2008.

This particular family happens to be black: "Cosby in NBC Series on a New York Family," *New York Times,* September 20, 1984.

same irritations and misunderstandings: "Cosby's Fast Track," *Newsweek,* September 2, 1985.

They're upper middle-class, not black: "White Racism and *The Cosby Show,*" *Jump Cut,* July 1992.

leave all of that anger and controversy: "Cos and Effect," *Los Angeles Times,* April 26, 1992.

began to lay it out and tell the truth: "Family, Not Race, Is Focus," *USA Today,* October 26, 1989.

201 episodes: Internet Movie Database.

wouldn't have happened if we weren't so rich: *Cosby Show* episode "Vanessa's Rich," aired on November 13, 1986.

deliver a riotous rap version: Linda K. Fuller, *The Cosby Show: Audiences, Impact and Implications,* 1992, p. 133.

assumed TV producers wanted from black actors: Ibid., p. 9, quoting "The Fall of the House of Huxtable," *Wall Street Journal,* April 18, 1988.

what you tend to think black families are like: *Enlightened Racism: The Cosby Show, Audiences, and the Myth of the American Dream,* 1992, p. 32.

I don't look at a black person: Ibid., p. 37.

as people regardless of their color: Ibid., p. 47.

half of the entire television audience: "Cos and Effect," *Los Angeles Times,* April 26, 1992.

$1.5 million in ad revenues per show: "'Cosby' Captioning Sparks Dispute," *New York Times,* January 6, 1986.

nineteen of the twenty-five most watched programs on television: Linda K. Fuller, *The Cosby Show: Audiences, Impact and Implications,* 1992, p. 32.

changing the white community's perspective: "Cosby's Fast Track," *Newsweek,* September 2, 1985.

Maryemma Graham and Amritjit Singh, *Conversations with Ralph Ellison,* 1995, p. 389.

most positive portrayal of black family life: "Cosby's Fast Track," *Newsweek,* September 2, 1985.

created opportunities for other blacks: "TV's Disappearing Color Line," *U.S. News and World Report,* July 13, 1987.

neither black nor white: "The Selling of Michael Jordan," *New York Times,* November 9, 1986.

not-so-nice blackness: *Enlightened Racism: The Cosby Show, Audiences, and the Myth of the American Dream,* 1992, p. 47.

"Does Obama Herald the End of Black?" *Ft. Lauderdale Sun-Sentinel,* January 11, 2009.

lunch-bucket ethic: "Our Ingrained Racism," *Rocky Mountain News,* May 14, 2008.

urban black youth robbing and raping: Herman Gray, *Watching Race,* 1995, p. 23.

solely responsible for their social conditions: "TV's Black World Turns—But Stays Unreal," *New York Times,* November 12, 1989.

artificial world of racial harmony: "Study: TV Avoids Racial Conflict," United Press International, April 22, 1989.

more important to black children's success: "Cosby Show's Values Lauded," *Washington Post,* May 31, 1986.

"Conservative Media Critic Applauds Prime-Time Television's Positive Portrayal of Black Families," Media Research Center press release, September 23, 1991.

the cause of alien oppression and distress: "When Will White People Stop Making Movies Like 'Avatar'?" io9.com, December 18, 2009.

movie about black suffering in which the hero is white: "In Cry Freedom, The Message Makes the Movie," *Miami Herald,* February 19, 1988.

pressures of a white family: "Out of Sight, Out of Mind," *Newsweek,* January 23, 1989.

viewers felt racism was a sin of the past: *Enlightened Racism: The Cosby Show, Audiences, and the Myth of the American Dream,* 1992, pp. 71–72.

overestimated black economic success: "Re-run Why So Many Americans Under 30 Are Greeting a Black President as Old News," *Boston Globe,* January 11, 2009.

four out of five whites: "Racism Rears Its Ugly Head Again," *Washington Post,* March 13, 1988.

a third supporting any congressional action: "White Racism and *The Cosby Show,*" *Jump Cut,* July 1992.

no longer feel blacks are discriminated against: "Questions of Color," *Los Angeles Times,* May 27, 1990.

black folks' worst nightmare: "A Decade of Pain and Gain," *St. Petersburg Times,* December 29, 1989.

strong right arm of the federal government "Blacks Feel the Brakes," *St. Louis Post-Dispatch,* December 31, 1989.

manages to accommodate individual people of color: Tim Wise, *Between Barack and a Hard Place,* 2009, p. 23.

we love Michael Jordan: "Reach Out and Touch Someone," *Sports Illustrated,* August 5, 1991.

racism masquerading as liberalism: *Enlightened Racism: The Cosby Show, Audiences, and the Myth of the American Dream,* 1992, p. 97.

different because he is a celebrity: Norman K. Denzin, "Representing Michael," from *Michael Jordan, Inc.,* 2001, p. 5, quoting Henry Louis Gates' 1998 *New Yorker* article, "Annals of Marketing: Net Worth."

either too black or not black enough: "Frustration at Obama's Nuanced Style on Race," *New York Times,* February 9, 2010.

"not listening" to African Americans: "Congressional Black Caucus: President Obama's Not Listening," *Politico,* March 11, 2010.

run from race like a black man runs from a cop: "Obama Needs to See Color on Some Issues," *Ft. Lauderdale Sun-Sentinel,* March 1, 2010.

stunningly similar to Martin Luther King: "How Barack Obama Is Like Martin Luther King, Jr.," *Nation,* January 17, 2010.

deal with more controversial issues: "The Real-Life Drama Behind Hit TV Show About a Black Family," *Ebony,* 4, 1985.

black enough to be an Uncle Tom: "Cosby Show: Black or White?" *Washington Post,* November 5, 1984.

not delving deeply enough into racial problems: "'Cosby Show' Gains Acceptance by Being Universally Identifiable," Associated Press, April 16, 1986.

no need to rap my show: "Cos and Effect," *Los Angeles Times,* April 26, 1992.

means that only white people: Linda K. Fuller, *The Cosby Show: Audiences, Impact and Implications,* 1992, p. 121, quoting *USA Today*'s article from August 31, 1987, headlined "Time Flies While Cosby, 50, Has Fun."

whenever there's a black person in the cast: "Eliminate the Negative," *Los Angeles Times,* April 3, 1985.

unspoken belief that white viewers don't want: "TV's Shame: Lack of Dramas on Black Life," *Los Angeles Times,* June 9, 1990.

We can't do *Do the Right Thing* every week: "Taking a Look at TV's Racial Picture," *Los Angeles Times,* August 23, 1989.

offending as few people and groups: "An Update on 'The Cosby Show,'" *New York Times,* January 21, 1988.

conspicuous absence of black Oscar winners: "'Murder She Wrote' Detective Has Clue to Tony Awards Show," *Orange County Register,* April 27, 1988.

his voting preferences: "Bull Market," *Washington Post,* February 9, 1992.

Republicans buy shoes, too: "Just Do It: If Michael Jordan Can Endorse a Sneaker, Why Not a Candidate?" *Washington Post,* June 16, 1996, quoting Sam Smith's 1995 book, *Second Coming.*

a pretty heavy downside: "Bull Market," *Washington Post,* February 9, 1992.

had to be fictionalized: "Fire This Time," *Time,* January 9, 1989.

commercial suicide: *Enlightened Racism: The Cosby Show, Audiences, and the Myth of the American Dream,* 1992, p. 4.

against the white race: Ibid., p. 106.

doesn't have the privilege to be that angry: "'Do the Right Thing': Issues and Images," *New York Times,* July 9, 1989.

left-liberals who grew up in the angry hothouse: "Setting Up Easy Targets for Karl Rove," *Time,* May 14, 2006.

very Huxtable: CNN, October 24, 2004.

like the Huxtables: "One First Is Celebrated. What About the Second?" *New York Times,* August 27, 2008.

reach Huxtable cult status: "Get Ready for 'Barchelle,'" *Politico,* February 14, 2007.

Huxtable voter: "Harnessing the Huxtable Vote," *Politico,* April 2, 2008.

Did you sell them to anyone: "Clinton Co-Chair Resigns Over Obama Drug Remark," ABCNews.com, December 13, 2007.

It took a president to get it done: "Defeat Forces New Strategy on Clinton," *Politico,* January 8, 2008.

doing something in the neighborhood: "Clinton Surrogate Makes Veiled Reference to Obama's Drug Use," ABCNews.com, January 13, 2008.

Obama ran a good campaign here: "Bubba: Obama Is Just Like Jesse Jackson," ABCNews.com, January 26, 2008.

branding Obama as "the black candidate": "Obama Wins South Carolina in Racially Charged Primary," Associated Press, January 27, 2008.

the country is caught up in the concept: "Geraldine Ferraro Lets Her Emotions Do the Talking," *Daily Breeze,* March 7, 2008.

if Jesse Jackson were not black: "Koch Endorses Gore; Jackson Parries Critics," *Washington Post,* April 15, 1988.

Anybody who knows the history of this country: Barack Obama, ABC's *Good Morning America,* March 12, 2008.

attacking me because I'm white: "Ferraro Defends Controversial Comments on Barack Obama," *Daily Breeze,* March 11, 2008.

apologize to me for calling me a racist: MSNBC.com, March 12, 2008.

pushing the Wright story: "Clinton Doesn't Deny Campaign Is Pushing Wright Story to Superdelegates," ABCNews.com, March 20, 2008.

the great whore: "Hagee Endorsement for McCain Comes Under Fire," ABCNews.com, February 29, 2008.

friendly with the Reverend Billy Graham: "Billy Graham: Hillary's Solace," *Time,* August 8, 2007.

caught on tape spewing rancid anti-Semitism: "Nixon, Graham Anti-Semitism on Tape," *Chicago Tribune,* March 1, 2002.

brought from Africa in slave ships: "A Brief for Whitey," Creators Syndicate, March 21, 2008.

between 10 percent and 20 percent: CNN's 2008 exit poll in Pennsylvania's Democratic primary found 12 percent of white voters said the race of the candidates was important to them—and Clinton won 76 percent of those voters; http://www.cnn.com/ELECTION/2008/primaries/results/epolls/#PADEM. CNN's 2008 exit poll in Kentucky's Democratic primary found 18 percent of white voters said the race of the candidates was important to them—and Clinton won 88 percent of those voters; http://www.cnn.com/ELECTION/2008/primaries/results/epolls/#KYDEM. CNN's 2008 exit poll in West Virginia's Democratic primary found 21 percent of white voters said the race of the candidates was important to them—and Clinton won 84 percent of those voters; http://www.cnn.com/ELECTION/2008/primaries/results/epolls/#WVDEM.

Clinton's 8-point margin of victory: Clinton won the Ohio Democratic primary by 8 points (53–45). In that election, CNN's exit poll found 20 percent of voters said the race of the candidates were important to them. Of those 20 percent of voters, 59 percent voted for Clinton. Fifty-nine percent of 20 percent is 12 percent of the total electorate.

not ready to vote for an African American candidate: "Gov. 'Blunt Talk' Rendell," *Pittsburgh Post-Gazette,* February 12, 2008.

hardworking Americans: "Clinton Makes Case for Wide Appeal," *USA Today,* May 8, 2008.

pro-America areas of this great nation: "Palin Apologizes for 'Real America' Comments," *Washington Post,* October 22, 2008.

allegations of madrassa indoctrination: "CNN Debunks False Report About Obama," CNN.com, January 22, 2007.

whispers about tapes of Michelle Obama: "Campaign: Michelle Obama Never Used Word 'Whitey,'" Associated Press, June 13, 2008.

act of racial solidarity and reverse racism: "Limbaugh Implies Powell Only Endorsed Obama Because He's Black," ABCNews.com, October 19, 2008.

from the bottom of the deck: "McCain Campaign Says Obama Is 'Playing the Race Card,'" ABCNews.com, July 31, 2008.

heated national conversation about race: "Let's Not, and Say We Did," *New York Times,* March 24, 2008.

is emancipating white voters: "Whites' Great Hope?" *Wall Street Journal,* November 10, 2007.

his own Bill Cosby moment: "Obama Assails Absent Black Fathers," *American Prospect*'s Tapped blog, June 16, 2008.

exists within segments of the white community: Barack Obama, March 18, 2008.

behave like a civil rights leader: "Post-Race," *New York Times,* August 10, 2008.

smart not to ballyhoo "a black agenda": "Frustration at Obama's Nuanced Style on Race," *New York Times,* February 9, 2010.

try to confine his racial references: "Obama Wades into a Volatile Racial Issue," *New York Times,* July 23, 2009.

stigmatized as a candidate mobilizing race: Interview with Charles Ellison and Manning Marable for Creators Syndicate column, "The Democrats Class War," February 8, 2008.

debate has heated up: "Before Obama, There Was Bill Cosby," *New York Times,* November 8, 2008.

a carryover effect: Ibid.

the end of black politics: "Is Obama the End of Black Politics?" *New York Times,* April 6, 2008.

myth of racism as a barrier: "President-Elect Obama," *Wall Street Journal,* November 5, 2008.

we've moved beyond: NBC News, November 4, 2008.

crucial that people don't see my election: "First Black President of School's Law Review Uninterested in a Cushy Job," Associated Press, April 16, 1990.

racial discrimination against blacks: CNN/Essence Magazine/Opinion Research Corp. poll, July 20, 2009.

ABC/Washington Post poll from January: "Fewer Call Racism a Major Problem," ABC News/Washington Post poll, January 19, 2009.

twice as large as the white unemployment rate: "For Blacks, Progress in Happiness," *New York Times,* September 14, 2010.

comparing blacks and whites of the same educational background: "In Job Hunt, College Degree Can't Close Racial Gap," *New York Times,* November 30, 2009.

black males now earn 12 percent *less:* "Economic Mobility of Black and Whit Families," Brookings Institution, November 2007.

quadrupling of the wealth gap: "Wealth Gap Nearly Quadrupled for Whites, Blacks," *San Francisco Chronicle,* May 22, 2010.

one in three chance of being discriminated against: Alfred W. Blumrosen and Ruth G. Blumrosen, "The Reality of Intentional Job Discrimination in Metropolitan America—1999," Rutgers University, p. xv.

same chance of getting a job as a black man: "This Is How We Lost to the White Man," *The Atlantic,* May 2008.

twice as likely to be unemployed: Marianne Bertrand and Sendhil Mullainathan, "Are Emily and Greg More Employable Than Lakisha and Jamal? A Field Experiment on Labor Market Discrimination," University of Chicago/ Massachusetts Institute of Technology, May 27, 2003.

has sought to transcend: "Obama Wades into a Volatile Racial Issue," *New York Times,* July 23, 2009.

chided his own attorney general: "Obama Gently Departs from Holder's Race Comment," Associated Press, March 7, 2009.

can't pass laws that say I'm just helping black folks: "Amid Criticism, Obama Reaches Out to Blacks," *Boston Globe,* December 26, 2009.

an incendiary issue in American politics: "Frustration at Obama's Nuanced Style on Race," *New York Times,* February 9, 2010.

race remains a factor in the society: Barack Obama, July 22, 2009.

Fox News chairman Rupert Murdoch: "Murdoch: Glenn Beck Was Right— Obama's a Racist," BusinessInsider.com, November 9, 2009, quoting Murdoch's SkyNews interview of the same day.

deep-seated hatred for white people: "Fox's Glenn Beck: President Obama Is a Racist," Associated Press, July 28, 2009.

black president trying to destroy a white policeman: "Obama-Haters Becoming Increasingly . . . Racial in Their Rhetoric," TPMDC.com, July 28, 2009.

an affirmative action appointment: Pat Buchanan, MSNBC, July 16, 2009.

affirmative action on steroids: "Reparations by Way of Health Care Reform," *Investor's Business Daily,* July 27, 2009.

six in ten whites openly admit: Tim Wise, *Colorblind,* 2010, p. 78.

less support for the exact same bill: "I'd Like the Same Plan Better If It Was Bill Clinton's," *Miller-McCune,* November 13, 2009, quoting a study by University of California psychologist Eric Knowles published in the *Journal of Experimental Psychology.*

disproportionately motivated by racial resentment: "Survey Finds that Racial Attitudes Influence the Tea Party Movement in Battleground States," University of Washington study by Christopher Parker, April 7, 2010.

rebuking former president Jimmy Carter: "Obama Rejects Race as the Lead Cause of Criticism," *New York Times,* September 19, 2009.

white, Christian, male power structure: Bill O'Reilly, Fox News, May 29, 2007.

long downward spiral: "That Bright, Dying Star, the American WASP," *Wall Street Journal,* May 15, 2010.

fear of going out at night: "Stumping with Mayor, Giuliani Stirs Old Fears," *New York Times,* October 18, 2009.

forgot he was black: MSNBC, January 27, 2010.

THE END OF HISTORY?

end point of mankind's ideological evolution: "The End of History? As Our Mad Century Closes, We Find the Universal State," *Washington Post,* July 30, 1989.

require a more positive portrayal: "Some Ins and Outs of Textbook Standards," *Dallas Morning News,* May 22, 2010.

The Culture of Narcissism: "The Culture of Narcissism," NYTimes.com, June 2, 2010.

another report on the growing sense of selfishness: "Empathy: College Students Don't Have as Much as They Used To," University of Michigan press release, May 26, 2010.

joining the speakers circuit: "Bristol Palin to Hit Circuit," Associated Press, May 19, 2010.

we couldn't wear our uniforms: "Candidate's Words on Vietnam Service Differ from History," *New York Times,* May 17, 2010.

$58.8 billion wartime spending bill: "War Funding Clears Senate," *Politico,* May 27, 2010.

expanding largely secret U.S. wars: "U.S. 'Secret War' Expands Globally as Special Operations Forces Take Larger Role," *Washington Post,* June 4, 2010.

people who have died for our country: "Keeping Pabst Blue Ribbon Cool," *Businessweek,* September 16, 2010.

some kind of diversity power struggle: "Altered Mural Fuels Racial Debate in Prescott," *Arizona Republic,* June 4, 2010.

right down to the shoes: MSNBC, April 22, 2010.

racial resentment toward whites: "New Arizona Law Targets Ethnic Studies," Associated Press, May 12, 2010.

what I call ethnic chauvinism: "In Defense of Arizona's Ethnic Studies Law," FoxNews.com, May 14, 2010.

supportive of genuine multiculturalism: "The Millennials: Confident. Connected. Open to Change," Pew Research Center, February 24, 2010.

more restrained use of force: "Joint Chiefs Chairman Mullen Outlines a More Restrained Art of War," *Washington Post,* March 5, 2010.

era of persistent conflict: "General Warns of Persistent Conflict, Toll on Soldiers," *Colorado Springs Gazette,* May 14, 2010.

plurality of Americans: "Americans More Divided on Strength of National Defense," Gallup.com, February 18, 2010.

Pentagon budget on the chopping block: "Robert Gates May Get Lift from Tea Parties," *Politico,* June 7, 2010.

Barack Obama, May 14, 2009, http://www.whitehouse.gov/the_press_office/ Remarks-By-The-President-At-Arizona-State-University-Commencement/.

observe the curfew and watch *The Cosby Show:* "Cosby's Last 'Show,'" *Entertainment Weekly,* May 3, 1996.

GLOSSARY

This limited glossary highlights the more obscure aspects of 1980s pop culture that are referenced but not fully explained in the text of the book. It is by no means a comprehensive list of every reference made in the book—only those references that are not self-explanatory and not considered universally known.

3-2-1 Contact Science-focused television show for children that aired on PBS from 1980 to 1988.

A Nightmare on Elm Street 1984 slasher flick about the ghost of a child rapist named Freddy Krueger haunting the dreams of kids.

The A-Team Prime-time television show about a group of Vietnam War veterans who fight crime while fleeing federal officials that have accused them of "a crime they didn't commit." The program ran from 1983 to 1987.

Action Jackson 1988 film about Detroit police officer Jericho Jackson's (Carl Weathers) investigation of a murderous businessman named Peter Dellaplane (Craig T. Nelson).

Adrian Zmed Actor who starred in *Grease 2* (1982) and *T. J. Hooker*, and who replaced Deney Terrio as the host of *Dance Fever* in 1985.

Afterburner Sega's 1987 video game simulation of air combat. The game is a near-perfect knock-off of rival Nintendo's game *Top Gun*.

Alex P. Keaton Elyse and Steven Keaton's conservative son played by Michael J. Fox in the hit television show *Family Ties*.

Alexander Haig Retired general who, before becoming the board member of a Hollywood studio, served as President Ronald Reagan's first secretary of state. Before that, Haig had served as President Richard Nixon's final chief of staff.

Alf Television show about a friendly Muppet-ish alien named ALF, short for Alien Life Form. The program aired from 1986 to 1990.

American Graffiti 1973 George Lucas film glorifying youth culture in the 1950s and early 1960s.

Andre Agassi Professional tennis player who became famous in the late 1980s for reaching the semifinals of the French and U.S. Opens as a teenager. He was also famous for his long dirty-blond hair.

Anthony Robbins Self-help guru and life coach who pioneered the use of infomercials to sell personal motivation tapes.

Apollo Creed The immediate preceding heavyweight champion to Rocky Balboa in the *Rocky* film series. Creed was played by Carl Weathers.

Apple IIe Apple computer model released in 1983 as the successor to the Apple II Plus and the immediate predecessor to the one-piece Apple Macintosh.

Arnold and Willis Jackson The two African American children adopted by the white Drummond family in the television show *Diff'rent Strokes.* They were played by Gary Coleman and Todd Bridges, respectively.

Arthur 1981 film about a drunk millionaire (Dudley Moore) who falls in love with a working-class woman (Liza Minnelli).

Asteroids 1979 Atari game in which players fly a spaceship through a cloud of asteroids.

Atari Computer-game company founded in the early 1970s by Nolan Bushnell and credited with creating the video-game boom of the early 1980s. Atari is most recognizable to children of the 1980s from its wood-paneled 2600 home unit.

Axel Foley The protagonist played by Eddie Murphy in the *Beverly Hills Cop* series. Foley is not, actually, a Beverly Hills police officer, as the movie might have you believe. Instead, he is a Detroit police officer who repeatedly freelances in Beverly Hills.

B-52s Retro rock band consisting of Fred Schneider, Cindy Wilson, Kate Pierson, Ricky Wilson, and Keith Strickland.

B.A. Baracus The member of *The A-Team* played by Mr. T.

Battlezone 1980 Atari arcade game that simulates tank warfare from the first-person perspective.

Benson Television series about an African American butler (Robert Guillaume) in the California governor's mansion who ends up becoming the state's lieutenant governor. The show aired from 1979 to 1986.

Betty White Longtime actress most famous in the 1980s for starring as Rose Nylund in the *The Golden Girls.*

Beverly Hills Cop 1984 film starring Eddie Murphy as a Detroit police officer who goes rogue by fighting crime outside his jurisdiction—specifically, in Beverly Hills.

Biff Tannen Chief bully, bad guy, and butthead in the *Back to the Future* films.

Big 1988 Penny Marshall film about twelve-year-old Josh Baskin making a wish to a carnival machine called Zoltar and waking up the next day as a thirty-year-old adult (Tom Hanks).

The Big Gulp A massive cup of fountain soda marketed as 7-Eleven's premiere product in the 1980s.

Big John Studd WWF pro wrestler known for his size, girth, and beard.

Bill Laimbeer The Detroit Pistons' center who the NBA Encyclopedia calls "one of the most notorious players ever to throw an elbow, thrust a hip, or feign being fouled." During a twelve-year NBA career that spanned almost the entire 1980s, the hulking Laimbeer was called, among other things, "the prince of darkness," "a street thug," "an ax murderer," and "His Heinous." The NBA Encyclopedia additionally notes that Laimbeer "was punched by some of the league's best players, including Robert Parish, Bob Lanier, Larry Bird and Charles Barkley."

Biloxi Blues The successor to *Brighton Beach Memoirs* and the second of Neil Simon's three semiautobiographical plays—this one about protagonist Eugene Jerome's time in World War II–era basic training in Biloxi, Mississippi. The Broadway play was turned into a movie starring Matthew Broderick and Christopher Walken in 1988.

Bo Jackson Heisman-trophy-winning running back for Auburn, and subsequently the first athlete to be named an all-star in both professional baseball (Kansas City Royals) and professional football (Los Angeles Raiders). He was the star of Nike's famed "Bo Knows . . ." commercials.

Bob Ross Bushy-haired host of *The Joy of Painting*, a television show that ran on PBS from 1983 to 1994. Ross is known for teaching viewers how to paint "happy trees," among other things.

Bon Jovi Band named for the singer, songwriter, and actor Jon Bon Jovi. The band is most famous for its penchant for livin' on a prayer; its willingness to criticize those who give love a bad name; its lead singer's hair; and its affiliation with the state of New Jersey.

Bonfire of the Vanities 1987 Tom Wolfe novel about a New York bond trader named Sherman McCoy who hits an African American youth with his car when he pulls off the highway in the Bronx. The event becomes the subject of a tabloid exposé, civil rights protests, and a municipal prosecution.

Booger Nickname of Dudley Dawson (Curtis Armstrong), a member of the Lambda Lambda Lambda fraternity at Adams College in the 1984 movie *Revenge of the Nerds.*

Boy George Androgynous lead singer of the band Culture Club.

Brantley Foster The protagonist of the 1987 film *The Secret of My Success.* Played by Michael J. Fox, Foster is a country boy who gets a job working in the mailroom of his uncle's New York City corporation. Unsatisfied with the job, he pretends to be an executive named Carlton Whitfield, ultimately orchestrating a hostile takeover of the company.

Brewster's Millions 1985 film starring Richard Pryor as a minor-league pitcher whose great uncle (Hume Cronin) offers him a $300 million inheritance if he can somehow spend $30 million in thirty days without accumulating a single asset.

Brighton Beach Memoirs The first of Neil Simon's three semiautobiographical plays, this one is about his time growing up in Brighton Beach, New York. The play became a film starring Jonathan Silverman and Blythe Danner in 1986.

Buck Rogers Protagonist of the show *Buck Rogers in the 25th Century,* a science-fiction television show running from 1979 to 1981. In the program, Captain

William Anthony "Buck" Rogers (Gil Gerard) is a NASA pilot whose 1987 space mission gets him accidentally frozen for more than five hundred years. The show takes place in the year 2491, when Buck is unfrozen and brought back to life.

Bud Fox Protagonist of Oliver Stone's 1987 film *Wall Street*. Played by Charlie Sheen, Fox is a lowly Wall Street trader who convinces corporate raider Gordon Gekko (Michael Douglas) to be his mentor.

Castle Wolfenstein 1980s World War II–themed video game challenging players to infiltrate a Nazi base called Castle Wolfenstein.

Clark Griswold Father of the Griswold family, played by Chevy Chase in National Lampoon's *Vacation* series.

Clash of the Titans 1981 film about the Greek myth of Perseus.

Cliff Clavin Mailman, Jeopardy contestant, best friend of Norm Peterson, and regular patron of the fictional Boston bar Cheers. Clavin was played by actor John Ratzenberger.

Close Encounters of the Third Kind 1977 Steven Spielberg film about an alien landing at Devil's Tower, Wyoming.

Cloud City Fictional mining colony featured in the 1980 film *The Empire Strikes Back*. The facility is administered by Lando Calrissian (Billy Dee Williams).

Clubber Lang Fictional Chicago boxer (Mr. T) who wins the heavyweight title from Rocky Balboa in 1983's *Rocky III*. Lang is later defeated by Rocky in a rematch, after Rocky trains with former champion Apollo Creed.

Cobra Fictional international terrorist organization that is the primary nemesis of American special forces in the cartoon/comic strip, *G. I. Joe: A Real American Hero*.

The Cobra Kai Dojo Fictional karate training center run by Vietnam veteran John Kreese in the film *The Karate Kid*. Among other moves, the Cobra Kai Dojo taught students to sweep opponents' legs—a maneuver considered unsportsmanlike when deployed against an opponent whose leg is already injured.

Combat Video-game cartridge included with the original Atari 2600. Each of *Combat*'s 27 games simulates a different form of military violence.

Coming to America 1988 film starring Eddie Murphy as an African prince looking for his bride in Queens, New York.

Commando 1985 film starring Arnold Schwarzenegger as a retired special forces officer who must use his military skills to save his daughter from kidnappers.

Cops Reality television series, first launched in 1989, that follows police officers on their nightly patrols.

Cry Freedom 1987 film about the real-life events surrounding South African black activist Steve Biko (Denzel Washington). The film tells the story through white journalist Donald Woods (Kevin Kline).

Dallas Television series about the Ewings, a Texas family that became rich and powerful in the petroleum and livestock industries. The program ran from 1978 to 1991.

Dance Fever Merv Griffin–produced dance-contest program airing in syndicated television from 1979 to 1987.

Danny Zuko Leather-jacketed protagonist of the musical *Grease*. In the 1978 film adaptation, the character is played by John Travolta.

David Robinson All-American center for the U.S. Navy's basketball team and all-star center for the NBA's San Antonio Spurs.

Dee Snider Lead singer for the band Twisted Sister.

Deion Sanders Flashy athlete who, following in Bo Jackson's footsteps, simultaneously played professional football and professional baseball.

Delta Force 1986 movie starring Chuck Norris and Lee Marvin as commanders of a special-forces squad charged with rescuing Americans taken hostage by Arab airline hijackers.

Deney Terrio Original host of the 1980s television show *Dance Fever.*

Devo 1980s band from Ohio best known for its boxy red "energy dome" hats, its yellow jumpsuits, and its 1980 single, "Whip It."

Die Hard 1988 action film starring Bruce Willis as John McClane, a New York police detective who attends his wife's office Christmas Party in Los Angeles—a Christmas party that ends up being the target of international bank robber Hans Grueber (Alan Rickman). *Die Hard* is often cited as the purest expression of the 1980s action-movie model.

Diff'rent Strokes Prime-time television series about a wealthy white family in Manhattan adopting Willis and Arnold Jackson (Todd Bridges and Gary Coleman). The program aired in prime time from 1978 to 1986.

Diner 1982 Barry Levinson film about twentysomethings hanging out at Baltimore's Fells Point Diner in the 1950s.

Dirty Dancing 1987 film about a young woman named Baby (Jennifer Grey) and her love affair with a professional dancer (Patrick Swayze) during an early-1960s vacation at a resort in the Catskill Mountains.

Do the Right Thing 1989 Spike Lee film about simmering racial tensions in Brooklyn.

Dominique Wilkins High-flying nine-time NBA all-star with the Atlanta Hawks.

Doom First-person-shooter video game originally released in 1993 by id Software. *Doom* is widely credited with popularizing the first-person-shooter perspective in modern video games.

Dr. J Nickname of Julius Erving, a Hall of Fame small forward for the ABA's New Jersey Nets and the NBA's Philadelphia 76ers.

The Dukes of Hazzard Television series about Bo and Luke Duke (John Schneider and Tom Wopat), who fight the crime in Hazzard County that (a) the corrupt Jefferson Davis "Boss" Hogg refuses to fight and (b) police officers Roscoe P. Coltrane and Enos Strate are too inept to stop.

Dungeons & Dragons Fantasy role-playing and dice game created by Gary Gygax in the mid-1970s and popularized in the early 1980s.

E.T.: The Extra Terrestrial 1982 Steven Spielberg film about a space alien inadvertently left on Earth and found by a young boy named Elliott.

Ed McMahon Television personality who rose to prominence as Johnny Carson's sidekick on *The Tonight Show*. In the 1980s, McMahon also was the host of the variety show *Star Search*.

The Electric Company Reading-focused television show for children that aired on PBS from 1971 to 1985.

The Empire Strikes Back 1980 film and second of the original *Star Wars* trilogy. The movie portrays Darth Vader at his most tyrannical and Luke Skywalker at his most whiny.

Ender's Game 1985 Orson Scott Card novel about a military program that trains children to be future military commanders.

Falcon Crest Television series about feuding families in the California wine industry. The show aired from 1981 to 1990.

Flux Capacitor The central component of Dr. Emmett Brown's Delorean time machine in the *Back to the Future* films. The Flux Capacitor is three glowing wires and requires 1.21 gigawatts of energy to function.

The Fonz Leather-jacketed tough played by Henry Winkler in the classic television series *Happy Days*.

Footloose 1984 film about a town that has followed the orders of a Bible-thumping minister (John Lithgow) and banned rock music and dancing.

G. I. Joe: A Real American Hero Mid-1980s line of syndicated cartoons, comic books, movies, and action figures documenting the adventures of an elite team of U.S. military specialists fighting the international terrorist organization known as Cobra.

Gary Hart Democratic U.S. senator who ran for president in 1984 and 1988 but was defeated in the latter contest after being caught in an extramarital affair.

Gene Simmons The bassist for the face-painted band Kiss.

General Lee The Dodge Charger owned by the *Dukes of Hazzard*'s Bo and Luke Duke. The vehicle's defining features are its bright orange color and the Confederate flag painted on its roof. Notably, access to the General Lee is limited to those who can climb through the car's windows, as the doors seem to be permanently welded shut.

George Gervin All-star NBA shooting guard for the San Antonio Spurs. He was nicknamed "The Iceman."

George McFly Father of Marty McFly, the lead character in the *Back to the Future* films.

Geraldine Ferraro Onetime New York congresswoman who became the Democratic vice presidential nominee in 1984.

Ghostbusters 1984 film about a group of Manhattan scientists who lose their university grants and are forced to continue their study of ghosts in the private sector. Fortunately for the Ghostbusters, their business venture begins just as the ghost Gozer the Gozerian and its henchmen (Zuul, Vinz Clortho, and the Stay Puft™ Marshmallow Man, etc.) are trying to take over New York City.

The Golden Girls Television comedy series about four female retirees living in South Florida. The program ran from 1985 to 1992.

Gordon Gekko The major bad guy in Oliver Stone's 1987 classic, *Wall Street*. Some believe his famous "greed is good" speech is based on a real-life speech by stock speculator Ivan Boesky, who said, "greed is healthy."

Great Balls of Fire 1989 biopic starring Dennis Quaid as singer-pianist Jerry Lee Lewis.

The Great Outdoors 1988 John Hughes film about the clash of two Chicago-area families as they jointly vacation in Wisconsin. The two enduring scenes of the movie are a family member eating a ninety-six-ounce steak and a grizzly bear's ass being shot by a rifle that also serves as a lamp.

Hamburger Hill 1987 film about a famous battle in the Vietnam War.

Hands Across America Fund-raising and publicity event on May 25, 1986, in which more than 5 million people formed a single human chain across the entire United States.

Hardcastle & McCormick Action-adventure television show about retired judge Milton Hardcastle's pursuit of criminals who escaped his sentencing on legal technicalities. Hardcastle's partner is Mark McCormick, a criminal who escapes sentencing in exchange for agreeing to help Hardcastle track down other criminals. The show aired on ABC from 1983 to 1986.

He–Man and the Masters of the Universe Mid-eighties cartoon based on Mattel's toy line, and the first major Program Length Commercial to air on American television. The plot centers around a prince named Adam who becomes a muscle-bound superhero anytime he holds his sword above his head and screams, "By the power of Grayskull!"

Heartbreak Ridge 1986 war film starring Clint Eastwood and Mario Van Peebles as American soldiers during the invasion of Grenada.

Helen Slater Actress most famous in the 1980s as the costar of the film *The Secret of My Success*.

Highway to Heaven NBC drama about an angel (Michael Landon) being driven across America by a wanderer (Victor French). The two help save people with various problems. The program aired from 1985 to 1989.

Hoosiers 1986 film starring Gene Hackman as the coach of a small-town Indiana basketball team that goes on to win the state championship in 1954. The story is based on the Milan High School Indians, who won the 1954 Indiana state championship. *Hoosiers* was recently named the top sports movie of all time by both *USA Today* and ESPN.com.

Huey Lewis Lead singer for the rock band Huey Lewis and the News, which is best known for its album *Sports* and its dominance of the *Back to the Future* soundtrack.

Hulk Hogan Blond professional wrestler who was the WWF's reining champion for much of the 1980s.

The Hunt for Red October 1989 film about a group of Soviet naval officers who seek to defect and turn over their superstealth submarine to the American government. The film is based on Tom Clancy's book by the same name.

Indiana Jones The protagonist in Steven Spielberg's *Indiana Jones* trilogy, this 1930s archaeologist discovers the Ark of the Covenant, the Sankara stones, and the

Holy Grail—all while singlehandedly defeating the Nazis and the Thugees with a bullwhip and a revolver.

The Iron Sheik Iranian evildoer who was one of the leaders of the bad guys in 1980s professional wrestling.

Isiah Thomas All-star guard for the Detroit Pistons, otherwise known as "Zeke."

Ivan Drago Fictional steroid-using Soviet boxer (Dolph Lundgren) who kills Apollo Creed and then is defeated by Rocky Balboa in *Rocky IV.*

Jack Ryan Fictional naval intelligence analyst and CIA agent who is the protagonist for many Tom Clancy novels. He first hit the silver screen in 1989's *The Hunt for Red October.*

James Tiberius Kirk Captain of the *Enterprise* in *Star Trek.*

Jerry Falwell Christian conservative evangelical leader who led a megachurch in Virginia; founded the religious college Liberty University; and created the political group the Moral Majority.

Jerry Seinfeld Comedian and lead in the eponymous television show *Seinfeld,* which premiered in 1989.

Jigowatt Key measurement of energy cited in calculations about time travel in the *Back to the Future* films. There remains some controversy about how to pronounce the word—the script of *Back to the Future,* for instance, spells the word "jigowatt" and the movie's characters therefore pronounce it with a soft "j" sound. The *New York Times,* however, notes that the word is actually spelled "gigawatt," not "jigowatt" and "since we pronounce gigabyte with a hard 'g,' it seems logical that gigawatt would follow suit." That said, there remains no debate over the amount of jigowatts/gigawatts (1.21) required to activate the Flux Capacitor—the device that makes time travel possible.

Jim Bakker Disgraced televangelist forced to resign from his ministry because of a sex scandal. Bakker later went to jail for accounting fraud and divorced his wife, Tammy Faye Bakker.

Jimmy "The Greek" Snyder Screen name of Demetrios Georgios Synodinos, a CBS football broadcaster fired in 1986 for making racist comments.

Jimmy Chitwood Fictional basketball player who led the Hickory high school basketball team to an Indiana state championship in the 1986 film *Hoosiers.*

Jimmy Swaggart Christian televangelist known for his on-camera sobbing. According to Swaggart's website, his television program was broadcast to three thousand stations and 500 million people worldwide in the 1980s.

John Hughes Filmmaker who wrote and directed some of the most commercially successful and culturally iconic movies of the 1980s. Hughes films were most often comedies about suburban families and suburban teenage life. Among his most famous 1980s productions were *National Lampoon's Vacation* (1983); *Sixteen Candles* (1984); *The Breakfast Club* (1985); *Ferris Bueller's Day Off* (1986); *Pretty in Pink* (1986), *Planes, Trains and Automobiles* (1987); and *Uncle Buck* (1989).

John McClane Fictional New York City police officer played by Bruce Willis in the *Die Hard* films.

John McEnroe Top-ranked professional tennis player in the 1980s known for his temper and for yelling at officials.

John Rambo Protagonist in the *Rambo* movies. Played by Sylvester Stallone, Rambo is a special forces veteran of the Vietnam War.

Joshua Fictional deceased son of Dr. Stephen Falken in the 1983 film *WarGames.* Falken also named his military computer program Joshua, in honor of his son.

The Karate Kid 1984 film about a high schooler named Daniel LaRusso (Ralph Macchio) who is taught tournament-winning karate by his apartment complex's diminutive Okinawan janitor, Mr. Miyagi (Pat Morita).

Kenny Loggins Singer famous in the 1980s for hits tied to major motion pictures. These included "Footloose" for the 1984 movie of the same name and "Danger Zone" and "Playing with the Boys" from 1986's *Top Gun.*

Knight Rider Prime-time television series about a privately funded vigilante named Michael Knight (David Hasselhoff) and his talking Trans Am, KITT, as they "champion the cause of the innocent, the helpless, the powerless, in a world of criminals who operate above the law." The program aired from 1982 to 1986.

L.A. Law Television drama about a Los Angeles legal practice. The show repeatedly dealt with cases involving the 1980s most controversial topics. The show aired from 1986 to 1994.

La Bamba 1987 biopic about Mexican American singer Ritchie Valens (Lou Diamond Phillips) growing up in the 1950s.

Lando Calrissian Original owner of the *Millenium Falcon;* administrator of Cloud City, a mining colony in *The Empire Strikes Back;* and key rebel pilot in the assault on the Death Star in *Return of the Jedi.*

Larry Bird All-star power forward for the Boston Celtics in the 1980s.

The Last Starfighter 1984 film about a high school video gamer who excels at an arcade game that is secretly a recruitment machine for an intergalactic army.

Lean on Me 1989 biopic about controversial New Jersey principal Joe Clark (Morgan Freeman) and his efforts to clean up an inner-city public school.

Lee Iacocca CEO of the Chrysler Corporation during the 1980s.

Lifestyles of the Rich and Famous Television series about very rich people and their extravagant lives. The show aired in syndication from 1984 to 1995 and was hosted by Robin Leach.

Live Aid Benefit concert held on July 13, 1985, in Philadelphia. Proceeds from the concert were donated to Ethiopian famine relief efforts.

The Lords of Flatbush 1974 film about a gang of greasers from the Flatbush section of New York City. The film was cowritten by Sylvester Stallone, who also starred in the movie alongside Henry Winkler (aka the Fonz from *Happy Days*).

The Lost Boys 1987 cult film starring Kiefer Sutherland as the leader of a gang of teenage vampires.

Lou Ferrigno Professional body builder who played the Hulk in Bill Bixby's television program *The Incredible Hulk.* The show aired from 1977 to 1982.

The Love Boat Television series about drama aboard a cruise ship called the *Pacific Princess.* The show ran from 1977 to 1986.

M.C. Hammer Rapper who became famous in the 1980s for his hit "U Can't Touch This" and his baggy pants.

MacGyver Action-adventure television program about Vietnam veteran Angus MacGyver (Richard Dean Anderson) solving seemingly impossible problems with preposterously limited resources. The show aired from 1985 to 1992.

Magic Johnson All-star point guard for the Los Angeles Lakers in the 1980s.

Magnum P.I. Television program about fictional private investigator Thomas Magnum (Tom Selleck) and his adventures in Hawaii. The show ran from 1980 to 1988.

Mars Blackmon Fictional basketball-loving character from Spike Lee's 1986 movie *She's Gotta Have It*. Blackmon, played by Lee, was later featured in Nike commercials with Michael Jordan.

Marty McFly Lead character played by Michael J. Fox in the *Back to the Future* films.

Maverick Call sign of the fictional naval aviator Pete Mitchell (Tom Cruise) in the 1986 film *Top Gun*.

Meatloaf Stage name for musician Michael Lee Aday.

Memory Children's card game made by Milton Bradley. The game asks players to try to match pairs of cards from memory.

Merv Griffin Television host, singer, and media-industry titan whose production company made many of the most famous game shows of the 1980s.

Miami Vice Television series about Miami police detectives Sonny Crockett (Don Johnson) and Ricardo Tubbs (Philip Michael Thomas). The show ran from 1984 to 1989 and is remembered for its high fashion, dark themes, and expensive cars.

Michael Milken Financial speculator famous in the 1980s for his controversial investments in junk bonds. Milken pleaded guilty to violations of securities laws in 1990.

Michael Ovitz Hollywood entertainment agent who cofounded Creative Artists Agency—one of the most influential talent agencies in the 1980s and beyond.

Missile Command 1980 Atari game (available as an arcade machine and Atari 2600 cartridge) that challenged players to shoot down warheads being dropped on American cities.

Mississippi Burning 1988 film based on a federal investigation into the murders of civil rights workers in Mississippi. The film starred Gene Hackman and Willem Dafoe.

The Money Pit 1986 film about lawyer Walter Fielding (Tom Hanks) and violinist Anna Crowley (Shelley Long) buying a house in the New York City suburbs that proceeds to fall apart and take much longer than two weeks to rebuild.

Moonlighting Television comedy-drama about fictional Blue Moon Detective Agency's two partners, Maddie Hayes (Cybill Shepherd) and David Addison (Bruce Willis). The show aired from 1985 to 1989.

Mr. Strickland Fictional vice principal and slacker-loathing disciplinarian at Hill Valley High School in the *Back to the Future* films.

Mr. T Screen name of the mohawked actor Laurence Tureaud, who played B.A. Baracus on *The A-Team* and Clubber Lang in *Rocky III*. Before becoming an actor, T was a professional bodyguard for, among others, Muhammad Ali.

Murphy Brown Television sitcom about an investigative reporter (Candice Bergen) working on a fictional CBS news program. The show aired from 1988 to 1998.

napalm in the morning The thing that fictional Lieutenant Colonel Bill Kilgore (Robert Duvall) most loves the smell of in the 1979 film *Apocalypse Now.*

Nikolai Volkoff 1980s professional wrestler whose defining feature was his allegiance to the Soviet Union.

Nintendo NES Bestselling home videogame system released by Nintendo in 1985. NES stands for "Nintendo Entertainment System." In terms of home video-game commercial success, the console is seen as the successor to the wildly popular Atari 2600.

Norman Lear Television writer and producer credited with politically controversial sitcoms such as *All in the Family, The Jeffersons, Good Times,* and *Sanford and Son.*

Norman Dale Fictional high school basketball coach played by Gene Hackman in the 1986 film *Hoosiers.*

Norman Schwarzkopf Barrel-chested army general who served as commander of U.S. forces in the 1991 Gulf War.

An Officer and a Gentleman 1982 film about the conflict between a U.S. naval aviation officer candidate (Richard Gere) and his sergeant (Lou Gossett, Jr.). The film also focuses on the officer candidate's love affair with a local woman (Debra Winger).

One to Grow On Educational "prosocial message" aired on NBC from 1983 to 1989 during Saturday morning cartoons.

Operation Wolf First-person military-themed shooter arcade game released by Taito in 1987. *Operation Wolf* was one of the first games to replace the traditional joystick with a lifelike console-mounted machine gun.

Orlando Woolridge High-scoring NBA power forward who rarely played for a winning team.

The Outsiders 1983 Francis Ford Coppola film based on the S. E. Hinton book about gang warfare during the early 1960s in Tulsa, Oklahoma.

Peggy Sue Got Married 1986 Francis Ford Coppola film about a woman who faints and finds herself back as a senior in high school in 1960.

Phil Knight Founder and CEO of the Nike Corporation.

Planes, Trains and Automobiles 1987 John Hughes film about a marketing executive named Neal Page (Steve Martin) trying to get home for Thanksgiving, and getting stuck traveling through various midwestern cities with a shower-curtain-ring salesman named Del Griffith (John Candy).

Poison 1980s hair metal band led by Bret Michaels. Among its best-known hits was its 1988 ballad, "Every Rose Has Its Thorn."

Predator 1987 film featuring Arnold Schwarzenegger and Carl Weathers as military commandos who get hunted in the jungle by an invisible extraterrestrial.

Project X 1987 film about a government facility that exposes primates to radiation as a means of testing whether human military pilots would be able to continue their missions during a thermonuclear war.

Raiders of the Lost Ark 1981 film directed by Steven Spielberg about archaeologist Indiana Jones's quest to find the Ark of the Covenant in Egypt during the 1930s. *Raiders* is the first of the Indiana Jones series.

Ray Parker, Jr. Singer who performed the theme song of the *Ghostbusters* films.

Reading Rainbow PBS reading program for children hosted by actor LeVar Burton. The show aired from 1983 to 2006.

Red Dawn 1984 film about a group of teenagers from the fictional town of Calumet, Colorado, who wage a guerrilla war against a Soviet invasion of the American homeland.

Remington Steele Television series starring Pierce Brosnan as a thief-turned-private-detective. The show aired from 1982 to 1987.

Rerun Stubbs Fictional character played by Fred Berry on *What's Happening!!* Rerun is most recognizable by his suspenders and red beret.

Return of the Secaucus Seven 1980 film about a reunion of friends at a weekend getaway in New Hampshire. Directed by John Sayles, the film has been compared to the 1983 film *The Big Chill*.

Revenge of the Nerds 1984 film about the fictional Lambda Lambda Lambda fraternity of nerds at Adams College.

The Right Stuff 1983 film based on Tom Wolfe's book about the beginnings of the U.S. space program in the 1950s and early 1960s.

Riptide Television detective series about private investigators who specialize in fighting crime at or near the Los Angeles waterfront. The show aired from 1983 to 1986.

Risky Business 1983 film about a high school senior (Tom Cruise) who starts a prostitution business when his parents leave town.

Robin Leach Loud British host of the syndicated television show *Lifestyles of the Rich and Famous*.

Robocop Paul Verhoeven's 1987 sci-fi film about a police officer who, after nearly being killed in the line of duty, is reconstructed as a cyborg.

Rocky Academy Award–winning 1976 film about a working-class Philadelphia boxer named Rocky Balboa (Sylvester Stallone) who is given a chance to fight for the heavyweight championship.

Rocky Balboa Fictional Philadelphia boxer played by Sylvester Stallone in the *Rocky* films. Otherwise known as "The Italian Stallion."

Rocky III 1982 film and third of the *Rocky* series. The movie features Rocky Balboa first losing his heavyweight championship belt to challenger Clubber Lang; then watching his trainer, Mickey, die from a locker-room heart attack; and then speaking Hebrew for the only time in the entire *Rocky* series (so far). Balboa ultimately reclaims the belt after his former nemesis, Apollo Creed, brings him to the Los Angeles ghetto and trains him for revenge in a series of homoerotic music montages, at least two of which feature splashing in the Pacific surf.

Roseanne Television series about a working-class family and starring Roseanne Barr and John Goodman. The program aired in prime time from 1988 to 1997.

Roy Tarpley Spectacularly talented NBA forward whose Dallas Mavericks career was cut short by drug-related suspensions.

Sergeant Slaughter Military-themed professional wrestler and G. I. Joe character who reached prominence in the 1980s.

Saturday Night Fever 1977 film starring John Travolta as a Brooklyn disco maven.

The Secret of My Success 1987 film about country boy Brantley Foster who starts in the mail room of a major New York City corporation and quickly works his way to the top.

Sesame Street PBS children's television show featuring famed puppet characters Big Bird, Mr. Snuffleupagus, Oscar the Grouch, Bert, Ernie, and the Cookie Monster.

Short Circuit 1986 film about a military robot named Johnny Five who suddenly becomes "alive" after a power surge overwhelms his circuits.

Silver Spoons Television comedy series starring Rick Schroeder as the son of a millionaire living in a vast mansion with his single father. The program aired from 1982 to 1987.

Simon & Simon Television program about a pair of brothers teaming up in a private detective business. The show ran from 1981 to 1989.

Sister Souljah Moment Term used to describe any event in which a politician attacks an individual or interest group perceived to be representative of that politician's natural electoral base. The term derives from Democratic candidate Bill Clinton criticizing African American rapper Sister Souljah during the 1992 presidential campaign.

Snow Cat G. I. Joe's snow-ready mobile missile-launching unit first released in toy stores in 1985. The Snow Cat was driven by the character Frostbite.

Socs (pronounced *so-shez*, for "Socials") Nickname for the preppy high school kids in the 1983 film *The Outsiders*. The Socs archenemies were the Greasers.

Some Kind of Wonderful 1987 John Hughes film starring Eric Stoltz as a reclusive high school senior who gets a date with the most popular girl in school (Lea Thompson) and then realizes he's actually in love with his best friend (Mary Stuart Masterson).

Space Invaders Arcade game and home video game first released by Taito in 1977. *Space Invaders* is considered one of the most successful Atari 2600 programs and was one of the first shooting video games.

Speak & Spell Talking computer console (with keyboard) that tested children's spelling abilities. The Speak and Spell was first released in 1978 by Texas Instruments, which sold additional modules for movie-themed spelling tests.

Spenser: For Hire Television drama starring Robert Urich as Spenser, a private detective. The program ran from 1985 to 1988.

Spies Like Us 1985 film starring Chevy Chase and Dan Aykroyd as unknowing decoys for actual CIA spies on a covert mission to show that a space-based missile defense system works.

Splash 1984 Ron Howard film starring Darryl Hannah as a mermaid who falls in love with a non-mermaid (Tom Hanks) in New York City.

Spud Webb Five-foot-seven-inch-tall NBA point guard for the Atlanta Hawks during the 1980s. He became famous for being able to compete in the dunk contest, despite his small size. He also starred in the music video for Paul Simon's 1988 song "Me and Julio Down by the Schoolyard."

Stand By Me 1986 film based on Stephen King's coming-of-age book *The Body*. The film follows a group of grade school boys who embark on a journey to find the corpse of another child.

Star Search Television variety show pitting entertainers in contests against each other for cash prizes. The program aired from 1983 to 1995 and was hosted by Ed McMahon.

Star Wars 1977 George Lucas film that launched an entire sci-fi–fantasy industry. If you don't know about *Star Wars,* you probably live in a cave.

Starman 1984 film starring Jeff Bridges as an extraterrestrial who visits Earth in the form of a woman's (Karen Allen) deceased husband.

Staying Alive 1983 Sylvester Stallone–directed sequel to the 1977 disco film *Saturday Night Fever.*

Stripes 1981 film about two goof-offs (Bill Murray and Harold Ramis) who enlist in the army and end up saving their fellow soldiers from the Soviet menace.

Super Mario Brothers Nintendo's psychedelic, mushroom-glorifying video game about two mustachioed brothers, Mario and Luigi. The game is not merely the most famous side-scrolling video game ever, but probably the most famous video game of the entire 1980s.

Superman 1978 film starring Christopher Reeve as the Man of Steele, Margot Kidder as Lois Lane, Gene Hackman as Lex Luthor, and Ned Beatty as Luthor's sidekick, Otis.

Superman II 1980 film that features Superman (Christopher Reeve) protecting the world from General Zod (Terrence Stamp), Ursa, and Non. The trio was originally sentenced to prison by Superman's father, Jor-El (Marlon Brando) before Krypton was destroyed. When they break out of prison, they travel to Earth looking for revenge on Jor-El's son, Kal-El (aka Superman).

Teenage Mutant Ninja Turtles Fictional squad of four anthropomorphized turtles who are in their mid-teens and who are karate masters. Named after four Renaissance artists (Leonardo, Michelangelo, Donatello, and Raphael), they became cartoon and toy hits in the late 1980s and beyond.

The Terminator 1984 film starring Arnold Schwarzenegger as a cyborg sent back in time to execute a child who will later grow up to lead a human resistance to Skynet, a computer that takes over the world.

The Equalizer Network television show about a former government spy who makes his private sector living helping people solve problems, right wrongs, and take revenge on criminals who have gone free. The show aired from 1984 to 1989.

The Fall Guy Action-adventure television show starring Lee Majors as a Hollywood stuntman who doubles as a bounty hunter. The program ran from 1981 to 1986.

thirtysomething Television series about a group of Philadelphia hippies-turned-yuppies struggling with the responsibilities of adulthood. The program aired from 1987 to 1991.

Thunder Road Abandoned roadway in the 1978 film *Grease* where rival gangs race their cars.

Tom Wolfe Famed author of many iconic novels, including the 1980s classic *The Bonfire of the Vanities.*

Top Gun 1986 film about naval aviators training in an elite Top Gun program in Miramar, California.

Total Recall 1990 Paul Verhoeven sci-fi classic starring Arnold Schwarzenegger as a man who has his memories retooled.

Toy 1982 comedy starring Richard Pryor as an out-of-work journalist who gets hired to befriend the son of a millionaire publisher (Jackie Gleason).

Trading Places 1983 film starring Eddie Murphy as an indigent street criminal named Billy Ray Valentine and Dan Aykroyd as an aristocratic financial speculator named Louis Winthorpe. The two are forced to trade life positions thanks to a $1 bet between Winthorpe's bosses, the Duke Brothers (Ralph Bellamy and Don Ameche).

Transformers Syndicated cartoon series that documents the war between the Autobots and the Decepticons, opposing factions of humanlike robots that can transform into various vehicles and objects. The series first ran from 1984 to 1987.

Trapper Keeper Plastic binder made by Mead, themed to various pop culture brands (movies, television shows, etc.) and marketed to tweens in the 1980s.

Tron Disney's 1982 film about a hacker (Jeff Bridges) who gets sucked into a mainframe computer and must fight the forces of evil in an electronic dystopia. This sci-fi classic is seen as one of the earliest allegories about the then burgeoning world of computers.

TRS-80 Boxy black personal computer made by the Tandy Corporation and sold in Radio Shack in the early 1980s.

Twiggy Fictional childlike robot sidekick of Buck Rogers (Gil Gerard) in the 1980s television show *Buck Rogers in the 25th Century.*

Uncle Buck John Hughes's 1989 film about an unrefined uncle who is asked to watch his nieces and nephew when his brother and sister-in-law must leave town because of an illness in the family.

up-up-down-down-left-right-left-right-B-A Sequence of joystick commands (technically called the Konami Code) that was required to make a player immortal in the Nintendo NES game *Contra.*

V 1984 miniseries about lizardlike aliens and their attempt to take over Earth.

WarGames 1983 film about a high school student (Matthew Broderick) who hacks into a military computer and inadvertently brings America to the brink of nuclear war.

Wayne Gretzky National Hockey League legend who played for the Edmonton Oilers and Los Angeles Kings in the 1980s. Gretzky is widely regarded as the best hockey player of all time.

We Are the World 1985 song written by Michael Jackson and Lionel Richie and performed by a large group of famous musicians. The proceeds of "We Are the World" were devoted to poverty relief in Africa.

We Didn't Start the Fire 1989 hit on Billy Joel's otherwise weak album, *Storm Front*. The song randomly lists headlines and events from the 1950s to the late 1980s.

Webster Television comedy series about a young African American child (Emmanuel Lewis) who is adopted by two white parents. The program ran from 1983 to 1987.

Who's the Boss? Television sitcom starring Tony Danza as a retired professional baseball player who becomes a housekeeper in ritzy suburban Connecticut. The show ran from 1984 to 1992.

William Shatner Actor who played, among others, *Star Trek*'s Captain Kirk, *T. J. Hooker*'s eponymous lead character, and *Airplane II*'s Commander Buck Murdock.

Witness 1985 film about an Amish child who witnesses the murder of a police officer in a Philadelphia train station.

Zelda (aka *The Legend of Zelda*) 1986 Nintendo game set in a medieval fantasy world and centering on a protagonist who must save Princess Zelda.

ZZ Top Rock trio known for its two bearded guitarists.

ABOUT THE AUTHOR

David Sirota is a journalist, nationally syndicated weekly news-
paper columnist, and radio host. His weekly column is based at
The Denver Post, San Francisco Chronicle, Portland *Oregonian,*
and *The Seattle Times* and now appears in newspapers with a
combined daily circulation of more than 1.6 million readers.
He has contributed to *The New York Times Magazine* and *The
Nation* and hosts the morning talk show on Denver's Clear
Channel affiliate, KKZN-AM760. He is a senior editor at *In
These Times* magazine and a *Huffington Post* contributor and
appears periodically on CNN, *The Colbert Report,* PBS, and
NPR. He received a degree in journalism and political science
from Northwestern University's Medill School of Journalism.
He lives in Denver with his wife, Emily, their son, Isaac, and
their dog, Monty.

www.davidsirota.com

ABOUT THE TYPE

This book was set in Bembo, a typeface based on an old-style Roman face that was used for Cardinal Bembo's tract *De Aetna* in 1495. Bembo was cut by Francisco Griffo in the early sixteenth century. The Lanston Monotype Company of Philadelphia brought the well-proportioned letterforms of Bembo to the United States in the 1930s.